Strategic Defense Initiative

About the Book and Author

The ballistic missile defense debate, which has permeated strategic discussion in the United States for nearly three decades, received an impressive stimulus when President Ronald Reagan addressed the nation on the evening of March 23, 1983. In that address, dubbed the Star Wars speech by the media, the president asked the scientific community to pursue research and development of hardware and software that would enable the nation to switch from the deterrence doctrine of Mutual Assured Destruction (MAD) to a policy based on the unilateral capability to physically defend the country against ballistic missile attack.

In conjunction with the third anniversary of the president's speech, Professor Lawrence has assembled approximately 1,000 citations-- including books, monographs, articles and government documents--that reflect the full spectrum of thought on the issue. Seminal references have been abstracted and divided into three sections: technical background of the debate, arguments in favor of the SDI, and arguments against the SDI. Each section contains an essay that integrates and amplifies the information presented in the abstracted materials.

Robert M. Lawrence is a professor of political science at Colorado State University, Fort Collins, and an affiliate of the Center for Space Law and Policy at the University of Colorado in Boulder. He is currently a visiting professor of political science at the University of Colorado, Boulder.

Published in cooperation with the
Center for Space Law and Policy,
University of Colorado at Boulder

Strategic Defense Initiative

Bibliography and Research Guide

Robert M. Lawrence

Westview Press • Boulder, Colorado

Mansell Publishing Limited • London

Copyright © 1987 by The Regents of the University of Colorado, on behalf of the Center for Space Law and Policy

Published in 1987 in the United States of America by Westview Press, Inc.; Frederick A. Praeger, Publisher; 5500 Central Avenue, Boulder, Colorado 80301

Published in 1987 in Great Britain by Mansell Publishing Limited, 6 All Saints Street, London N1 9RL

Library of Congress Cataloging-in-Publication Data
Lawrence, Robert M.
  Strategic defense initiative: bibliography and research guide.
  1. Strategic Defense Initiative--Abstracts.
2. Strategic Defense Initiative--Study and teaching.
I. Title.
UG743.L38   1987   358.1754'07   86-7811
ISBN 0-8133-7229-1

British Library Cataloguing in Publication Data
Lawrence, Robert M.
  Strategic Defense Initiative bibliography and research guide.
  1. Strategic Defense Initiative
  I. Title
  358'.8'0973   U393
  ISBN 0-7201-1868-9

Composition for this book was provided by the author.

Printed and bound in the United States of America

∞   The paper used in this publication meets the requirements of the American National Standard for Permanence of Paper for Printed Library Materials Z39.48-1984.

4/88

Contents

viii / Contents

Foreword

When future generations look back upon the
1980s, they will remember the decade as one of
triumph as well as tragedy in space. The success
of the Voyager-Uranus encounter and Halley's
missions stand out as significant triumphs; the
loss of the Challenger and crew was a tragedy.
Somewhere along this continuum will lie the
Strategic Defense Initiative, or Star Wars.

The issues surrounding the SDI program are
complex and, for the layperson, often confusing.
It is for this reason that the University of
Colorado Center for Space Law and Policy, in
cooperation with Dr. Robert M. Lawrence,
developed this book. The Strategic Defense
Initiative: Bibliography and Research Guide
should prove a valuable companion to laypersons
and experts alike. Those unfamiliar with the
contesting sides of the SDI debate should find
the introductory essays on the general background
of the ABM debate, the technical background of
SDI, and the cases for and against the SDI
particularly instructive. Those knowledgeable in
the field should find the book's extensive
bibliography extremely useful.

The purpose of this project is similar to that
underlying many of the other research and
education programs at the Center: to stimulate
discussion, debate, research, and education
concerning policy, business, and legal issues
related to space. I believe that Dr. Lawrence's
book takes a significant stride in that direction
and I am pleased that the Center is now able to
offer it, through Westview Press, to the general
public.

S. Neil Hosenball
Director
Center for Space
Law and Policy

ix

Preface

The debate over ballistic missile defense, which has ebbed and flowed in the United States for nearly three decades, received an impressive stimulus when President Ronald Reagan addressed the nation on the evening of March 23, 1983. In that address, popularly referred to as the Star Wars speech, the president called for the nation's scientific community, some of whom had helped invent nuclear weapons, to respond again to the government's request for assistance. Mr. Reagan asked scientists to develop the means that would enable the country to replace the policy of mutual assured destruction (MAD), along with its deterrent threat to kill millions of Soviets should the Soviet Union first strike the United States, with the capability to physically defend the nation against ballistic missile attack. The president's address triggered a torrent of writing from both those who opposed and those who supported the Strategic Defense Initiative (SDI), as his plan became named.

Given the potential that the SDI may hold for either great harm or enormous benefit, depending upon one's point of view, it seems important that thoughtful citizens become informed on the subject. Accomplishment of that task is the objective of this book.

Approximately 1,000 citations have been collected that reflect primarily the spectrum of American thought on the subject of the SDI since the president's address. These appear alphabetically in the bibliography.

Eighty-four of the references contained in the bibliography were identified as having a seminal character because they contain the basic perspectives that are influential in the current

debate on ballistic missile defense. Each of
these has been summarized into an extended
abstract and categorized according to whether it
provides a technological background about the
SDI, favors construction of the SDI, or opposes
construction of the SDI. On the basis of these
materials, three essays were written. The
first provides an introduction to the technical
background of the SDI; the second essay
summarizes the arguments in favor of the SDI, and
the third summarizes the arguments against the
SDI. These essays are preceded by a historical
introduction that highlights the debates over
strategic defense prior to the president's
speech, and they are followed by a short chapter
noting the various concepts to be watched for as
the SDI debate evolves.

The portion of the president's speech that
contains his SDI proposal is reproduced in
Appendix A, as are the texts of five arms
control treaties related to the SDI program.

To assist those unfamiliar with strategic
terminology a list of acronyms and a glossary of
terms taken from official usage are provided in
Appendix B.

In any project such as this, there is a
supporting cast known initially only to the
author. The members of this cast deserve thanks.
As in previous writing efforts, my wife, Elaine
was patient and supportive. At Colorado State
University, Earlene Bell, Pat Maxey, and Patsy
Smith typed rough drafts into final copies. At
the University of Colorado's Center for Space Law
and Policy, Marta Luce contributed where she was
asked to help. Rebecca Smith cheerfully checked
proofs and made corrections. Mark Turnoy spent
hours entering bibliographic citations into his
computer. The Center's assistant director,
Jefferson S. Hofgard, offered substantive
comments, assisted with the administration of the
project and provided technical support. The
Center's director, S. Neil Hosenball, was
generous in providing financial support.
Representing the university's highest administra-
tive echelon, Donald Hearth, director of the
Office of Space Science and Technology, gave
support from the "Top."

Len Ackland, Barry Daniel, Michael Grant, Liz Moore, and Robert Ristinen offered constructive criticism. At Westview Press Alice Levine, Chris Arden, Bev LeSuer, and Kellie Masterson provided editorial assistance.

Special thanks are saved for Sally Reynolds, a tireless and multitalented student who contributed on a number of fronts, from orchestrating the bibliographic search to making useful editorial suggestions.

The above-named persons should share in any useful consequences of this book. Fault found with the book is, of course, solely the responsibility of the author.

Robert M. Lawrence
Boulder, Colorado

1

General Background

Before one can appreciate the literature on strategic defense, it is necessary to review the origins and evolution of the perspectives for and against President Reagan's proposal to defend the United States against missile attack. One view is that in the nuclear age, the only realistic strategy is to deter an attack on the United States by threatening an unacceptable retaliation against the Soviet Union. The contrasting view is that while deterring an attack may be preferable, it is also necessary to prepare defenses against the possibility that deterrence will fail and an attack will follow.

CHANGES IN CONVENTIONAL MILITARY THINKING BROUGHT ABOUT BY THE NUCLEAR AGE

Scholars who have studied the nature and history of war have noted the oscillation over time between the superiority of offense and the superiority of defense--a phenomenon that has often reflected the introduction of new tactics or, in particular, new weapons systems. For example, the offensive strength of the regimental cavalry in the early and mid-nineteenth century was largely destroyed with the advent of artillery and rapid-firing weapons protected by fortifications. In turn, the defensive superiority of the redoubt fell to the offensive power and maneuverability of tanks. In pre-nuclear times, aerial warfare and the development

1

of anti-aircraft weaponry tended to foster the belief that for every weapon a counterweapon could be developed. Through the long and unfortunate history of warfare, that belief has been borne out time after time. But on August 6, 1945, the belief in this conventional military wisdom would change dramatically. On that day a single B-29 bomber carrying a single atomic bomb, small by today's standards, largely devastated the Japanese city of Hiroshima. Three days later another solo plane carrying one bomb destroyed much of a second Japanese city, Nagasaki. The nuclear era had arrived, and with it came widespread questioning of the conventional wisdom.

With the beginning of the atomic age, the oscillations between offense and defense that had typified previous periods of warfare appeared to be a thing of the past: There could be no defense against "the bomb." This view was expounded in 1946 by Bernard Brodie, one of the leading pioneers in nuclear strategic thought, in his book, The Absolute Weapon: Atomic Power and World Order.1 Brodie believed that little could be done in the future by way of active defense to protect a nation's society from the effects of nuclear weapons, which he characterized as both enormously destructive and capable of being delivered with unprecedented suddenness. His perspective suggested that the Battle of Britain, in which the German Luftwaffe was turned back by the Spitfires and Hurricanes of the Royal Air Force, would be the last example of defensive superiority in a strategic context. The message behind Brodie's analysis was clear: "Thus far the chief purpose of our military establishment has been to win wars. From now on its chief purpose must be to avert them. It can have almost no other useful purpose."2

THE NEW WISDOM OF THE NUCLEAR AGE

Since the bombing of Hiroshima and Nagasaki, the view that has become prevalent in the United States and elsewhere is that peace at the nuclear level has the best chance of being maintained if

the two most powerful nuclear weapons states--the
United States and the USSR--adopt a policy of
nuclear deterrence, not nuclear defense. Such a
policy requires that a nation seek to deter a
nuclear attack by (1) building nuclear
retaliatory forces that could not be destroyed by
an enemy's first strike, and (2) credibly
promising that a first strike would be followed
by a nuclear retaliatory counterattack surpassing
in horror any loss and any possible gain anticipated by the initiator.

During the first years of the cold war confrontation between the United States and the
Soviet Union, the nuclear balance of terror
heavily favored the United States. It was said
during those times that while the Soviet Union
was able to cripple the United States in a first
strike, the latter nation could destroy the
former in a retaliatory blow. It was further
assumed in Washington that, under such
circumstances, a nuclear peace would prevail. In
the 1960s Secretary of Defense Robert McNamara
referred to the U.S. capability as "assured
destruction."

In time the Soviet Union obtained the
capacity to match the United States in nuclear
destructive capacity, and the grim prediction of
early U.S. nuclear weapons physicists became a
reality. The United States and the Soviet Union
could be seen as two scorpions in a bottle, both
immobilized by virtue of their own, and their
antagonist's, fatal power. In light of the
Soviets' increasing capability to match the
Americans' nuclear prowess, McNamara's assured
destruction was transformed into "mutual assured
destruction," or MAD. The essence of the deterrence doctrine of MAD, many thought, was nowhere
more clear than in the everyday meaning of the
acroynym itself-MADness.

Concerns about MAD

MAD seems to have worked effectively thus far
in maintaining the nuclear peace between the
United States and the Soviet Union. Still,
various misgivings about the policy's long-run

utility and safety have developed over the years,
even predating President Reagan's recent criticisms. Some analysts have objected to the MAD
policy on moral grounds: How can a nation that
espouses Judaic and Christian values threaten to
destroy the society and population of the Soviet
Union as well as those unfortunate enough to live
downwind from the nuclear targets? According to
Secretary of Defense Caspar Weinberger, the
Reagan administration's policy is that under no
circumstances may such nuclear weapons be used
deliberately for the purpose of destroying populations.

We can place Secretary Weinberger's statement
in the proper context by citing a passage in a
letter from former National Security Advisor
William Clark to Joseph Cardinal Bernardin, who
was assisting with the writing of the National
Conference of Catholic Bishops' Pastoral Letter
on War and Peace. In answer to the cardinal's
request for clarification on the government's
policy of using nuclear weapons, Clark wrote:

> For moral, political and military
> reasons, the United States does not target
> the Soviet civilian population as such.
> There is no deliberately opaque meaning
> conveyed in the last two words. We do not
> threaten the existence of Soviet
> civilization by threatening cities. Rather
> we hold at risk the warmaking capability of
> the Soviet Union--its armed forces, and the
> industrial capacity to sustain war. It
> would be irresponsible for us to issue
> policy statements which might suggest to the
> Soviets that it would be to their advantage
> to establish privileged sanctuaries within
> heavily populated areas, thus inducing them
> to locate much of their war-fighting
> capability within those urban sanctuaries.[3]

Others have criticized MAD as an inappropriate
strategy of defense in which one's security is
entirely hostage to the good judgment and
behavior of one's purported enemy. A further

concern is that the threat to retaliate would not prevent human error, miscalculation, or a technical malfunction capable of provoking an accidental attack that would trigger more exchanges with consequences potentially as awful as those proceeding from the intentional use of nuclear weapons. A related worry is that MAD constitutes no safeguard against the so-called suitcase A-bomb--that is, terrorists willing to strike with nuclear weapons. And, of course, there is the constant concern that MAD may not deter a Soviet first strike on the United States, which in turn would result in a U.S. retaliation upon the Soviet Union, the combined consequences of which would be catastrophic.

Alternatives to MAD

Despite the uncertainties and shortcomings of MAD, the policy has remained intact and, to some, still appears preferable to several alternatives. One of these is what has come to be known as "finite deterrence." The concept behind finite deterrence is that an aggressor can be deterred with a minimum nuclear capacity. For instance, the United States might effectively deter the Soviet Union by maintaining the capacity to destroy twenty of the largest Soviet cities. The basis of this reasoning resides in the dramatic destructivess of nuclear weapons themselves. According to this scenario, the Soviet Union might gain a decisive numerical superiority in terms of nuclear weapons should the United States reduce its arsenal to a finite deterrence level; but would Moscow be willing to commence war with that kind of advantage under the threat of losing 25-30 million persons? Those believing in finite deterrence would answer in the negative, meaning that strategic nuclear war would not occur.

A second alternative to MAD that in recent years has gained grass-roots support, particularly in Europe, is unilateral disarmament. Advocates of this concept contend that MAD serves only to reinforce mutual suspicions and thereby prolongs the nuclear arms competition. They argue that by taking a bold step toward removing suspicion through unilateral disarmament, the "raison d'etre" of the arms race is, in turn, eliminated. Unilateral disarmament has been attacked on several fronts, but, in general, its greatest flaw appears to be that it is an idealistic solution for very real problems and fails to take into account the multiplicity of vested interests and complex security requirements that must, at a minimum, be maintained.

A third option, mutual arms control, enjoys considerable support and, in some instances, has proven useful. The 1963 Partial Nuclear Test Ban Treaty, which prohibits nuclear tests except those conducted underground, and the 1967 Outer Space Treaty, which contains a provision banning the stationing of nuclear weapons in space, are often cited as arms control measures that have been relatively successful. On the other hand, the Reagan administration frequently cites the Anti-Ballistic Missile Treaty, which is intended to place constraints upon ABM system deployments, as being ignored by the Soviet Union.

Depending upon one's perspective, real reductions in U.S. and Soviet nuclear arsenals have failed because of the intransigence of the Soviets, because of the intransigence of the Reagan and past administrations, or both. At the time of this writing, the Soviet Union has introduced a new proposal in the Geneva talks, aimed at eliminating all nuclear weapons by the year 2000. Although some have hailed the approach as a potential "new beginning," others describe it as "old ideas in new wrapping." Again, only time will tell whether this latest arms control initiative will flourish or fail.

Although the objections to the policy of MAD appear reasonable and well founded, none of the alternatives mentioned above have garnered the necessary support or commitment in the United States or the Soviet Union to replace MAD. The results have been twofold. First, while MAD continues to play a prominent role in strategic theory, the search for alternatives is becoming increasingly more prominent. The growing threat of nuclear war is fueled by expanding arsenals on both sides of the ocean, and it has aroused international concern to the point where the United States and the Soviet Union must not only listen but also, some believe, act. Second, frustration with MAD has sparked a renewed interest in the strategy of nuclear defense in contrast to offense. Although President Reagan's Star Wars speech of March 23, 1983, provided a great boost to proponents of nuclear defense, his support for strategic defense is merely the culmination of nearly three decades of thinking about the subject, together with constant technical evolution. Within the context of this essay, it is now useful to elaborate on the development of anti-ballistic missile defense conceptualization in the United States as it has occurred over the past thirty years.

Early ABM Development

The German development of the V-2 rockets, which were designed to traverse a ballistic trajectory from the continent to impact upon England, came too late to change the course of World War II. This fortunate circumstance resulted primarily from the fact that the Germans had not been able to develop nuclear weapons to place on their missiles. Nevertheless the German invention, though unimportant in the war effort, set the technological stage for the subsequent development of long-range nuclear delivery systems called intercontinental range ballistic missiles, or ICBM's. These missiles travel the 5,000 to 6,000 miles between Eurasia and North America, or the reverse route, in approximately thirty minutes and reach altitudes of a few hundred miles over the North Pole.

In 1957 the Soviet Union launched the first earth satellite, thus indicating that Moscow had developed a missile that would also be capable of hurling a nuclear warhead across the arctic to hit the United States. Shortly thereafter the United States countered with its own version of the ICBM, called the Atlas. Since that time both nations have deployed successive iterations of ICBMs. Each has also deployed a smaller version

of the ICBM--a missile carried aboard submarines
--known as the submarine-launched ballistic
missile, or SLBM. The United States and the
Soviet Union also maintain a bomber force for
nuclear weapon delivery. However, over the years
missiles have grown to be the most prominent of
the nuclear delivery systems for both nations.

After World War II the United States began
development of two types of ground-based,
defensive missiles. Success came relatively soon
to the effort to build and deploy surface-to-air
missiles, called SAMs, which were designed to
destroy enemy aircraft. The other defensive
missile effort, an attempt to develop and deploy
missiles to shoot down other missiles, or the
warheads they propel, has had a much different
history. Although the anti-ballistic missile, or
ABM programs produced the Nike-Zeus and Nike-X
systems, neither have been added to the U.S.
arsenal. But before it was finally canceled, the
Nike-X ABM program had grown to include an
extensive array of early warning, target
acquisition, and tracking radars, as well as two
missiles. The Spartan was a nuclear-tipped
missile with a range of more than 100 miles,
designed to intercept Soviet warheads as they
descended into U.S. airspace. The Sprint was a
nuclear missile with rapid acceleration
capabilities designed to intercept at relatively
close range the warheads that the Spartans failed
to destroy. Later the Sprint was replaced by an
improved short-range missile known as the Low
Altitude Defense System, or LOADS.

The Early ABM Debates

A year before the Soviets demonstrated that
they could fire a warhead to a point 5,000 miles
away, the Department of Defense ordered that the
Nike-Zeus system be developed. The rationale was
that it would be needed for defense against a
Soviet ICBM attack when the Soviets acquired such
a capabililty. Although the Nike-Zeus ABM was
developed, it was not deployed during the
Eisenhower administration.

A recent chronicler of the nuclear weapons evolution, Fred Kaplan, describes the early and successful arguments against the Nike-Zeus in his book, The Wizards of Armageddon.4 According to Kaplan, the first ABM debate took place in the spring of 1958. A panel of Pentagon technical experts, called the Reentry Body Identification Group, concluded a report with the opinion that Nike-Zeus would not be effective against a determined Soviet ballistic missile attack. The basic argument, which created doubts about the effectiveness of an ABM in the late 1950s, was similar to a primary technical argument made against President Reagan's Strategic Defense Initiative in the 1980s--namely, that the defense would be too easily defeated by any of a number of Soviet actions. Among these potential actions might have been (1) an increase in the number of warheads with which the defense would have to contend; and (2) a saturation of the defense with various kinds of decoys, which would be difficult to distinguish from actual warheads. It was also believed that the radars crucial in guiding defensive missiles would be subjected to direct nuclear attack from which they could not be adequately protected. In this connection, it had been discovered that high-altitude, high-yield, nuclear detonations could "black-out" radar systems for several minutes. Finally, it was noted that even if the Soviets did not begin their attack with black-out detonations, the explosions of the nuclear warheads fired aloft by the Nike-Zeus would have the same deleterious effect upon U.S. radars.

Kaplan further notes that the reservations of the Reentry Body Identification Group were corroborated in a classified report by a prestigious panel from Eisenhower's Presidential Science Advisory Committee. This group included some individuals still active as participants in the current strategic defense debate-that is, scientists such as Hans Bethe, director of the Theoretical Physics Division at Los Alamos during the war; Wolfgang Panofsky, director of the High-Energy Physics Laboratory at Stanford; Harold Brown, formerly the director of the Livermore

Laboratory, and Jerome Wiesner and Jerrold Zacharias of the Massachusetts Institute of Technology.

But the rejection of the proposal to deploy Nike-Zeus during the Eisenhower administration is not the only background detail relating to the reexamination of defenses against ballistic missiles in the 1980s. On January 17, 1961, four days before turning over the presidency to John F. Kennedy, Eisenhower delivered a farewell message in which he issued a warning frequently recalled by contemporary opponents of ballistic missile defense. In such recollections special weight is often attached to Eisenhower's words because the president was a former five-star general--a fact noted by those who cite him to indicate that Eisenhower would not recklessly attack the United States military.

The retiring president stated that the United States had entered a period during which the presence of the Soviet threat required a massive military establishment to be maintained over an unprecedented length of time. He was therefore concerned about the possibility that during a long period the military might thirst for too much power, and that the corporate management which sells weapons to the military might exploit its opportunities for profits--all in a way that could subvert the legitimate ends of the national defense establishment. The most quoted passages from Eisenhower's warning refer to this potential for harm:

> This conjunction of an immense military establishment and a large arms industry is new in the American experience. The total influence--economic, political, even spiritual--is felt in every city, every state house, every office of the federal government. We recognize the imperative need for this development. Yet we must not fail to comprehend its grave implications. Our toil, resources, and livelihood are all involved; so is the very structure of our society.
>
> In the councils of government we must guard against the acquisition of unwarranted influence, whether sought or unsought, by

the military-industrial complex. The
potential for misplaced power exists and
will persist.
We must never let the weight of this
combination endanger our liberties or
democratic processes. We should take nothing
for granted. Only an alert and
knowledgeable citizenry can compel the
proper meshing of the huge industrial and
military machinery of defense with our
peaceful methods and goals, so that security
and liberty may prosper together.[5]

The Kennedy administration also decided against
the deployment of the Nike-Zeus ABM, on the basis
of much the same kind of reasoning as was
persuasive during the Eisenhower administration.
The transmission of the anti-ABM arguments to the
new president was accomplished by several
advisors. Particularly prominent, writes Kaplan,
was Jerome Wiesner, former chairman of
Eisenhower's Presidential Science Advisory
Committee, who became Kennedy's science advisor,
and Jack Ruina, formerly a member of the Reentry
Body Identification Group, who became the
director of the Pentagon's Advanced Research
Projects Agency in the Kennedy administration.[6]

Despite presidential rejection of ABM
deployment, research and development on ABM
technologies continued as a hedge against an
uncertain future. For example, Richard Foster,
formerly the director of the Strategic Studies
Center at the Stanford Research Institute, led
his staff for years in classified ABM studies for
the Army. The late Herman Kahn, the founder of
another think tank, the Hudson Institute, wrote
of coupling the mutual reduction of ballistic
missiles with ABM defenses and an extensive civil
defense program.[7] The latter was intended to
protect the population against the percentage of
warheads expected to penetrate the defenses.

Here and there in the defense community novel
ideas were discussed. One idea concerned the
spreading of foreign material in the path of
incoming warheads so that they would be destroyed
by the kinetic force of impact. Another, called
BAMBI, for Ballistic Missile Boost Intercept, was

a plan to destroy ICBMs as they rise from their launch sites, at a time when they are particularly vulnerable. This concept failed to warrant action because technology was not available at the time to permit the United States to attack ICBMs being fired from the Soviet Union. In 1967 a prominent writer on military affairs, J. S. Butz, suggested that it might be possible to detonate large nuclear explosions high above the earth, thereby inducing radiation belts around the globe that could prove lethal to ICBM warheads.[8] Another Hudson Institute researcher, the late Don Brennan, wrote in 1967 that consideration should be given to a mutual freeze on offensive strategic forces coupled with the open-ended construction of strategic defensive systems.[9]

Near U.S. Acceptance of ABMs

The vision of a defense against ballistic missile attack using ABMs has come close to realization three times during the past two decades. In the summer of 1967 Secretary of Defense Robert McNamara announced that the United States planned to deploy an improvement to the Nike-Zeus, called Nike-X. McNamara referred to the Nike-X as the Sentinal program and stated that its purpose was to provide protection to the nation against what was termed a "light attack." This term was used in reference to the possibility of an attack from an emerging nuclear power, such as the People's Republic of China. Fred Kaplan provided an interesting commentary on McNamara's position.[10] He wrote that the secretary of defense was opposed to the ABM, but that he was under considerable political pressure to take some kind of positive action on the Sentinal system. His solution to this dilemma was to announce an ABM deployment that could be easily criticized and was limited in scope.

In 1968 the Johnson administration was replaced by that of Richard M. Nixon. Early in 1969 the White House announced that the Sentinal system would be succeeded by a new program dubbed "Safeguard." Using the same Spartan and Sprint

ABMs, the Safeguard system differed from Sentinal only in its purpose. The Nixon administration wanted to deploy ABMs near ballistic missile sites such as the underground steel and concrete silos that house Minuteman ICBMs. Such "hard-point" sites are easier to defend against attack than are "soft" targets such as cities. The administration argued that defending ICBM silos was less disruptive to the stability of deterrence established in the MAD policy than defending cities would be. The first deployment of the Safeguard system was scheduled for the Minuteman missile fields at Grand Forks, North Dakota, and Malstrom, Montana.

Before Safeguard could become operational, President Nixon, assisted by his national security advisor, Henry A. Kissinger, had negotiated the Anti-Ballistic Missile Treaty with Soviet ruler Leonid Brezhnev. Treaty proponents believed that the concluding of the ABM agreement legitimized the doctrine of MAD, from both the U.S. and the Soviet points of view. A supporting concept was that by abandoning programs aimed at defending cities from nuclear attack, the United States and the USSR would remain equally vulnerable to nuclear destruction and would thus maintain the deterrence posture of MAD, not so much out of preference as out of necessity. Further, the ABM Treaty was seen as a means to prevent additional increases in both defensive and offensive arms deployments.

Under the terms of the 1972 ABM Treaty, and its 1976 Protocol, each nation could choose either to deploy the agreed limit of 100 ABMs around the national capital or to protect an ICBM field. The United States decided to deploy the limited Safeguard system at the Grand Forks site. By 1975 this deployment was ready, but the following year the Congress refused to fund the program for a number of reasons. These reasons were similar to those that had prevented ABMs from being deployed in the Eisenhower and Kennedy years; primary among them was the belief that the system would not work in the face of Soviet efforts to defeat it.

Eventually, the Grand Forks installation was dismantled. For their part the Soviets deployed approximately 64 ABMs (called Galosh missiles) in the vicinity of Moscow. The initial Galosh missile appeared similar to the U.S. Spartan.11

Changes in the ABM Debate

Roughly coincident with the nearly successful efforts to deploy an ABM system late in the 1960s and into the 1970s, a significant change occurred in the way the ABM subject was handled. The debate became public, and a contrasting view to that presented by the Department of Defense received prominent attention. In May 1968 Hans Bethe and Richard Garwin, men who had long been associated with the nation's nuclear weapons program, wrote an anti-ABM article for Scientific American.12 They explained to the public the arguments made in the late Eisenhower years regarding why an ABM would fail (i.e., owing to the vulnerability of radar to black-out) and the likelihood that the Soviets could defeat a defensive system by adopting a variety of countermeasures. Later that same year a group of senators from both political parties worked together in nearly defeating a funding request for the ABM. This group included such well-known members of the Senate as Mike Mansfield, John Sherman Cooper, Philip A. Hart, Gaylord Nelson, Clifford Case, Albert Gore, Jacob Javits, Charles Percy, Frank Church, Edward Kennedy, and Stuart Symington.

Early in 1969 Senator Kennedy asked Abram Chayes of the Harvard Law School and Jerome Wiesner, then provost of the Massachusetts Institute of Technology, to prepare a nongovernmental evaluation of the ABM system under consideration in the Nixon administration. Kennedy noted that previous decisions on major and expensive weapons systems had been made in the context of the Pentagon's perspective of the issue only--that is, in the absence of an alternative view. The Massachusetts Senator put it this way: "There is nothing sacrosanct about the recommendations of the Department of Defense. The Congress should put them to the same scrutiny it applies to all other government programs." 13

Kennedy appeared sensitive to criticisms that what he was preparing to do might be thought by some as being unpatriotic. He responded by writing:

> The suggestion is often made that it is unpatriotic to question recommendations of the Defense Department. This, of course, is folly. Our military men, who have led our armed forces with skill, imagination and courage down through the years, are trained how to wage war. But it is not their job-- nor is it within their competence--to weigh in the balance the diplomatic and domestic implications of deploying new strategic weapons systems.[14]

Seventeen scholars, scientists, and former government officials responded to Kennedy's call for the ABM evaluation. The general thrust of the resulting book, entitled ABM, was reminiscent of the earlier objections to the ABM during the Eisenhower years; it was also predictive of the objections to ballistic missile defense today. As Chayes and Wiesner, the book's editors, wrote:

> Our principal conclusion is that there is no need for a decision to deploy the Sentinal/Safeguard ABM system at this time. We believe that the system, even if considerably expanded and upgraded over the years following initial deployment, cannot perform effectively the missions suggested for it.[15]

In the same year nine national security scholars, all of whom were associated in some fashion with the Hudson Institute, published chapters in a book entitled Why ABM?, which is broadly supportive of the general ABM concept. Particularly relevant to the current evaluation of ballistic missile defense are the chapters by Herman Kahn, in which he advocates what was then called a Thin System; by Don Brennan, in which he advances the case in support of population defense; and by Albert Wohlstetter, in which he argues for exclusive defense of strategic nuclear offensive forces such as ICBMs.[16]

Many of the arguments in Why ABM? are similar
to those being made today by supporters of
President Reagan's Strategic Defense Initiative.
These arguments center on the need to take
prudent protective action in the face of both an
apparently hostile and unpredictable opponent
and the proliferation of nuclear weapons. It
was further argued in Why ABM? that a thin or
light ABM defense for the nation would prove
useful in case of a small and unsophisticated
attack by nations other than the Soviet Union.
Such a system was also touted as providing
effective defense from the effects of a small and
accidental launch by any nation. It was noted
that even a less than perfect ABM would
nevertheless cause problems and uncertainties for
Soviet planners that would thus augment
deterrence, and that if deterrence failed and a
nuclear attack occurred many civilians would be
saved. And, finally, it was argued that
protection of U.S. ICBM fields would be both
possible and supportive of deterrence by denying
the Soviets a first-strike disarming capability.
    Then, as now, the policy of MAD was viewed
critically. As Don Brennan wrote:

> It seems to me there is little doubt
> about which way the policy process in the
> U.S. ought to evolve in relation to BMD.
> The American body politic is unlikely to
> judge that pursuit of 'Assured
> Vulnerabililty' is a proper objective of
> the Department of Defense.[17]

Although it constituted a public precursor to
the ballistic missile defense arguments of the
mid-1980s, debate in the late 1960s differed in
two important respects from the current one.
Back then there was some emphasis given to
defending the United States from an attack by
China. This concern was grounded in the belief
that China was a rogue nation whose rulers might
view their enormous population as insurance
against the effects of nuclear retaliation.
Since the Chinese had only relatively primitive
offensive nuclear capabilities, the argument was

made that while an ABM might not be effective against a massive and sophisticated Soviet attack, it would successfully stop a Chinese one. After the political break between Peking and Moscow and the diplomatic efforts of President Nixon and Professor Kissinger to normalize U.S.-Chinese relations, however, the fear of a Chinese missile attack greatly receded.

The other difference between the previous debate and the 1980s argument concerns the consequences resulting from the evolution of technology during the intervening years. The exotic ballistic missile defense weapons currently being researched, such as lasers, particle beams, and electromagnetic rail guns, are further along toward possible development and, hence, figure prominently in ballistic missile defense discussions. In the mid-1960s, however, the primary mechanism for destroying an incoming warhead was another nuclear warhead carried by a defensive missile of relatively short range and relatively slow speed. In the future, should the exotic weapons prove feasible, ballistic missiles and their warheads may be attacked at the speed of light, immediately after they lift off from launching areas.

THE RESURGENCE OF BALLISTIC MISSILE DEFENSE

After the Congress withdrew support from the Grand Forks deployment, ABM advocates continued to promote the idea that an active ballistic defense was technically possible and strategically desirable. One of the most outspoken defense proponents was General George Keegan, a retired officer who had served as chief of Air Force Intelligence. Keegan toured the country, visiting universities and participating in forums, warning that the Soviets had not accepted the American perspective that in an era of one-warhead, one-city destroyed, MAD was preferable to the construction of ineffective ballistic missile defenses.

General Keegan charged that the Soviets were taking advantage of developments in many areas of technology, the most promising and potentially

dangerous being directed-energy beams, which
Keegan argued could serve as part of a Soviet
ballistic missile defense. As Keegan put it:

> High energy lasers and particle beam
> weapons--both pioneered by the Soviets--are
> the revolutionary new tools of space
> warfare. They will neutralize America's
> strategic deterrent and invalidate most
> of the free world's conventional land, sea,
> air and logistic forces as currently
> structured and deployed.[18]

In 1976 an organization called the Committee on
the Present Danger was formed. Among its members
were former high-ranking government officials
such as David Packard, Eugene V. Rostow, and Paul
Nitze. They were joined by Harvard professor
Richard Pipes; the director of the national
security program at the University of Southern
California, William Van Cleave; and retired
Admiral William R. Zumwalt, Jr. These prominent
figures, and others who constituted the 141-
member group, reflected much of the conservative
thinking that would become associated with the
Reagan presidency in the 1980s. In 1978 the
Committee on the Present Danger charged that the
Soviets had rejected MAD as a basis for a
relationship with the United States. Moscow, it
was alleged, had signed the ABM Treaty merely to
stall the more advanced U.S. ABM program, so that
the Soviets could catch up and prepare to surpass
the United States. The Committee warned:

> There is a significant risk that at some
> time in the future the Soviets will believe
> their ABM technology has reached a point at
> which it might be useful for them to
> "break out" of the Treaty by deploying ABM
> radars and missiles (including perhaps the
> upgrading of new, high-technology air
> defense missiles to an ABM capability)
> so rapidly that the United States would not
> be able to match their move.[19]

As the 1970s merged into the 1980s, another retired military officer, Army Lt. General Daniel O. Graham, who had served as director of the Defense Intelligence Agency, advanced the proposition that technology had reached the point where the United States was able to build non-nuclear defenses against ballistic missile attack. Graham cited developments in kinetic kill technologies and in the fields of lasers and particle-beam weapons, which could be incorporated into an active space-based defense. To further promote his ideas, Graham founded High Frontier, Inc., a private organization. The main thrust of the organization's conceptualization can be found in a book written by Graham, We Must Defend America--and Put an End to MADness. [20]

Others questioned the validity of MAD and suggested a search for alternatives. Among them was the physicist Edward Teller, a man who could trace his national security contributions back to the atomic bomb project during World War II. Consistently suspicious of Soviet motives and always urging greater vigor in U.S. responses to the Soviet threat, Teller suggested that new advances in physics might provide the extraordinary amounts of energy necessary for a ballistic defense system.

ENDORSEMENT OF STRATEGIC DEFENSE AGAINST BALLISTIC MISSILES

The vision of a defense against ballistic missile attack received an enormous boost on the evening of March 23, 1983, when President Reagan addressed a national television audience on "Defense Spending and Defensive Technology." The address was dubbed the "Star Wars speech" by the media.

The president stated his preference for replacing the policy of mutual assured destruction with the capability to physically defend the United States from ballistic missile attack. Put another way, President Reagan called for a renewed effort directed toward defense of the nation by killing missiles and nuclear warheads rather than by threatening to kill human beings.

In apparent anticipation of the major arguments to be raised against his proposal, the president stated:

> I clearly recognize that defensive systems have limitations and raise certain problems and ambiguities. If paired with offensive systems, they can be viewed as fostering an aggressive policy, and no one wants that. But with these considerations firmly in mind, I call upon the scientific community in our country, those who gave us nuclear weapons, to turn their great talents now to the cause of mankind and world peace, to give us the means of rendering these nuclear weapons impotent and obsolete.[21]

President Reagan held out no hope for easy or early realization of his vision, stating in the same speech:

> I know this is a formidable technical task, one that may not be accomplished before the end of the century. Yet, current technology has attained a level of sophistication where it's reasonable for us to begin this effort. It will take years, probably decades of effort on many fronts. There will be failures and setbacks, just as there will be successes and breakthroughs. And as we proceed, we must remain constant in preserving the nuclear deterrent and maintaining a solid capability for flexible response. But isn't it worth every investment necessary to free the world from the threat of nuclear war? We know it is.[22]

Near the end of his speech President Reagan told his audience:

> I am directing a comprehensive and intensive effort to define a long-term research and development program to begin to achieve our ultimate goal of eliminating the threat poised by strategic nuclear weapons.[23]

Then the president concluded his speech with
the words:

> My fellow Americans, tonight we're
> launching an effort which holds the
> promise of changing the course of human
> history. There will be risks, and
> results take time. But I believe we can
> do it. As we cross this threshold, I ask
> for your prayers and your support. Thank
> you, good night, and God bless you.[24]

It should be noted that the president did not
specifically include the nuclear weapon delivery
systems called "air-breathers" in his category of
weapons that might be rendered "impotent and
obsolete" by his Strategic Defense Initiative.
Air-breathers are vehicles such as cruise
missiles and bombers that operate in the
atmosphere, at times only a few tens of feet
above the earth's surface. As Defense Secretary
Caspar Weinberger stated in 1985, however,
defenses against air-breathers would have to be
improved to complement the defenses being
contemplated against ballistic missiles. Nor did
the president describe in his speech how the
United States might defend itself against the
various weapons that could be introduced into the
nation clandestinely, such as "suitcase A-bombs"
and nuclear weapons hidden aboard ships, trucks,
and planes.

In the months following the president's speech,
many of the nation's scientists, some of whom had
worked on the World War II atomic bomb project,
not only refused to answer the president's call
to assist in researching the possibilities of his
proposal, but actively lobbied against the
president. One of the most prominent opponents
was Hans Bethe, the Nobel Laureate in physics who
wrote against the ABM concept in 1968.

Beyond individual opponents, the president's
proposal has sparked opposition from
organizations composed mainly of scientists such
as the Federation of American Scientists, which
is headed by an early-day associate of Herman
Kahn--namely, the mathematician named Jeremy
Stone; and the Union of Concerned Scientists,

whose board of directors is chaired by Henry W. Kendall, professor of physics, at the Massachusetts Institute of Technology.

Persons not belonging to these organizations also began writing in opposition to the Strategic Defense Initiative, or what the Pentagon calls the SDI and what opponents came to call, with a note of derision, Star Wars. Others, many of whom had previously supported the general idea of defense against ballistic missile attack, now joined the president in advocating the SDI.

The debate triggered by President Reagan is, for better or worse, quite different from the discussions and analyses that preceded the development of the atomic bomb. The latter decision was made by only a few men within the government, without the benefit of a prolonged and informed public examination of the issue. By contrast, in the three years since President Reagan's speech, the SDI has been the subject of extensive discussion both within and outside the government. The extent of this public debate is indicated by the bibliography contained in this volume.

NOTES

1. Bernard Brodie, ed., The Absolute Weapon, New York, Harcourt, Brace, 1946.

2. Ibid., p. 76.

3. Caspar Weinberger, Annual Report to the Congress, Washington D.C.: Government Printing Office, February 1, 1983, p. 5; and The Challenge of Peace: God's Promise and Our Response, Publication No. 863, Washington, D.C.: United States Catholic Conference, May 3, 1983, p.56.

4. Fred Kaplan, The Wizards of Armageddon, New York: Simon and Schuster, 1983. See particularly Chapter 24, "The ABM Debate."

5. U.S. Office of the Federal Register, Public Papers of the Presidents, Dwight D. Eisenhower, 1960-61, Washington, D.C.: Government Printing Office, 1961, p. 1038.

6. Kaplan, p. 345.

7. Paul R. Williamson, ed., On a New Arms Control Strategy, Harmon-on-Hudson, N.Y.: Hudson Institute, 1966.

8. J. S. Butz, Jr., "The Myth of Technological Stalemate," Air Force and Space Digest, March 1967, p. 50.

9. Donald D. Brennan, "New Thoughts on Missile Defense," Bulletin of the Atomic Scientists, July 23, 1967, pp. 10-15.

10. Kaplan, pp. 346-348.

11. U.S. Department of Defense, Soviet Military Power, Washington, D.C.: Government Printing Office, 1984, pp. 67-68.

12. Richard L. Garwin and Hans A. Bethe, "Anti-Ballistic-Missile Systems," Scientific American, March 1968, pp. 21-31.

13.   Abram Chayes and Jerome Wiesner, eds., ABM, New York: Harper and Row, 1969, p. xiv.

14.   Ibid.

15.   Ibid. p. xi.

16.   Johan J. Holst and Willaim Schneider, Jr., eds., Why ABM?, New York: Pergamon Press, 1969. See particularly Chapter 4: Herman Kahn, "The Case for a Thin System"; Chapter 5: Donald Brennan, "The Case for Population Defense"; and Chapter 6: Albert Wohlstetter, "The Case for Strategic Defense."

17.   Holst and Schneider, p. 17.

18.   David Baker, The Shape of Wars to Come, Cambridge, England: Patrick Stephens, 1981. In particular, see the Foreword by George F. Keegan, Jr., p. 6.

19.   Eugene V. Rostow, et al; Is America Becoming Number 2?,   Washington, D.C.: Committee on the Present Danger, October 5, 1978, p. 16.

20.   Daniel O. Graham, We Must Defend America-- and Put an End to MADness, Chicago: Regnery Gateway, 1983.

21.   U.S. Department of State, Department of State Bulletin 83, (April 1983), pp. 13-14.

22.   Department of State Bulletin, pp. 13-14.

23.   Department of State Bulletin, pp. 13-14.

24.   Department of State Bulletin, pp. 13-14.

2

Technical Background

This essay was written to acquaint the reader with the general technical context within which a defense against ballistic missile attack would probably occur, and with the technologies that might constitute the several layers of defense currently being studied by the Strategic Defense Initiative Organization within the Department of Defense. Thus prepared, the layperson should be able to make more informed judgments regarding the arguments for, and against, the Strategic Defense Initiative that are summarized in Chapters 3 and 4.

The literature that supplies background information on the technical context of strategic defense may be categorized into three main subject headings: (1) the ballistic trajectory that would be followed by an ICBM and its payload launched from a site in the Soviet Union against a target in the United States; (2) the technologies that might be employed by the United States to defend itself against a ballistic missile attack; and (3) the electronic network designed to alert U.S. forces to an attack and then to coordinate the defensive efforts involved.

Broad coverage of the technical background to the Strategic Defense Initiative can be found in a number of sources. A basic study produced in 1985 by the Office of Technology Assessment, a research arm of the Congress, is <u>Ballistic</u>

Missile Defense Technologies. This volume was
combined with a study of anti-satellite weapons,
issued in 1986 by the Princeton University Press
under the title Strategic Defenses. In the
spring of 1985 the New York Times published a
series of six articles entitled "Weapons in
Space--The Controversy over 'Star Wars.'" A
follow-up series appeared late in the year
containing three additional articles, again
called "Weapons in Space." One of the New York
Times reporters, William Broad, also wrote Star
Warriors in 1985. Broad examines portions of the
SDI through interviews with researchers at the
Lawrence Livermore National Laboratory. The
Christian Science Monitor published six articles
in the fall of 1985 entitled "Star Wars Will It
Work?". The September 1985 issue of Discover
carried a special section on the SDI: Fredrick
Golden, "Star Wars: The Research Heats Up," and
Meredith Hamilton and Michael Killian,
"Battleground in the Heavens." The September
1985 issue of IEEE Spectrum also contained a
lengthy examination of the subject: "Star Wars--
SDI: The Grand Experiment," by John Adam and
Mark A. Fischetti. Representative of college
textbooks that have begun to introduce undergrad-
uates to the subject of strategic defense is
Science, Technology, and the Nuclear Arms Race,
by Dietrich Schroeer. The Wizards of Armageddon,
by Fred Kaplan provides a historical analysis of
the nuclear era by focusing upon the
personalities involved in U.S. nuclear
development; it also includes a chapter on the
early ABM debates, part of which were technical
in character.

THE TRAJECTORY OF A BALLISTIC MISSILE
AND ITS PAYLOAD

In order for a nuclear warhead launched from
the Soviet Union to hit the United States, a
number of sequential events must occur within
approximately thirty minutes. Thus a half-hour
is the time frame within which U.S. strategic
defenses would be required to recognize that a
ballistic missile attack had been launched and to

respond effectively to it. For purposes of understanding and analysis, the thirty-minute flight time is divided into four segments, or phases.

Phase One

The first phase of the flight trajectory is called the boost phase. The boost phase of the Soviet ICBMs currently deployed lasts for approximately five minutes. During this time a three-stage ballistic missile (carrying in its nose cone a much smaller post-launch vehicle called a bus, which in turn carries a number of decoys as well as warheads that are individually targeted) is launched by a first stage rocket booster. The initial booster soon exhausts its fuel; then a second stage booster is ignited, followed by a third. When the rocket engines burn out they separate from the bus, which continues along the trajectory, and the boost phase has been completed. As noted in Chapter 3, the boost phase of an ICBM's flight trajectory looms large in contemporary SDI plans to fashion an effective defense because a missile is particularly vulnerable during this phase.

Phase Two

The second phase of the flight trajectory begins when the third stage engine and fuel tank separate, propelling the bus onward into space. The bus contains nuclear warheads and various defense penetration aids, such as dummy warheads and other kinds of decoys meant to confuse SDI defenses. The bus is steered by small jets as it dispenses the warheads and penetration aids. This phase lasts for about five minutes and represents the last opportunity for the defense to destroy more than one warhead with a single hit.

Phase Three

The third phase of the flight trajectory is called the midcourse phase. Warheads and decoys that survive the boost and the post-boost defenses will spend nearly twenty minutes traveling through space in the midcourse phase of their flight. In the jargon of ballistic missile defense, objects that pass through one defensive layer into the next are said to have leaked into the next defensive zone; hence the process is known as leakage.

Phase Four

The fourth and final segment of the flight trajectory is called the terminal phase. Depending upon the point at which one defines the beginning of this phase, it lasts for from one to several minutes. In this phase warheads and decoys slam into the atmosphere, and several events occur within a relatively short space of time. The decoys are destroyed by the reentry forces. The warheads continue toward their targets unescorted and emit detectable infrared radiation caused by the heat resulting by the friction of reentry.

COMPARATIVE ANALYSES OF SDI TECHNOLOGIES

Much of the case made in favor of the Strategic Defense Initiative is based upon optimistic expectations that new weapons technologies, frequently called exotic technologies, will be developed and integrated into a comprehensive defense system. In fact, a substantial portion of the current SDI research effort is directed at answering President Reagan's question: Can such technologies be utilized for the SDI? Those opposing the SDI have made various criticisms of the exotic technologies, and much of their case rests upon pessimistic assumptions about the technologies.

Kinetic Kill Vehicles

Kinetic kill technology achieves its destructive capacity by direct-impact collision between a projectile and its target, such as an enemy warhead. There is thus no need for kinetic kill weapons to employ an explosive warhead. When the projectile collides with its target the force of the collision shatters the warhead.

One kinetic kill technology under investigation is the electromagnetic railgun. This device would use large amounts of electricity to produce electromagnetic forces that, like the chemical explosion in an artillery piece, would hurl projectiles forward. SDI enthusiasts have suggested that railguns can be made that will fire projectiles at ten to twelve miles per second.

After leaving the railgun, the projectiles must then hit a target that may be many miles away and traveling at a high rate of speed. Proponents of SDI hope to solve targeting problems by equipping the railgun projectile with some type of guidance system, possibly a heat--seeking capability. If perfected, this kind of projectile could live up to its nickname, "smart rocks."

A second type of kinetic energy kill vehicle was successfully demonstrated by the United States in June 1984. Termed the "Homing Overlay Experiment," or HOE, the test involved a modified ICBM fired from the Kwajalein Missile Test Range in the far Pacific and a dummy warhead fired from California. The defensive ICBM lofted a second interceptor missile above the atmosphere, where it separated from the booster rocket. The interceptor missile then used heat sensors and an onboard computer to locate and track the target. Just before impact, the interceptor missile unfurled a netlike apparatus to widen its destructive radius. Both the intercepting missile and the dummy warhead were destroyed by the subsequent collision.

Rockets carried aboard satellites would also constitute kinetic kill vehicles, in that they could be fired at Soviet ballistic missiles rising from their launching areas during the boost phase, or subsequently at the bus.

The swarmjet is another example of a potential kinetic kill vehicle. In this concept, a large number of small rockets are fired from the ground in the direction of an incoming warhead, when the warhead is close to the target being defended. Because the projected intercept point is close to the ground, the accompanying decoys would have burned up because of friction within the atmosphere as they reenter, leaving the warheads more easily detected.

Lasers

It is generally agreed that some of the kinetic kill technologies, such as the one demonstrated in the HOE test, are among the SDI weapon possibilities closest to deployment. It is also generally agreed that next in line, in terms of research and development, are a family of kill mechanisms called lasers. The acronym stands for Light Amplification by Simulated Emission of Radiation.

A laser is a device that produces a coherent beam of electromagnetic radiation in either the infrared, visible, ultraviolet, or x-ray regions of the electromagnetic spectrum. A laser beam travels at the speed of light, which is 186,000 miles per second. If a laser beam dwells for a long enough time on a surface, it can burn a hole in the object. Or if the laser energy is "pulsed," it may push a shock wave through the target, much like hitting it with a heavy object.

There are several types of lasers that could have SDI applications. The chemical laser obtains its energy from the chemical interaction of gases. The free-electron laser uses a large particle accelerator to generate electrons which in turn are then passed through a magnetic field and emitted as ultraviolet light. An excimer laser uses rare gases in addition to chlorine or fluorine to produce a laser beam.

Because of weight considerations and energy requirements, some laser weapons, such as the free-electron laser and the excimer laser, would probably have to be ground-based. As their beams cannot be bent around the curvature of the earth to focus upon ICBMs rising from the Soviet Union, novel techniques for using these lasers are needed. One solution under investigation is to direct the beams from lasers based in Alaska toward high-altitude satellites carrying mirrors, which, in turn, would relay the beams to aiming mirrors on other satellites over the Soviet Union. These would focus the beams upon the ICBMs in the boost phase. Other lasers might be carried by satellites and aimed directly at their targets from space.

The nuclear-pumped x-ray laser is another type of potential SDI weapon that, through a combination of technologies, is intended to avoid the possible problems associated with lasers requiring mirror satellites or lasers carried on board satellites, both of which can be shot down or disabled by the Soviets. A vehicle containing a thermonuclear bomb is fired aloft, or poped-up, when warning satellites detect the launch of Soviet ICBMs. Once the vehicle has cleared the atmosphere that it must do in order for an x-ray laser beam to operate effectively, and once it has risen above the curvature of the earth to permit line-of-sight propagation of the beam to its target, a nuclear explosion occurs. The energy thus produced is emitted by lasing rods in the form of x-ray laser beams before the device is destroyed by the explosion.

It is generally agreed that the nuclear-pumped x-ray laser vehicles would be utilized from one of two types of deployment locations. They would be shot aloft either from bases in allied nations, if such nations would accept them, or from U.S. submarines in the Indian Ocean and other locations near the Soviet Union.

Particle Beams

Least understood of the new SDI technologies is the particle beam. This potential weapon relies on tiny particles of matter fired at close to the speed of light by a particle accelerator. The most likely candidate for weapons application at this time is the neutral particle beam composed of hydrogen atoms. Such a beam would not be bent by the earth's magnetic field, as is the case with the other particle beams. It would have to be used above the atmosphere because passage through the atmosphere would convert the beam to charged particles that would be subject to magnetic bending. Thus, like the nuclear-pumped x-ray laser, the neutral particle beam is limited to use in space--a place in which Soviet warheads and decoys enjoy substantial advantages.

Unlike the typical laser, which deposits energy on the surface of a target, a neutral particle beam penetrates the target vehicle and interferes with the internal electronics. It is in this context that a neutral particle beam is said to render a warhead "stupid."

Ultra-Advanced Concepts

In U.S. national weapons laboratories, even more advanced concepts are being studied. Two that appear a very long way from being transformed into weapons are gamma-ray lasers and "plasmoids". The former, possibly more lethal than x-ray lasers, would be produced by a nuclear explosion. A plasmoid defense would involve hurling clouds of energized atomic nuclei and electrons into the path of incoming warheads. There is also the concept of laser/charged particle beam which calls for a laser to ionize a channel in the atmosphere along which a charged particle beam could travel to its target. In this way the beam would be protected from the interference it would otherwise encounter from passing through the atmosphere. Finally there is the Advanced Test Accelerator research. At the Lawrence Livermore Laboratory scientists have been able to create a kind of synthetic lighting from pulses of electrons, a procedure that may have a weapons capability.

Nuclear-Armed ABMs

Should the SDI weapon technologies prove ineffective, and/or if the nation is willing to abandon the generally nonnuclear characteristics of SDI technologies, the United States could return to the ABM technology of the late 1960s. The Office of Technology Assessment describes such technology as mature and states that ABMs equipped with nuclear warheads could be deployed relatively soon. These weapons would be capable of being fired at Soviet warheads that were in the terminal phase, and of destroying some of them with nuclear explosions.

Underground Nuclear Detonations

If national policy did revert to permitting nuclear defensive systems, there is another potential weapon that would at least protect hard-site targets such as U.S. ICBM silos. This system would involve radars identifying warheads in the terminal phase that threaten particular silos. Just before the warhead passes overhead on its way to a silo, nuclear explosives buried underground north of the silo would be detonated. The column of earth blown upward by the explosion would then destroy the warhead as it passed through the dust and debris, through kinetic impact.

BATTLE MANAGEMENT OF THE SDI

Given the enormous amount of complex data that must be handled within a time frame calculated in minutes, human minds are woefully inadequate for the direct, and real-time, battle management of any SDI system. Therefore, computers, and the software by which they are programmed, are expected to play a central role in all SDI efforts. Two cryptic terms are used in reference to the battle management task facing an SDI: C^3I and SATKA. The former refers to the command, control, communications, and intelligence network that is designed to electronically orchestrate the entire SDI battle from the first moments after warning of an attack is received, to the point at which the final battle assessment is completed. SATKA refers to a set of interconnected functions performed by space and

ground-based computers, as well as associated
sensors, which are necessary for a successful SDI
response to a Soviet missile attack.

The S in SATKA stands for the constant
surveillance of Soviet ICBM fields by early
warning satellites in geosynchronous orbit. Such
orbits, at approximately 22,300 miles in
altitude, synchronize the satellite's orbit with
the rotation of the earth so that the former
appears to remain in the same place in relation
to a point on the earth's surface. The
geosynchronous satellites would be designed to
provide nearly instantaneous warning of a missile
launch by detection of the infrared emissions
from the ICBM rocket engines.

The A in SATKA stands for the acquisition by
radars of the potential targets that have been
identified by the early warning satellites. The
T stands for the tracking of targets as they move
through the four phases of the ballistic missile
flight path. The KA stands for the kill
assessment that determines which warheads have
been destroyed or rendered inoperative. The kill
assessment is a continuing process conducted as
the battle moves from one phase of the ballistic
trajectory to the next one.

A fully developed SDI envisions at least four,
possibly more, layers of defense through which
the Soviet attack must penetrate. Thus it will
be necessary for SATKA data to be "handed over"
from one layer of defense to the next so that
defensive fire may be continued throughout the
entire ballistic flight path.

Although the exact architecture of the C^3I and
SATKA structures is not entirely clear at this
time, a general outline has been presented in the
background literature on the SDI. This outline
suggests that the primary components would
include the following: (1) Early warning
satellites in geosynchronous orbit would be
designed to hover over the equator, where their
sensors would be directed at the Soviet ICBM
fields to the north. These might be augmented by
satellites in elliptical orbits, thus permitting
them to dip down over the Soviet Union from as
far up as 24,000 miles to as low as fewer than
500 miles. Satellites in low earth orbits that

pass directly over the Soviet Union at several hundred miles in altitude could also be utilized. (2) Space and ground-based computers whose purpose is to review stored information regarding optional responses to attack would be designed to direct the defensive fire against the ICBMs and their payloads. (3) As the battle moves into the terminal phase of the ballistic missile flight path, aircraft flying near or above the United States would contribute radar, infrared sensors, and on-board computers to the final effort to intercept and destroy the surviving warheads. The aircraft capabilities would be complemented by ground-based radars.

It is expected that the computer complex having centralized authority over an SDI battle will be based at the Consolidated Space Operations Center in Colorado Springs, Colorado. Suitable backup facilities located elsewhere will provide redundant capacity in case the primary computer center is attacked or malfunctions.

SUMMARY

The background literature about the SDI suggests the existence of several observations that would have widespread, though not unanimous support. Not necessarily in order of importance, these observations follow: (1) The effort to build the SDI will be a technical task of unprecedented proportions. Whether it can be accomplished or not has yet to be determined. (2) The SDI technology closest to deployment is based upon the ABM development of the 1960s and 1970s. Potentially the most successful example of that technology would be ABMs which carry nuclear warheads. (3) The most difficult of the many SDI tasks may be building a battle management system that can operate effectively in a short period of time, as well as handle enormous amounts of data, in an environment made hostile by Soviet actions.

ABSTRACTS

1. Adam, John A., and Mark A. Fischetti. 1985. Star Wars--SDI: the grand experiment. IEEE Spectrum, 22 September, 33-64.

This comprehensive article, written by a team led by the cited authors, has as its focus the battle management of strategic defense, the exotic weapons technologies being proposed for the SDI, and a comparison of the arguments for and against the SDI. It is illustrated with artists' conceptions of what various components of the SDI would look like in battle, and with several charts that assist the reader in understanding (1) the technologies under investigation in terms of their strengths and weaknesses, (2) the defensive weapons and the Soviet countermeasures, and (3) the more generalized arguments in favor of the SDI together with those in opposition. Considerable explanation of the technical background is provided for each of the basic weapons technologies found in the contemporary SDI program of research.

2. Broad, William J. 1985. Star Warriors. New York: Simon and Schuster.

Broad weaves together a history of the Lawrence Livermore National Laboratory, strategic defense technology, and vivid portraits of young Star Wars weapons designers. He describes the recruitment and retention of promising young scientists by Lowell Wood, a protege of Edward Teller. Wood directs the Lawrence Livermore "O-Group", and helps to select the recipients of fellowship funds for the conservative Hertz Foundation which supports graduate students in the applied sciences who accept the requirement that they "morally commit themselves to make their skills and abilities available for the common defense, in the event of national emergency" (p. 29).

Broad examines the political and personal motivations of Wood and the physicists and computer scientists working on "third generation" nuclear weapons such as the x-ray laser. Mingled among accounts of his week-long visit with the O-Group personnel are Broad's explanation of SDI weaponry and arguments for and against the president's proposal.

The author records an interview with Edward Teller. The nuclear physicist is reported as being concerned that many more Soviet scientists are working on the Soviet version of the SDI than are working on the American SDI. Broad concludes with the observation that the enthusiasm of Wood's group stems from a combination of patriotism, defense ideology, and a desire to work with the big physics machines at Lawrence Livermore on the forefront of science.

3.   Dietrich, Schroeer. 1984. Science, technology, and the nuclear arms race. New York: John Wiley and Sons.

The referenced chapter in this textbook is a good example of how ballistic missile defense (BMD) issues can be related to the more comprehensive whole of national security studies. It will be particularly useful in the growing number of national security courses being offered at the college and university levels. The author has two primary objectives. First he relates the history of the Safeguard ABM during the Nixon administration to illustrate the pro and con arguments for ABMs in general. Then he explains the basic principles involved in directed-energy weapons for students not versed in advanced technology.

4.   Golden, Frederic. 1985. Star Wars: the research heats up. Discover, September, 28-40.

This is a spritely written, even humorous, highly generalized account of where the SDI program stands circa 1985. It is sprinkled with quotations from scientists working on various

aspects of laser and particle-beam research.
These quotations make the point that although the
scientists are enthusiastic about the task before
them, they do not underestimate the extraordinary
difficulty of the technical feats they have been
asked to examine. Included in the article are
colored photographs of the giant devices at such
national laboratories as Lawrence Livermore,
Sandia, and Los Alamos to illustrate the hardware
currently in use for SDI research. The author
writes in an even-handed fashion, balancing
points made by SDI proponents with counterpoints
by opponents. As if to remind readers that the
Gee Whiz, Buck Rogers photographs and weapons
proposals are still far from reality, the author
concludes with cautionary statements by senior
officials close to the SDI program. Lt. General
James A. Abrahamson, director of the SDI
organization, is quoted to the effect that the
program is now solely research oriented, designed
to "answer the fundamental scientific and
engineering questions." The famous two questions
that Paul Nitze, senior arms control advisor to
the president, says must be answered before SDI
proceeds to actual development are noted: Will
the defensive program be invulnerable to Soviet
attack? And if the Soviets improve their
offensive forces, can SDI adequately respond for
less than it costs the Soviets?

5. Grier, Peter, and Scott Armstrong. 1985.
Star Wars: will it work? Christian
Science Monitor issues dated November 4, 5,
6, 7, 8, and 12.

In this six-article series, the authors
sequentially set forth some of the early history
of ballistic missile defense, then methodically
examine in balanced fashion the 6 categories of
the SDI debate suggested by the issue titles:
Race for the High Ground; Canons in Space;
Battling with Beams; The Challenge of Mission
Control; The Soviet Strategy; and The Politics of
Space. The series is well illustrated with black
and white graphics of the four phases of a
ballistic missile flight path and with

illustrations meant to convey to the reader some
appreciation of how various weapons would be used
in the layered defense concept of SDI. The six
articles are peppered with quotes from proponents
and opponents as well as from scientists making
observations on technical facets of the SDI
issue. Many of the most common arguments for and
against SDI are set forth in chart form for ready
assimilation.

6.   Hamilton, Meredith, Michael Killian, Joe
      Lertola, and Robert McCall. 1985.
      Battleground in the heavens. Discover,
      September, 43-62.

In this article the major SDI weapons being
proposed--including excimer and free-electron
lasers, neutral particle beams, pop-up x-ray
lasers, chemical lasers, electromagnetic
railguns, and other kinetic kill vehicles--are
portrayed in full-page, colored artists'
renditions, together with brief descriptions of
the weapons and some of their technical
liabilities. The four phases of a ballistic
missile's flight from the Soviet Union to the
United States are also portrayed. Unfortunately,
the likely Soviet countermeasures are neither
depicted visually nor described verbally. This
portion of the article is followed by short
essays written by Edward Teller, in support of
strategic defense as a replacement for MAD, and
by Carl Sagan, who argues for better politics and
less technology.

7.   Kaplan, Fred. 1983. The wizards of
      Armageddon, New York: Simon and Schuster.

This book focuses on the members of the U.S.
scientific and strategic elite who have shaped
the nuclear weapons policies. Chapter 24
provides technical and political background to
the SDI debate taken from the days of the first
ABM debates. Kaplan describes the role of PSAC
(the President's Scientific Advisory Council) and
that of other scientific advisors in the
administrations of Eisenhower, Kennedy, and

Johnson; he also discusses the preponderance of technical advice given to those chief executives--advice that was negative regarding the Nike Zeus and Nike-X ABM systems. The general arguments in the 1960s and 1970s against the ABM defense were that the efforts to protect population would probably fail, owing to both the immense destructiveness of nuclear weapons and the countermeasures that the Soviets would likely adopt.

An interesting account is given of the political pressures on Secretary of Defense Robert McNamara that resulted in his announcement of the first U.S. ABM deployment decision, in his San Francisco speech of September 18, 1967, when he justified a light ABM deployment on the basis of a purported missile threat from Red China. According to Kaplan, McNamara was resisting an ABM program by casting it in a context he believed to be intellectually unsupportable on the grounds that no realistic Chinese ballistic threat existed. Kaplan recalls for the reader that the two scientists who first spoke out publicly against ABM in 1968 are the same as the two current leading opponents of SDI, Hans Bethe and Richard Garwin. Kaplan credits their May 1968 article in Scientific American, "Anti-Ballistic-Missile Systems," with helping to move the ABM debate out of government confines and into the unclassified public area. He chronicles the formation of a successful effort by senators of both parties to seek scientific advice on the ABM. Such senators as John Sherman Cooper, Philip Hart, Edward Kennedy, William Fulbright, Albert Gore, Jacob Javits, Charles Percy, Mike Mansfield, George McGovern, Frank Church, Mark Hatfield, and Stuart Symington contacted equally prominent scientists for their views, which were generally negative on ABM. The scientists included Bethe, Garwin, Jerome Wiesner, Sidney Drell, Wolfgang Panofsky, Paul Doty, Jack Ruina, George Rathjens, James Killian, and George Kistiakowsky. Kaplan extends his account of the ABM debate back to the Nixon administration, to the decision to change the name of United States' ABM system from Sentinel to Safeguard, and to the decision to deploy the ABMs of the former

system around hard silos of an ICBM field near
Grand Forks, North Dakota--a change in policy the
ABM opponents found more difficult to argue
against on technical grounds.

8.   "Weapons in space--The controversy over
      Star Wars," New York Times issues dated
      March 3, 1985: Leslie H. Gelb, "Vision of
      space defense posing new challenges"; March
      4, 1985: William J. Broad, "Reagan's Star
      Wars bid: many ideas converging"; March 5,
      1985: Wayne Biddle, "Star Wars technology:
      it's more than a fantasy"; March 6, 1985:
      Charles Mohr, "What Moscow might do in
      replying to Star Wars"; March 7, 1985:
      Philip M. Boffey, "Dark side of Star Wars:
      system could also attack"; March 8, 1985:
      Philip M. Boffey, "Star Wars and mankind:
      consequences for the future."

These six articles cover the basic technology
of the SDI proposal with appropriate photographs
and graphics depicting the technological
processes involved. Two particularly interesting
articles are those by William J. Broad and Philip
M. Boffey. In the article of March 4, the author
sets forth the linkage of thoughts, persons, and
events that influenced President Reagan prior to
his Star Wars speech of March 23, 1983. In the
March 7 article, the author explores the
possibilities of using some of the SDI weapons
technologies for strategic offensive purposes,
the most impressive of which would be in support
of a U.S. first strike on Soviet strategic
forces.

9.   Weapons in space, New York Times issues
      dated December 5, 1985: Leslie H. Gelb,
      "Star Wars advances: the plan vs. the
      reality"; December 16, 1985 William J.
      Broad, "Science showmanship: a deep Star
      Wars rift"; and December 17, 1985: Charles
      Mohr, "Star Wars in strategy: the Russian
      response."

These three articles were written as follow-up
pieces to the six articles published in March
1985 (discussed in item 8 above). Using their

access to high administration officials, some of
whom are named and some who remain anonymous, the
Times reporters analyze the arguments over SDI
within the administration, and between the
administration and Star Wars critics circa late
1985. Gelb writes that the arguments over using
the SDI to defend people or missiles, and the
criteria for making judgments about SDI prospects
and arms control, "have reached a kind of
equilibrium. Neither side prevails. The result
is that the established policy and the programs
chug right along, more slowly than if there were
unity, but forward nonetheless." In his article
Broad reports that there is concern, even among
some government scientists, that the selling of
SDI is relying on "exaggerated assertions,
hyperbolic tests and costly public-relations
razzle dazzle." Several tests ballyhooed by SDI
officials are described in less than sensational
terms in the article. Broad notes that in one
case researchers became so upset with exaggerated
reports of an SDI test that they broke security
laws to give a different interpretation of the
demonstration. Mohr chronicles the efforts
within and outside government to assess both the
most likely Soviet response to an SDI deployment
and the real military value of SDI to the United
States. On the first point he reports general
agreement that the Soviets will probably deploy
more offensive missiles equipped with
countermeasures, in addition to an enlarged but
traditional ABM deployment, and that they will
possibly break the ABM Treaty. Mohr also writes
that there is substantial thinking within the
administration that even a leaky SDI will be
useful in enhancing deterrence by creating
greater uncertainty in the minds of Soviet
strategic planners regarding the effectiveness of
a first strike.

10.   U.S. Office of Technology Assessment. 1985.
      Ballistic Missile Defense Technologies.
      Washington, D.C.:   U.S. Government Printing
      Office, September.

It should be explained initially that the
Office of Technology Assessment (OTA) was created
in 1972 as an independent and analytical arm of

the Congress. The OTA's basic responsibility is to assist legislators in analyzing the many ways in which technology may impact upon society. In this volume the OTA has provided by far the most extensive analysis of BMD technical parameters yet to appear in the unclassified literature. In addition to a comprehensive study and evaluation of BMD technologies, this OTA document contains a quantity of useful information in the appendix, such as the texts of the 1972 ABM Treaty and 1976 Protocol; data regarding the interfaces between BMD and existing arms control treaties; a list of Reagan administration statements on BMD together with excerpts from administration officials; excerpts from Soviet statements on BMD; and a glossary of acronyms and terms.

Four chapters providing background information precede a technical chapter on ballistic missile defense technologies, feasibility studies, alternative BMD future scenarios, and alternative research and development programs. Also featured are a 34-page executive summary and a 9-page introduction to the BMD issue, as well as a number of charts and artists' renditions of various components of BMD systems.

The OTA analysis led to the issuance of eight findings: (1) To date in the nuclear age, strategic offensive technologies have had a fundamental advantage over defensive technologies. Unless this imbalance is resolved, strategic defense may be plausible for limited purposes such as defense of ICBM silos or the complication of enemy attack plans, but not for the more ambitious goal of ensuring the survival of U.S. society. (2) The assured survival of the U.S. population appears impossible to achieve if the Soviets are determined to deny it. (3) If the Soviets agree to cooperate in the transition to a mutual assured survival relationship, the United States and the Soviet Union would probably find it necessary to negotiate verifiable agreements on reducing present and restricting future offensive forces, and on the manner, effectiveness, and timing of defensive deployments--all of which will be difficult. (4) There is considerable uncertainty about the strategic situation that would arise should BMD

deployment take place in the absence of any
agreement to reduce mutually offensive forces as
defensive forces increase. (5) Now at hand is
technology that should promise to protect a
substantial portion of the U.S. ICBM force when
combined with rebasing. (6) It is not possible
now to state how effective an affordable BMD
system would be. (7) The question as to whether
to push SDI vigorously or to scale it back
involves balancing opportunities against risks in
a context of considerable uncertainty. The
opportunities involve great technological
advancements combined with the willingness of the
Soviets to cooperate. Although this scenario may
be attractive to Americans, there is no guarantee
that the Soviets will perceive it that way. The
risks are that SDI research could provoke an
offensive/defensive arms competition and that
actual deployment of SDI could create severe
instability. (8) It would be prudent to pursue
U.S. BMD research in such a way as to minimize
the incentives to the Soviets for deploying their
BMD beyond the limits of the ABM Treaty, before
the final U.S. decision is made.

3

The Case in Favor of the Strategic Defense Initiative

In President Reagan's speech of March 23, 1983, he called for research that might lead to the most fundamental change in U.S. defense policy since the use of nuclear weapons against Japan. This potential change of policy surprised many, including some within the Reagan administration. The thoughts expressed that night did not spring from a vacuum, however; nor were they lost in a void after their utterance. Three articles and a book describe the immediate background of the program that has officially become known as the Strategic Defense Initiative. They help explain why a goodly number of citizens and government officials, some quite prominent, have responded positively to the president's call for the development of a defense against strategic ballistic missiles.

BACKGROUND TO THE PRESIDENT'S SPEECH

In a New York Times article, William J. Broad (1985) provided background on the interactions between Mr. Reagan, then governor of California, and various scientists and conservative groups, among whom were persons concerned about the Soviet threat and confident that the United States' vaunted technology could supply an appropriate response to that threat. Broad reported that Edward Teller, who traces his work on U.S. nuclear weapons programs back to the development of the atomic bomb in the Manhattan

45

Project, was among the most influential of the
scientists. After World War II, several well-
known nuclear physicists, including Robert
Oppenheimer, director of the Manhattan Project,
voiced concern over the moral implications of
their work. Teller, however, lobbied instead for
development of a significantly more powerful
weapon--the thermonuclear or H-bomb. This weapon
was developed in the early 1950s with Teller's
substantial involvement.

An appreciation of Teller's contribution to the
U.S. nuclear weapons arsenal may be gained by
comparing the destructive effects of the atomic
bomb, upon which he merely worked, to those of
the H-bomb, for which he is responsible to a
large degree. The explosive power for each of
the two bombs dropped on Japan was equivalent to
that of nearly 12,000 tons of TNT (expressed as
12 KT in the vocabulary of the nuclear age). The
largest H-bomb ever tested was detonated by the
Russians in the early 1950s. It had a
destructive force equivalent to approximately
58,000,000 tons of TNT, or 58 megatons (58 MT).

Over the years Teller became the best-known
American scientist combining a theoretical
knowledge of nuclear physics and a "hands-on"
acquaintance with nuclear weapons with the call
for constant vigilance against the Soviet threat.
Broad records that Mr. Reagan was the first
California chief executive to visit the Lawrence
Livermore National Laboratory at Livermore,
California, where extensive nuclear weapons
research is conducted. The laboratory was
founded by Teller, and the eminent physicist was
the future president's host for the tour.

Thus began Mr. Reagan's exposure to advanced
science, which might have offered solutions to
two problems that concerned him, even before he
entered the presidency: the dangers of nuclear
weapons, and the intentions of the Soviet Union,
a nation he has called an "evil empire." Broad
suggests that Mr. Reagan gradually became
intrigued with the possibility that one of the
United States' major assets, prominence in basic
science and applied technology, would in fact be
able to solve the problems with nuclear weapons
and the Soviets.

As the president's interest in technology grew, so too did a new notion--namely, the then highly classified project for a nuclear-pumped x-ray laser, a concept attributed to Edward Teller. In concluding his article Broad notes:

> A lingering question no one can answer is whether "Star Wars" would have happened in the absence of the X-ray laser. Mr. Reagan was obviously ripe for the idea of strategic defense. And so it seemed was a variety of new technologies, Dr. Teller's among them.

THE STAR WARS SPEECH

On March 23, 1983, President Reagan expressed to the American people not only his concerns over nuclear weapons and the Soviet Union but also his enthusiasm for new technology:

> Now, thus far tonight I've shared with you my thoughts on problems of national security we must face together. My predecessors in the Oval Office have appeared before you on other occasions to describe the threat posed by Soviet power and have proposed steps to address that threat. But since the advent of nuclear weapons, those steps have been increasingly directed toward deterrence of aggression through the promise of retaliation.
>
> This approach to stability through offensive threat has worked. We and our allies have succeeded in preventing nuclear war for more than three decades. In recent months, however, my advisers, including the Joint Chiefs of Staff, have underscored the necessity to break out of a future that relies solely on offensive retaliation for our security. Over the course of these discussions, I've become more and more deeply convinced that the human spirit must be capable of rising above dealing with other nations and

human beings by threatening their existence. Feeling this way, I believe we must thoroughly examine every opportunity for reducing tensions and for introducing greater stability into the strategic calculus on both sides. . . .

After careful consultation with my advisers, including the Joint Chiefs of Staff, I believe there is a way. Let me share with you a vision of the future which offers hope. It is that we embark on a program to counter the awesome Soviet missile threat with measures that are defensive. Let us turn to the very strengths in technology that spawned our great industrial base and that have given us the quality of life we enjoy today. .

What if free people could live secure in the knowledge that their security did not rest upon the threat of instant U.S. retaliation to deter a Soviet attack, that we could intercept and destroy strategic ballistic missiles before they reached our own soil or that of our allies?

I know this is a formidable, technical task, one that may not be accomplished before the end of this century. Yet, current technology has attained a level of sophistication where it's reasonable for us to begin this effort. . . . But isn't it worth every investment necessary to free the world from the threat of nuclear war? We know it is. . . .

I call upon the scientific community in our country, those who gave us nuclear weapons, to turn their great talents now to the cause of mankind and world peace, to give us the means of directing a comprehensive and intensive effort to define a long-term research and development program to begin to achieve our ultimate goal of eliminating the

threat posed by strategic nuclear
missiles.

The entire text of the conclusion of President
Reagan's Speech on "Defense Spending and
Defensive Technology" is in Appendix A.

In the aftermath of the president's speech,
many scientists refused to respond positively to
the call for researching the SDI technologies.
Some even formed groups to lobby against the
president and his proposal. Other scientists
responded enthusiastically. A similar split in
opinion occurred in other professional groups,
such as those composed of former military
officers, civilian national security specialists,
politicians, and the business community, as well
as among the general public.

The reasons the president's SDI proposals were
so well received by many are suggested by a
review of the writings of two retired generals
and a scientist who joined the SDI Organization.
Like the president, Army Lt. General Daniel O.
Graham had become concerned about the strategic
nuclear relationship existing between the United
States and the Soviet Union. In his book, We
Must Defend America, Graham was particularly
critical of the strategy that sought to protect
the United States from nuclear attack by
promising an even more devastating nuclear
retaliation upon the Soviet Union--the policy
known as mutual assured destruction, or MAD.
Graham saw two problems with MAD. First, its
success depended upon the Soviets' acceptance of
MAD and cooperation in its implementation, a
proposition Graham thought unlikely and
dangerous. Second, if MAD failed to deter war,
the result would be "indescribable disaster for
everyone, which is all that our present sole
emphasis on offensive forces had to offer" (p.
23).

These concerns about the utility of MAD
occurred in the context of Graham's overarching
worry that the military balance was steadily
tipping in favor of the Soviet Union because too
many Americans were blind to the Soviet threat.
To Graham, the late 1970s and early 1980s were
reminiscent of the years prior to World War II,

when England failed to perceive the approaching danger from Nazi Germany. He wrote:

> We are witnessing an eerie and tragic repetition of history. The United States, today's leader of the opposition to the powerful totalitarian Communist system, is following in the footsteps of Great Britain, yesteryear's leader of the opposition to Nazism. The stench of appeasement, pacifism, self-flagellation, and abandonment of principle hangs heavy over our land. (p. 11)

Further, Graham stated that Americans who warn about not provoking the Soviets, who are concerned with maintaining stability, and who think increased defense spending will hurt domestic social programs remind him of the English appeasers, Stanley Baldwin and Neville Chamberlain, who argued against the military preparedness suggestions of Sir Winston Churchill.

To remedy the defects in MAD, and to respond effectively to the growing Soviet threat, Graham suggested adding new technology to the ABM work of the 1960s and 1970s. He argued that the result would be a non-nuclear ballistic missile defense for the United States, the first iteration of which he termed Global Ballistic Missile Defense I. The conceptual heart of this plan would be the deployment of 432 satellites, each carrying 40 to 50 non-nuclear rockets. These would be fired at Soviet ICBMs to destroy them by impact. Later, laser and particle beam weapons could be added to Graham's system. Graham's concern about the Soviet threat and Moscow's perfidy reflects the perspectives of those Americans who were ready and waiting for President Reagan's Star Wars speech.

John C. Toomay is a retired Air Force major general who served on the Defensive Technologies Study Team, the so-called Fletcher panel, which was established after the 1983 speech to advise the president on SDI technologies. According to Toomay, (Summer 1985), the perceived deterioration in the nuclear deterrence relationship existing between the United States and the Soviet Union was a major cause for the broad appeal of SDI. In his view, the strategic nuclear relationship, in which U.S. forces had been dramatically superior to those of the Soviets, has evolved into rough parity: "The Soviets have matched the U.S. in numbers of strategic warheads, and exceed the U.S. in the total amount of explosive power" (p. 221).

Exacerbating the situation is the fact that the Soviets

> have maintained and are now improving their ABM system around Moscow; their air defense network is extensive; Soviet civil defense preparations are vastly greater than our own; and they are pressing ahead with advanced ballistic missile defense technologies. (p. 221).

Toomay also noted that the various efforts to counteract the Soviet strategic buildup over the past twenty years, including the Strategic Arms Limitation Talks (SALT) negotiations, have not been fruitful. SALT diverted but did not, in his opinion, serve to halt the momentum of Soviet deployments. Toomay then summed up the concerns and frustrations that make SDI the choice of many:

> As things stand, we are frustrated in our dealings with the Soviets, we have no consensus at home about what our policy should be, and our media's recent focus on the horrors of nuclear war has unsettled us. What we are in need of is a new approach, one that might allow us to escape our current dilemmas while still preserving viable strategic forces. The addition of strategic defenses to our national policy serves just this function. (p. 222).

Gerald Yonas (Spring 1985) is another advocate of SDI. He was a member of the Fletcher Panel and is now chief scientist for the Strategic Defense Initiative Organization in the Department

of Defense. Yonas corroborated Toomay's view
that the decade of the 1980s is the right time
for SDI.

Yonas chronicled the disappointment for many
that the 1972 ABM Treaty has not opened the door
to more impressive means of limiting strategic
nuclear forces. Adding to that concern has been
the worry over the decreasing survivability of
U.S. ICBM silos, given the growing Soviet
capacity to target them accurately with high-
yield warheads. These concerns have been
heightened by the United States' difficulty in
developing a secure basing mode for the MX, the
current replacement for the Minuteman ICBM.
Yonas noted further that those people who worked
in the nuclear weapons field became increasingly
aware in the early 1980s of social pressures
across the nation that were generating doubts
about the country's strategic nuclear posture.
The Nuclear Freeze movement, for example, called
for halting the production and testing of nuclear
weapons. And in their Pastoral Letter on War and
Peace (The Challenge of Peace: God's Promise and
Our Response), The American Catholic Bishops
raised troublesome moral questions concerning the
use of any nuclear weapon. Over it all hung
concern about the general deterioration in U.S.-
Soviet relations, which reflected growing
suspicion and mistrust on both sides. Yonas
recalled that "many were beginning to question
whether civilization could survive indefinitely
in this condition" (p. 74). Of those so
described, some were ready for the way out
promised by SDI.

Following the president's 1983 speech,
publications from three primary sources sought to
expand, explain, and justify his SDI vision.
Much of the writing came from high-ranking
officials, both civilian and military, within the
Reagan administration. Such materials include
General James A. Abrahamson's "The Strategic
Defense Initiative," and "The Impact of Space on
Arms Control," by Kenneth Adelman, director of the
Arms Control Agency. The leader of the so-called
Fletcher Report made at the request of the
president summarized his thinking in "The
Technologies for Ballistic Missile Defense"; his

counterpart [in regard to the Hoffman Report],
Fred S. Hoffman, presented his views in a paper
entitled, "Active Defense and Western Security."
At the time he wrote Security and Stability:
The Role for Strategic Defense, George Keyworth
II was the science advisor to President Reagan.
Senior Arms Control Advisor Paul Nitze's address,
"The Objectives of Arms Control," appeared in the
Department of State Bulletin; and Abraham D.
Sofaer, legal advisor to the Department of State,
is quoted in The ABM Treaty and the SDI Program.
Government documents include Ballistic Missile
Defenses and U.S. National Security (the Hoffman
Report); Soviet Military Power (1984, 1985, and
1986); Soviet Strategic Defense Programs; The
Strategic Defense Initiative Defensive
Technologies Study (the Fletcher Report); The
Strategic Defense Initiative; The President's
Strategic Defense Initiative; and Report to the
Congress on the Strategic Defense Initiative.
A number of persons who have either been in the
government or have served as consultants to
government agencies have written in support of
various facets of SDI. They include Harold
Brown, former secretary of defense, "Is SDI
Technically Feasible?"; Joseph D. Douglas and
Samuel T. Cohen, "SDI the Hidden Opportunity";
Colin Gray, "SDI Necessary for National
Security"; the Fusion Energy Foundation, Beam
Weapons--An Alternative to Nuclear Destruction;
Robert Jastrow, "Reagan Vs. the Scientists: Why
the President Is Right about Missile Defense";
and How to Make Nuclear Weapons Obsolete; Thomas
Krebs, "BMD: Soviet Countermeasure Strategies";
Keith Payne and Colin Gray, "Toward Ballistic
Missile Defense," in Charles W. Kegley, Jr., and
Eugene R. Wittkopf, eds., The Nuclear Reader;
Edward Teller, "Science and Technology in SDI";
and an interview in Discover; and William Van
Cleave, Fortress USSR.

PROPOSITIONS SUPPORTING THE SDI

Acting upon the fears and uneasiness suggested
by Broad, Graham, Toomay, and Yonas, the Reagan
administration laid out a $26 billion research

program for the first five years of the SDI era. One justification for such an effort can be found in an intellectual elaboration by SDI proponents of the major points made by the president in his 1983 speech and subsequently. For study and evaluation their case in favor of the SDI may be separated into six major propositions:

1. Regardless of the original value imputed to mutual assured destruction, that policy is now so fatally flawed as to demand replacement if technically possible.

2. The logical policy-of-choice to initially augment, and possibly replace, MAD is an orchestration of ballistic missile defenses far more comprehensive and exotic than the ABM programs of the late 1960s and 1970s.

3. A safe transition can be made from the current MAD regime to one characterized by nuclear retaliatory forces and an incrementally growing component of sophisticated strategic defense.

4. Patience and financial support are needed for research on technologies that might produce the needed ballistic missile defense at an undetermined future date. Requests for such support frequently appear in the context of two criteria, which must be met in order for the SDI to move from research to deployment. First enunciated by Paul Nitze, the president's senior arms control advisor, the criteria are as follows: that the strategic defense initiative will move into a deployment mode only if defensive systems can be made survivable to Soviet attack, and if they are cost-effective at the margin.

5. Pervasive Soviet cheating in regard to various arms agreements is placing the United States at risk.

6. The Soviet Union is developing a strategic defense effort that demands a response from the United States.

Before we turn to the following introduction to
the pro-SDI literature that has developed since
the president's speech, we must note a curious
facet of the Strategic Defense Initiative: In
the case of SDI, the president first set forth a
policy, which then required that hardware be
developed to meet its demands.   Historically,
however, the technology-policy sequence has been
the reverse;   technical development usually
occurred first, with a subsequent demand for
changes in strategy and doctrine to guide its
use. For example, airplanes were invented before
the policies describing their use in war appeared
from Billy Mitchell, Giulio Douhet, and others.
Although physicists were aware of the potential
for destruction inherent in nuclear weapons, the
invention of nuclear weapons preceded any
systematic development of a strategy for their
integration into a national defense posture.

MAD IS MORALLY AND FATALLY FLAWED

In his 1983 speech President Reagan agonized
over the moral deficiencies of mutual assured
destruction. Elaboration of this critique of MAD
is a ubiquitous theme among those who favor SDI.
For example, two months after the president's
speech, Republican Congressman Ken Kramer from
Colorado's 5th Congressional District led eleven
House members in cosponsoring H.R. 3073, called
the People Protection Act. This bill responded
positively to Mr. Reagan's concerns that the MAD
policy leaves the American people unprotected.
The bill would have required Congress to
"encourage the President to implement those
measures needed to protect people and to reduce
dependence on nuclear retaliation strategies."
The bill further called for the creation of a
unified organizational approach to the
development of directed-energy weapons and the
transfer of space activities needed for military
space purposes to the Department of Defense. An
assessment of the role for strategic defense
within the context of the ABM Treaty and other
international conventions was also required. The
Republican Senator from Colorado, William

Armstrong, introduced the same proposal in the Senate. To date, neither bill has become law.

Edward Teller (April/May 1985), writing in support of SDI, listed as his first reason for opposing MAD the fact that it is morally bankrupt. This judgment was issued in the context of Teller's claim that he has opposed deterrence based upon weapons of mass destruction from the day he first heard of the concept. Further buttressing his stance against MAD, Teller expressed his belief that the American people are uncomfortable and unhappy with MAD for presumably the same moral reasons as his.

Robert Jastrow is another prominent scientist who has joined Teller in speaking out in support of SDI. A professor of Earth Sciences at Dartmouth, Jastrow served as the first chairman of NASA's Lunar Exploration Committee; he also founded NASA's Institute for Space Studies. He opens his book, How to Make Nuclear Weapons Obsolete (1983), with a statement apparently intended to shock the reader: Jastrow claims that since the ABM Treaty was signed, it has been the policy of the U.S. government to deprive the American population of defenses against a Soviet nuclear attack. He writes of the troubling inhumanity of MAD and concludes that the president's statement (that relying on the specter of nuclear retaliation is a sad commentary on the human condition) contains "the essence of the moral dilemma posed by the doctrine of MAD" (p. 14). To Jastrow, the fact that MAD was invented by intellectuals who probably never killed any human being does not prevent the policy from being a cruel one. His moral evaluation becomes a dual critique: MAD deliberately exposes the American people to nuclear attack without protection while offering only the subsequent incineration of the Soviet people as a possible deterrent.

George Keyworth II (1985), who recently resigned as President Reagan's science advisor, writes of the "inherent unacceptability--or immorality, if you will--of mutual assured destruction as a guarantor of the world's future" (p. 2). Keyworth is almost apologetic about the legitimization of the MAD relationship through its incorporation into international law via the 1972 ABM Treaty. He explains that the adoption of the treaty prohibiting significant defenses was a "default option," accepted at the time because no defense was technically feasible and because there were high expectations that the treaty would lead to the build-down of nuclear weapons. In his view, the treaty was a test to determine whether it is possible to reduce armaments if defenses are limited. Keyworth writes that the results of this test "were most discouraging" (p. 2).

Moral dilemmas associated with the MAD doctrine are explored in a series of chapters in Charles W. Kegley, Jr., and Eugene Wittkopf, The Nuclear Reader. The chapter titles are suggestive of the perspectives aired: "MAD versus NUTS: Can Doctrine or Weaponry Remedy the Mutual Hostage Relationship of the Superpowers?" (Spurgeon M. Keeny, Jr., and Wolfgang K. H. Panofsky); "Nuclear Strategy and the Challenge of Peace: Ethical Principles and Policy Prescriptions" (National Conference of Catholic Bishops); "Bishops, Statesmen, and Other Strategists on the Bombing of Innocents" (Albert Wohlstetter); "MAD Is the Moral Position"(Paul M. Kattenberg); "The Madness Beyond MAD: Current American Nuclear Strategy" (Robert Jervis); "When a Nuclear Strike Is Thinkable" (Pierre Gallois and John Grain); and "Strategies for Making a Nuclear Strike Unthinkable" (Earl C. Ravenal).

THE PROBLEM OF FAILURE

Closely allied with concerns about the moral deficiencies of MAD is the argument that, should nuclear deterrence fail, the consequences of the resulting war would be catastrophic. Colin S. Gray, (February/March 1985), one of the most prolific writers on SDI in or outside the government, puts the matter succinctly when he notes, "Deterrence through offensive retaliation is fine as long as it is not tested severely" (p. 14). He considers a recent government state- ment to be accurate: "If deterrence were to fail, without a shield of any kind, it could cause the

death of most of our population and the
destruction of our nation as we know it" (p. 18).
Gray further observes that the perspective
provided by history suggests that eventually all
security systems will either malfunction in some
fashion or will be transformed by altered
conditions.

It is thought by many that a failure of MAD
would leave between 120 and 150 million dead in
the United States. Such figures are relatively
unimpressive, however, when compared with the
worldwide death rates predicted in studies of the
hypothesized phenomenon known as Nuclear Winter.

Accidents, Third Nations, and Terrorists

There is yet another problem with MAD that
while perhaps less serious than the potential for
system failure, is still troublesome in terms of
the carnage that could occur: the inability of
MAD to protect against accidental and other
"small" nuclear attacks. Accidental attack could
be caused by human error of omission or
commission, electronic malfunction or mechanical
failure. Currently, even one ballistic missile
mistakenly sent on its flight could not be
stopped. Such an accidental launch could deliver
ten or more warheads, each one much larger than
the bombs used against the Japanese cities.

Conscious attacks with similar consequences
could be initiated by "third nations" or by
terrorist groups in the unlikely event that they
could obtain and launch a missile. Kenneth
Adelman (April/May 1985), director of the U.S.
Arms Control and Disarmament Agency, took note
of the accident scenario: "Would we not all be
better off if we did not have to accept that form
of nuclear terror, no matter how remote it might
appear" (p. 46).

MAD and NATO

For some years the relationship between the MAD
doctrine and North Atlantic Treaty Organization
(NATO) policy has been referred to as "extended

deterrence." According to this strategy, U.S.
strategic nuclear forces are expected to extend
deterrence protection to American allies, such as
the Western European nations and possibly Japan,
and to all U.S. forces stationed overseas. In
another article Colin Gray (April/May 1985),
contends that this mission is politically one of
the most stressful demands placed upon U.S.
strategic forces (pp. 26-40). Gray's point is
that as assured destruction gradually became
mutual (i.e., shared by both the United States
and Soviet Union), the coupling of the U.S.
strategic nuclear forces to distant battlegrounds
became less credible. The question is this: If
Moscow should invade West Germany, would the
United States faced by massive Soviet strategic
nuclear forces, retaliate against the Soviet
Union, thus inviting a nuclear strike on the
United States? Further, Gray maintains that the
ability of SDI to enhance extended deterrence may
erode when the Soviets build their own SDI. He
writes, "A weaponized SDI that could protect
offensive forces and defend cities to some extent
would be greatly supportive of U.S. 'extended
deterrence,' if only it were not for the certain
fielding of new Soviet defenses" (p. 32).

MAD and the Soviet Union

The Soviet Union has accepted the premises
neither of MAD nor of related arms control
measures, and Moscow is systematically using both
to erode the security of the United States.
While this type of allegation is typically made
by SDI enthusiasts outside the government, the
seriousness of the charge and its central role in
the SDI debate are also fundamental to the
government's support of SDI. A good example of
how seriously the government views the allegation
is found in a document released by the Department
of State, The Strategic Defense Initiative.
In what amounts to an official indictment of
Soviet behavior, the State Department has made a
number of charges:

1.   The Soviet Union has failed to demonstrate
the restraint in regard to strategic offensive
and defensive forces that Washington hoped would
be the case when the SALT process began in the
early 1970s.

2.   Improvements made by the Soviet Union in
its ballistic missile force, such as increasing
their missiles' hard-target kill capability,
threaten the survivability of U.S. silo-based
ICBMs, whose purpose is to deter aggression.
Further, the improved Soviet ballistic missile
capacity also threatens fixed installations in
the United States and among its allies, and this
threat extends to the leadership structures.

3. Simultaneous with its offensive force
buildup, the Soviet Union has pursued strategic
advantage through the development and improvement
of its active strategic defense forces. Such
activity is steadily providing the Soviet Union
with the ability to counter U.S. and Allied
retaliatory forces, and this will be especially
true should U.S. forces be degraded by a Soviet
preemptive first strike. It is further alleged
that only the Soviet Union has deployed an
anti-satellite (ASAT) weapon, and that such an
ASAT puts U.S. space-based assets at risk.
According to the State Department, the advantage
held today by the Soviet Union could, through
logical evolutionary improvement, "provide the
foundation of decisive advantage in the future"
(p. 2).

4.   The Soviet Union is spending substantial
sums to improve the survivability of its own
military forces, its command structure, and its
national leadership. The Soviet Union has been
pursuing a wide range of research on strategic
defense over the years, augmented by research in
many of the same technologies being studied by
the U.S. SDI program. According to the State
Department, the Soviet research, if not met by
equivalent work in the United States, will
further erode the effectiveness of U.S.
retaliatory forces.

5. The Soviet Union is not complying with the arms control agreement covering both strategic offensive and strategic defensive systems. Specifically, the State Department charges the Soviet Union with direct violation of the ABM Treaty in its construction of a phased-array radar at Krasnoyarsk.

From the Reagan administration's perspective, the problem with the Krasnoyarsk radar is twofold: (1) It violates the ABM Treaty requirement that such radars be placed on the nation's periphery, and (2) it violates the prohibition that radars should not be focused on a nation's interior. The intent of the ABM Treaty is to prevent the construction of radars that could direct ABM fire at warheads that have penetrated over a nation's borders. The administration has also charged that the Soviets engage in actions designed to impede U.S. verification of treaty compliance. An example given is the Soviet use of encryption of telemetry during tests of various weapons to disguise their performance characteristics.

In an effort to document the magnitude of Soviet strategic defensive expansion, including Moscow's violations of arms control agreements, the State Department and the Defense Department jointly issued an unusual booklet entitled <u>Soviet Strategic Defense Programs</u>. Beginning with an introduction signed by Secretary of Defense Caspar Weinberger and Secretary of State George Shultz, the publication contains a detailed accounting of activities viewed by the U.S. government as endangering its strategic retaliatory capability, which is the heart of the MAD doctrine.

These Soviet activities include development of potential laser, particle beam, and kinetic kill weapons that are similar to, but in some instances more advanced than, technologies under investigation by the U.S. SDI program. The booklet includes an artist's rendition of the directed energy research and development site at Sary Shagan, including a laser beam aimed heavenward in a test. The explanation associated with the drawing is that the Soviet laser program is much larger than the U.S. one, given the Soviet Union effort involving over 10,000 scientists and engineers located at more than six major facilities and test ranges. The extensive Soviet infrastructure for defense against air-breathing delivery systems, such as cruise missiles and bombers, is also explained and depicted in drawings. In addition, the document contains allegations of cheating on arms control agreements, ranging from charges of potential violations in regard to mobile land-based ABM systems to the familiar charge of direct ABM Treaty violation represented by the radar installation at Krasnoyarsk.

Many nongovernment persons also believe that the Soviets have rejected the MAD doctrine. A good example is Edward Teller. In an interview with Discover (1985), he flatly asserted that the Soviet leadership has never accepted the operating principles of MAD (pp. 67-74). Teller supported his contention by noting that the Soviets, unlike the United States, chose to deploy around Moscow the ABM system that was allowed by the ABM Treaty. Further, Teller claimed that the Soviets augmented their ABM defense by constructing and maintaining an extensive civil defense system for their population. In comparison, Teller noted that the United States decided to dismantle its one ABM installation permitted by the ABM Treaty, and that civil defense has never constituted a major effort in the United States. Emphasizing the disparity between the civil defense efforts of the two nations, Teller cited the figure of $13 per capita spent on civil defense in the Soviet Union compared with 78 cents in the United States. The noted physicist also cited evidence that the Soviets have proceeded along a very different track while the United States clung to MAD. Finally, he claimed that some of the ingenious new possibilities for defensive systems being developed by researchers at the Lawrence Livermore National Laboratory were actually based on insights gained from Soviet sources.

SDI IS THE ALTERNATIVE OF CHOICE TO MAD

SDI Is Morally Superior to MAD

Those who contend that the policy of MAD is basically immoral also argue that an effective SDI is moral. A strong case is presented by Kenneth Adelman (1985), who has written that the ethics of morality of U.S. reliance on nuclear deterrence is "one of the most critical issues of our times" (p. 46), and that if defense systems that reduce the risk of nuclear war can be developed, they would be morally justified. Elaborating upon a prominent theme in the president's Star Wars speech, Adelman stated: "We cannot simply sit back and forever assume that the only deterrent is the threat of mutual annihilation, a markedly depressing condition which today drives humanity toward some inevitable psychic breakdown" (p. 48).

Adelman then drove home his point by citing clergy. From a petition signed by more than 1,000 clergymen who have publicly endorsed SDI research he quoted: "that if a non-nuclear, genuinely defensive system is feasible, then its deployment. . . is not only morally justifiable, but perhaps even obligatory for the American people and their government" (p. 48). Adelman also quoted the Catholic Bishop of Peoria, Illinois, to the effect that destroying unmanned missiles far removed from populations would be vastly superior to nuclear deterrence.

SDI Is Valuable in Preventing a Soviet Disarming First Strike

An argument favoring SDI is that it will significantly reverse the claimed erosion of U.S. strategic offensive forces that has been caused by the increasing capability of Soviet offensive forces. This basic theme is found frequently in pro-SDI literature. For example, there is the article written by Joseph D. Douglass, Jr., a former deputy director of the Tactical Technology Office within the Defense Department's Advanced

Research Projects Agency, and Samuel Cohen, the originator of the concept that led to enhanced radiation weapons. Recalling the advice of the ancient Chinese strategist, Sun Tzu, to the effect that successful strategy defeats the enemy without war, Douglass and Cohen (1985), suggest that SDI be used in a similar fashion. To them the Soviet strategy for war is the execution of a surprise first strike. Their objective is to destroy the majority of our forces before we can successfully mount an organized and powerful counter-strike. (p. 6).

Thus it appears to Douglass and Cohen that to seriously diminish Soviet confidence in the success of a first strike constitutes a substantial contribution to deterrence. So strongly do they hold this perspective that they have written that eliminating the chances of a Soviet first strike against U.S. strategic forces is the "sine qua non" of U.S. deterrent strategy. Accordingly, they have urged that SDI should initially be developed and deployed to optimize U.S. capability to strike back during, or at the beginning of, a Soviet first strike.

If Deterrence Fails, SDI Is to Be Preferred to MAD

It is not known in this country whether the Soviet Union has purposely targeted the urban centers of the United States with the intent to kill the greatest number of civilians. Such a strategy could be in place now. Although a leaky SDI might not prove particularly effective in preventing such a population-killing attack, there are other kinds of attacks against which a leaky SDI would prove useful in protecting our civilian population. An example is given in a paper written by Fred Hoffman, chair of the Reagan administration's Ballistic Missile Defenses and U.S. National Security Study Team, "Active Defense and Western Security" (1984). Hoffman suggests that there could be a range of strategic Soviet attacks on U.S. military targets that are colocated with population centers. He also argues that if SDI were sufficiently effective to prevent the Soviets from hitting the military targets, and if the United States retained the capacity to hit back at Soviet cities in retaliation for the loss of American cities, denial of the Soviet ability to achieve specific military objectives "would contribute powerfully to deterring attack by them" (p. 6) and the result would be the sparing of the colocated cities.

SDI Has a Good Chance to Limit Damage from Accidents, Third Nations, and Terrorists Substantially

Almost by definition, any SDI effort with some capability to defend against a Soviet attack would have a capacity against a small launch, whether by accident or by Third World nations. In "Toward Ballistic Missile Defense," Keith Payne and Colin Gray suggest that protection for both sides against an accident would be preferable to the current condition, which carries a very high risk that disastrous consequences would follow from any such mishap. The problem here is that there are other ways for Third World nations and terrorists to deliver a weapon to the United States. To be foolproof, an SDI would therefore have to incorporate some kind of increased air defense against cruise missiles and bombers. It appears that SDI alone will have no capability to protect the United States against clandestinely introduced nuclear weapons.

SDI Is Preferred over the Other Alternatives

SDI is not the only alternative to MAD vying for the nation's support. Only recently the Nuclear Freeze movement evoked substantial interest around the country when it appeared as a proposition on local and state ballots and was lobbied with considerable success in the Congress. The movement stalled, however, partly because of opposition to it from the Reagan administration. Proponents of SDI argue that the problem with the Freeze is that, if implemented, it would freeze into place serious Soviet superiorities, particularly with regard to strategic offensive and defensive forces. SDI advocates also argue that such a freeze cannot be verifiable, thus preventing U.S. advancements while providing a cover for Soviet development.

Another alternative to MAD opposed by SDI supporters is a dramatic increase in U.S. strategic offensive forces. Proponents of such an increase argue that in this way the expanded Soviet offensive forces would be given more targets to hit, and in a U.S. retaliatory attack their defenses would be overwhelmed. The basic argument against this alternative is that it merely compounds all the undesirable features of MAD, and that it contributes to the kind of world future President Reagan would like to use SDI to prevent. As Jastrow points out in his book, How to Make Nuclear Weapons Obsolete (1983), it would be an unstable world (p. 40).

Still another alternative to MAD is actually just a modification of the MAD strategy: to move up the alert status of U.S. offensive forces so that they would be capable of being launched "on warning" or "under attack." The argument contends that, with this change in strategy, there would be only empty silos by the time the Soviet warheads arrived on target. This scheme has never enjoyed great popularity. Its hairtrigger characteristic is troublesome: as noted by Jastrow, there are too many scenarios in which war is begun accidentally when a false warning is amplified into nuclear exchanges (p. 38).

SDI Is Advantageous to U.S. Allies

Like its opposite number--the contention that MAD is disadvantageous to extended deterrence for NATO--this argument is murky. According to Caspar Weinberger, as quoted by Colin Gray (April/May 1985), "There's not the slightest possibility that America would be decoupled from Europe by the pursuit of this vital initiative [SDI]." However, as Gray has pointed out, if both the United States and the Soviet Union had space-based defenses, nuclear threats would "lose technical credibility" (p. 32) and NATO might then be required to make some changes if extended deterrence was less a factor under SDI. By way of response, Gray's suggestion is that NATO should make some long-overdue military adjustments along the lines of modernization and force expansion, whether SDI is deployed or not.

The White House is advocating a kind of mini-SDI for its European allies. In The President's Strategic Defense Initiative, the president states that the United States will carefully examine "technologies with potential against shorter-range ballistic missiles," such as the Soviets have deployed against NATO (p. 6). The president then goes on to say, "An effective defense against shorter-range ballistic missiles could have a significant impact on deterring aggression in Europe" (p. 6). He also points out that Soviet doctrine stresses the use of ballistic missiles with conventional warheads for quick attack on NATO targets throughout Europe. Thus the argument is that a European derivative of SDI could also be useful in deterring conventional attacks as well as nuclear ones. The government pledges to work with the NATO allies on the various SDI possibilities.

SDI Addresses the Alleged Soviet Rejection of MAD and Will Lead Both Nations into a Reciprocal Strategic Defense Relationship

According to The President's Strategic Defense Initiative, Soviet SDI research is so advanced that concerns have been raised about Moscow's capability to "break out" of the ABM Treaty with the deployment of a nationwide ABM system within the next ten years. The seriousness of this concern is indicated by the president's statement that "were they to do so, as they could, deterrence would collapse, and we would have no choices between surrender and suicide" (p. 4). Responding with an American SDI program is, in the view of the United States government, a means to provide an appropriate response to the growing Soviet threat. If cooperation with Moscow is achieved, an SDI will, or at least could, permit both nations to proceed on roughly parallel paths with strategic defense. Regarding this last possibility, "because we have no ambitions in this regard [establishing military superiority], deployments of defensive systems would most usefully be done in the context of a cooperative, equitable, and verifiable arms control environment that regulates the offensive and defensive developments and deployments of the United States and the Soviet Union." (p. 5). Scientists who are proponents of SDI also agree that the creation of a mutual SDI regime would be as beneficial to the United States as to the Soviet Union. As Robert Jastrow (January 1984) has noted:

> If the Soviets acquire an effective defense against American missiles, so much the better. They will not even have to steal it. The president has suggested that his successor can give the new technology to the Soviet Union, just to prove that there is no point in both sides' keeping bulging warehouses of these deadly weapons any longer. (p. 31)

SAFE TRANSITION FROM MAD TO THE SDI

Assuming that some or all of the technologies being examined by the SDI Organization work effectively, the question arises: How will the transition be made to the world envisioned by President Reagan, where nuclear-tipped ballistic missiles are no longer useful? Addressing this question in 1986 is in a sense "getting the cart before the horse." But government documents look forward with some confidence to a transition period, and some civilian strategists have started to consider it. Notable among these are Keith Payne and Colin Gray. According to Payne and Gray (Spring 1984), the transition period could take up to twenty years, starting with the deployment of hard-point, non-nuclear terminal defenses late in this decade, and followed by exotic spaced-based defenses much later. The two warn that the transition era, particularly the earlier phases, could hold dangers for the United States unless care is taken to maintain political and strategic stability. For example, it would be possible for the Soviet Union to gain an initial advantage during the transition period because of its already-existing network of radars and "a rapidly deployable ground-based BMD" (p. 203). Further, the authors suggest that a unilateral Soviet BMD deployment would be highly destabilizing because it would be added to existing Soviet air defenses, the Soviet civil defense network, and the large Soviet ICBM force, which has first-strike potential. Worse, according to Payne and Gray, is the possibility that a combination of Soviet first-strike capacity and a Soviet BMD could be used against a substantially degraded U.S. counterattack. They paint a bleak scenario:

> This combination of Soviet offensive and defensive capabilities could increase first strike incentives during a crisis if Soviet leaders were persuaded that the U.S.S.R.'s defenses might be capable of largely absorbing the much diminished U.S. retaliatory capability. (p. 204)

To compensate for this potentially unstable period, Payne and Gray have two suggestions: the early deployment of defenses to protect U.S. ballistic missiles (to give pause to Soviet planners) and the addition of more penetration aids to U.S. ICBMs (making it easier for them to pass through a Soviet BMD). The reader may recall that Douglass and Cohen also advocated early construction of defenses to protect U.S. strategic offensive forces in order to deny the Soviets a cheap first-strike option.

Because of what they claim is the crucial role of U.S. retaliatory forces during the transition period, Payne and Gray urge that the force modernizations currently under way be carried to fruition. According to them, this would involve phasing in MX and Midgetman ICBMs, cruise

missiles, B-1 bombers, and additional Trident
submarines carrying ballistic missiles (SLBMs).
They further note that Soviet leaders may also
use the same means to obtain stability.

Payne and Gray suggest that the transition to a
comprehensive defense system for the United
States will require support from many
presidential administrations as well as major
advancements in appropriate technology. They
warn that a transition could be stymied because
of problems in either politics or technology.
For these reasons, they argue, SDI should be
incrementally deployed, and each component should
be both valuable in its own right and
complementary to any following deployments.

Payne and Gray analyze the array of potential
Soviet responses that would occur if the United
States begins a transition to SDI. While
acknowledging the extensive Soviet investment in
defense, the writers try to second-guess the
Soviet leadership. Their conclusion is that
Moscow will not attempt a "breakout" from the
constraints of the ABM Treaty. Their logic is
threefold. First, it is to the Soviets'
advantage to adhere to the Treaty, which permits
Moscow to gradually increase its air defense and
to achieve increased BMD capacity without
triggering a strong reaction from the United
States. Second, the Soviets may prefer to wait
for the United States to initiate a change in the
ABM Treaty, thus making propaganda points,
possibly with the West Europeans, by noting that
it was the United States that first tried to
weaken or negate the Treaty. Third, the Soviets
probably realize that a "breakout" would
galvanize Washington into deploying terminal
hard-point defenses "within our [U.S.] grasp" (p.
210), which in turn would negate the money the
Soviets have poured into SS-18s and SS-19s to
threaten U.S. ICBMs.

PATIENCE AND FINANCIAL SUPPORT FOR RESEARCH ON
SDI TECHNOLOGIES

Appearing in government document after document
is the statement that SDI is currently only a

research program designed to analyze the technologies that might be melded together to form a comprehensive, layered strategic defense against ballistic missile attack. The inference is that this will take considerable time. Thus there is an implicit request by the executive branch of government for time, patience, and money to enable it to undertake a complex number of investigations that could eventually lead to the decision either to continue or to stop the SDI program. A typical example of the government's position appears in Report to the Congress on the Strategic Defense Initiative:

> It should be stressed that the SDI is a research program that seeks to provide the technical knowledge required to support a decision on whether to develop and later deploy advanced defensive systems. It is not a program to deploy those systems. (p. 7) [original emphasis]

Frequently, government discussion of the SDI contains a reference to a statement by Paul Nitze made in a speech entitled "The Objectives of Arms Control" (May 1985). Nitze, senior arms control advisor to the president, stated that to be considered for deployment, any SDI system would have to meet two criteria: The system must be survivable against Soviet efforts to destroy it; and the system must be cost-effective at the margin. The first requirement is designed to prevent the Soviets from believing they could first strike vulnerable parts of an SDI system. The second requirement is intended to ensure that a U.S.-deployed SDI would not trigger an offensive buildup by the USSR; if such a response were to cost the Soviet Union more than the additional defensive capacity to defeat it would cost the United States, presumably Moscow would decline that kind of competition.

Since the president's speech in early 1983, a number of government documents have appeared in addition to articles authored by senior officials, that make the argument that sufficient promise of the new SDI technologies has been demonstrated, or theorized, to warrant asking the public to support SDI research with funding over a period of some considerable time. Perhaps the best example of this approach is an article by the man President Reagan appointed as the first director of the Strategic Defense Initiative Organization, Air Force Lt. General James A. Abrahamson. This article, "The Strategic Defense Initiative" (August 1984), is a readable introduction to the SDI program for persons relatively new to the field of national security studies.

Seeking to build public support for SDI, General Abrahamson has criss-crossed the nation with the message contained in this article. He begins by explaining that the purpose of SDI is to defend people and military forces, and that these objectives may be achieved by conducting research on a number of technologies. Success with the SDI would enable the United States to remove the threat of a preemptive first strike designed to disarm U.S. strategic offensive forces. By reducing the military value of ballistic missiles, a successful SDI would also create the military and economic pressures that would contribute to a negotiated force reduction regarding ballistic missiles with the USSR.

The general explained the multilayered SDI concept in terms of a hypothetical four-tiered system, each layer of which could be targeted upon one of the four phases of a ballistic missile flight trajectory. He notes that if each of the four U.S. defensive layers allowed only 10 percent leakage rate of vehicles to pass through to the next layer, the total leakage after four layers would be only one-hundredth of 1 percent. He points out that the advantage of such a multilayered system is that the attacking nation will need to devise multiple strategies and hardware to penetrate each defensive layer, thus complicating its task and making attack a far less attractive option.

Key elements in a layered defense would involve accomplishment of the following functions according to General Abrahamson:

1. Rapid and reliable early warning that an attack is underway and information as to the size

of the attack, based upon constant surveillance
of all ballistic missile launch areas; Early
destruction of booster missiles and post-boost
vehicles, thus minimizing the proliferation of
warheads and penetration aids;

2. Quick and efficient discrimination of
of lightweight decoys from warheads, thus forcing
the offense to use heavy and sophisticated
decoys, which in turn will detract from the
effective payload of any given missile;

3. Complete "birth-to-death" tracking of all
potentially threatening objects, together with
effective "hand-over" of responsibility for the
objects from one layer of defense to the next;

4. Low-cost interception of targets in the
midcourse flight phase;

5. High-altitude interception of warheads in
the terminal phase to preclude collateral damage
from salvage-fused warheads; and

6. The orchestration of early warning, acquisition, tracking, data management and
communications into a rapid functioning battle-
management whole.

A special point to be emphasized is the
importance to a fully developed SDI of taking
advantage of the missile vulnerabilities found in
the boost phase of ballistic flight. These are
four in number.
The first is that at the moment of first-stage
engine ignition the missile clearly identifies
its location and the fact that it is being
launched by the large flame that spurts from the
engine nozzle. This flame becomes a long plume
of fire emitting infrared radiation, which is
easily detected and which enables the missile to
be tracked. The plume trails the missile until
the end of the boost phase.
A second vulnerability during the boost phase
occurs at the time of lift-off, when the missile
is moving very slowly as it gradually gains
sufficient momentum to complete the flight.

A third vulnerability is caused by the fact that at lift-off the missile is full of fuel, which comprises approximately 70 percent of its total take-off weight. The fuel can be exploded if the fuel tank is pierced or ruptured in some fashion.

The fourth boost-phase vulnerability is that during this phase the missile offers a larger target than it does later, when it has proliferated into tens of warheads and hundreds of decoys.

It is extremely important that the missile vulnerabilities in the boost phase be successfully exploited. In fact, most analysts concede that much of the projected success of a fully deployed SDI will be dependent upon achieving a relatively high kill rate against Soviet missiles while they are in the boost phase. Or, put another way, many believe that should the United States be unable to destroy large numbers of Soviet missiles in this phase, the chances for success by the other layers of defense, working with substantially fewer advantages, will be dramatically reduced or perhaps made impossible. These observations apply most directly to an SDI designed to protect cities, and less so to an SDI limited to the protection of hardened targets buried underground and constructed of steel and concrete.

Apparently sensitive to concerns voiced about the possibility of a president's delegation of firing orders to SDI computers that can be programmed incorrectly or make mistakes, General Abrahamson has suggested that varying degrees of system activation and automation could be developed. He states that to guard against accidental and confused responses, the degree of automation would be inversely related to the severity of the crisis. In this context he notes that C^3I for non-nuclear weapons--such as those generally planned for the SDI, which do not directly harm persons--can be different from those for nuclear weapons.

A private group, the Fusion Energy Foundation, has published a book explaining the various SDI technologies. The title is <u>An Alternative to Nuclear Destruction</u> (1984).

Thomas Krebs (1985) points out that while Moscow may attempt to degrade and destroy SDI components with countermeasures, there are costs to the Soviets in such a strategy. The penalties that must be paid are reduced weight for the payload if countermeasures are added, the extra economic cost of developing and deploying countermeasures, and perhaps some loss in accuracy.

For the more technically sophisticated reader there are several government documents that reflect the evolution of the SDI concept since President Reagan suggested the Strategic Defense Initiative. These documents resulted from the formation, immediately after the president's speech, of two study efforts: (1) the Defensive Technologies Study to review the technologies that might be used against ballistic missiles and to recommend specific long-term programs for technical advancement; and (2) the Future Security Strategy Study to assess the role of defensive systems in future U.S. security planning. The latter study was divided between two teams: an interagency group headed by Franklin C. Miller, whose report has not been released; and a collection of outside experts headed by Fred S. Hoffman, whose report has been made public.

1. The Defensive Technologies Study, produced the so-called Fletcher Report, entitled The Strategic Defense Initiative Defensive Technologies Study, published by the Department of Defense. This report is cast in a technically optimistic framework. In the letter of transmittal written by R. D. DeLauer, assistant secretary for research and engineering, the sttement is made that despite uncertainties, "new technologies hold great promise for achieving the President's goal of eliminating the threat of ballistic missiles to ourselves and our allies." The report sets forth a technical program for the SDI based upon motivating innovation, focused technology, and the technical demonstration of concepts. A further elaboration of the Fletcher Report may be obtained from the leader of the

group, James C. Fletcher (1985) in "Ballistic Missile Defense: The Technologies," Issues in Science and Technology.

2. The Future Security Strategy Study, produced the so-called Hoffman Report, a summary of which is entitled Ballistic Missile Defenses and U.S. National Security. The thrust of this report is suggested by the following quotation:

> The new technologies offer the possibility of a multilayered defense system able to intercept offensive missiles in each phase of their trajectories. In the long term, such systems might provide a nearly leakproof defense against large ballistic missile attacks. However, their components vary substantially in technical risk, development lead time and cost, and in the policy issues they raise. Consequently, partial systems, or systems with more modest technical goals, may be feasible earlier than the full system. (p. 2)

The subject of the last sentence in the above quotation from the Hoffman Report--that a partial SDI would be reasonable earlier than a fully deployed system, has for practical purposes divided the original SDI into two versions. What could be called SDI I is President Reagan's vision of "rendering nuclear weapons impotent and obsolete." SDI II would be the use of technologies much closer to development for protecting hard-site targets.

Writing in the 1985 "America and the World" issue of Foreign Affairs, published early in 1986, Harold Brown, a scientist and former secretary of defense, adds substance to the general statement in the Hoffman Report. According to Brown, ABMs that are more advanced that the Spartan and Sprint of the 1960s and 1970s could be deployed in fewer than fifteen years if a decision to do so were made now. If the ABMs were non-nuclear, then the time required for deployment would be several additional years.

Brown writes that such a partial SDI would be
capable of defending hard targets such as ICBM
silos. The more exotic technologies will only be
available, if ever, much later than the ABMs.
Brown sums up his perspective by writing:

> The near-term prospects for ballistic
> missile defense capabilities are
> reasonably well known. Technically, they
> appear cost-effective for defense of some
> kinds of strategic retaliatory forces.
> For defense of populations against a
> responsive threat, they look poor through
> the year 2010 and beyond. (p. 454)

In the spring of 1984, Secretary of Defense
Caspar Weinberger released a study that
incorporated the work of both the Defensive
Technologies Study team and the Future Security
Strategy Study group. Published by the
Department of Defense, it is entitled Defense
Against Ballistic Missiles--An Assessment of
Technologies and Policy Implications. This
document also contains a set of questions and
answers about SDI as well as a number of sections
in which the interface between SDI, arms
control, and SDI and the concerns of U.S. allies
are examined.

For the reader who wants a detailed examination
of SDI technologies set forth in more readable
form, a book already cited is available--namely,
How To Make Nuclear Weapons Obsolete, by Robert
Jastrow. The tone of this book is generally
supportive of the president's vision regarding
SDI, and it has a ring of authority derived from
the author's recognized scientific credentials.

Those who are curious about what the average
citizen may read about SDI should consult the
Reader's Digest for February 1986. The magazine
contains a condensed article, by Robert Jastrow,
that first appeared in the American Legion
Magazine.

THE COST OF THE SDI

Those interested in the long-term anticipated
costs of SDI must probably wait a number of years

for definitive estimates on a deployed system. The problem with estimating costs for SDI is twofold. First, how can one estimate the costs for technologies that have yet to be made into weapons? Second, who can predict the amount of inflation, and the cost of money (i.e., interest rates) for an unknown future date when the various components of the SDI may be capable of being integrated into an operating system? Cognizant of these problems, the Department of Defense has stated in Report to the Congress on the Strategic Defense Initiatives that "because this information will not be available until more is known about the potential of the technologies involved and the course of future arms control negotiations, long-term defense costs estimates are not feasible at this time" (p. C-24).

It is much easier to project the costs of SDI research and development out to fiscal year 1987. For the various technologies now under investigation, such cost projections are scattered throughout the above-referenced report.

SOVIET CHEATING ON ARMS CONTROL AGREEMENTS

The Report to Congress cited above also contains allegations of Soviet cheating on arms control agreements, ranging from charges of potential violations with regard to mobile land-based ABM systems to the familiar charge of direct ABM Treaty violation resulting from the radar installation at Krasnoyarsk.

One of the most outspoken of the civilian analysts alleging that the Soviet Union cheats on arms control agreements is William Van Cleave, the director of the Defense and Strategic Studies program at the University of Southern California. In fact, Van Cleave devotes an entire chapter of his book, Fortress USSR, to the subject of Soviet cheating.

Van Cleave criticizes President Reagan for being inconsistent in charging the Soviets with cheating, yet continuing U.S. observance of the very agreements Moscow is accused of breaking. His recommendation to the president is this:

If the administration is serious about strategic defenses--even about research and development of them, since so much development is constrained by the ABM Treaty,--its only choice is to act decisively and declare the ABM Treaty void by reason of Soviet nonobservance; or, even more to the point, because it is contrary to U.S. national security interests. (p. 37)

The charge that the Soviet Union is cheating on the ABM Treaty brings up the subject of the U.S. interpretation of the Treaty. There is a dispute on the matter. The argument turns on whether defensive systems based on physical principles other than those understood in 1972, when the Treaty was signed, are restricted by the Treaty. The so-called restrictive interpretation of the Treaty holds that such exotic technologies as are now under investigation are covered. However, what is termed the broad interpretation holds that references to ABM systems in the Treaty do not pertain to future technologies, except as found in Agreed Statement D, which calls only for discussion regarding limitation of systems based upon future technologies.

State Department Legal Advisor Abraham D. Sofear is quoted in a State Department publication, The ABM Treaty and the SDI Program, as to the Reagan administration's policy in 1985:

Notwithstanding our belief in the merits of the broader interpretation, the President has decided to pursue the SDI program as currently structured, which can be accommodated within the confines of the "restrictive" interpretation-- namely, research into, but not development or testing of, systems or components based on future technology and capable of substituting for ABM interceptors, launchers, or radars. (p. 3)

SOVIET PROGRESS IN SDI RESEARCH

The increasing concern of the Reagan administration over Soviet progress in SDI research and development can be gauged from a series of documents published by the Department of Defense entitled Soviet Military Power. Published annually since 1983, these books chronicle through words, photographs, and artists' sketches the advancing Soviet military potential.

The 1983 version of Soviet Military Power contains relatively brief mention of Soviet space activity. The 1984 issue carries four paragraphs under the heading Directed Energy (p. 106). In the 1985 edition there is a 17-page chapter devoted to Soviet SDI, ASATs, and air defense against air-breathing delivery systems. In the same chapter there are several artists' renditions of a Soviet space shuttle that appears to be a near-replica of the U.S. craft, and the reader is informed that such space ships are "in the final stages of development" (p. 57). The 1985 version of Soviet Military Power also carried an extensive discussion of Soviet BMD activity similar to that being projected for the United States SDI, in addition to the following warning:

> By the late 1980s, the Soviets could have prototypes for ground-based lasers for ballistic missile defense. Testing of the components for a large-scale deployment system could begin in the early 1990s. The many difficulties in fielding an operational system will require much development time, and initial operational development is not likely in this century. However, with high priority and some significant risk of failure, the Soviets could skip some testing steps and be ready to deploy a ground-based laser BMD by the early-to mid-1990s. (p. 44)

In the 1986 issue of <u>Soviet</u> <u>Military</u> <u>Power</u> a chapter entitled "Strategic Defense and Space Operations" contains ominous statements by the Department of Defense. For example:

> The USSR already has ground-based lasers--capable of interfering with some US satellites and could have prototypes for ground-based lasers for defense against ballistic missiles by the late 1980s. (p. 41)

And:

> In the Soviet view, the USSR could best achieve its aims in a nuclear war if it attacks first, destroying much of the US and allied capability for retaliation. Defensive measures, both active and passive, would in turn prevent those enemy forces that survived a Soviet first strike from destroying targets in the USSR. (p. 42)

Van Cleave writes that the real Star Wars effort is Russian, not American, and that the entire Soviet space program is predominantly military in character. He warns that through propaganda and disinformation the Soviets are attempting to convince the world that Moscow's space program is civilian, peaceful, and scientific, none of which is true.

By way of emphasizing his contention that it is the Soviet Union that threatens Star Wars, not the United States, Van Cleave refers to the SDI as the SDR--Strategic Defense Response.

SUMMARY

The case favoring the Strategic Defense Initiative that has been made in the past three years generally follows the original outline set forth by President Reagan on March 23, 1983. The SDI is offered as the preferable alternative to the policy of mutual assured destruction, which, it is argued, is immoral and catastrophically dangerous in the event of its failure.

Much of the hopes for the SDI rest upon the potential development of new and exotic technologies that were not available when the first ABM debates occurred nearly thirty years ago. As questions about the effectiveness of the new technologies can be answered only with the expenditure of money during an extensive period of time, SDI proponents spend much of their effort asking for research money and patience from the population.

A noticeable departure from President Reagan's proposal can be seen in the fact that some SDI supporters have shied away from his suggestion that cities could be protected from nuclear attack. In fact considerable discussion has occurred among SDI advocates about this issue. A number of them believe the more technically likely possibility is that terminal defenses will prove practical in the near term for defending sites that have been hardened against the effects of nuclear blast (e.g., the underground silos housing U.S. ICBMs and certain command centers).

A continuing theme in the pro-SDI literature is that the Soviets have rejected the tenets of MAD and that this fact is exercabated by Moscow's persistent cheating on the ABM Treaty. The consequence of these actions, as seen by those favoring SDI, is that the Soviet Union is amassing a huge nuclear offensive force that threatens the United States, coupled with the move toward a Russian SDI. In this set of circumstances SDI proponents suggest that the United States has no option but to move ahead rapidly on its SDI.

It is frequently emphasized that development of a successful SDI will not mean the elimination of the U.S. strategic offensive forces. That outcome could be contemplated only if the Soviets agreed to mutual and balanced reductions of their offensive capacity.

Government officials argue for the so-called broad interpretation of the ABM Treaty. Their point is that the exotic technologies being examined for the SDI do not fall under ABM Treaty restrictions, which pertain to 1972 technologies. But government spokesmen have stated that for the SDI research currently contemplated it is not necessary to interpret the Treaty broadly. They say that the United States will live within the so-called restrictive interpretation of the Treaty, meaning that the SDI effort will engage in research into, but not development or testing of, the exotic technologies.

The administration has acknowledged, however, that should SDI technologies prove to be effective, their deployment would be a subject of discussion with the Soviet Union. Implicit in the SDI/ABM Treaty context is the possibility that at some future date the United States may need to consider withdrawal from or renegotiation of the ABM Treaty.

It should be noted that on two important points, substantial agreement exists between those who support and those who oppose the SDI: (1) that the SDI should not be deployed unless its components can be made survivable against Soviet efforts to destroy them in a first strike, and (2) that the SDI must be cost-effective in comparison with the costs to the Soviets of their activity to destroy or erode the SDI.

ABSTRACTS

1. Abrahamson, Lt. General James A. 1984. The
    Strategic Defense Initiative. _Defense_ **84**,
    August, 3-11

In this article the director of the SDI Office
within the Pentagon provides a succinct
explanation of the SDI objective, as follows:
"The purpose of the Strategic Defense Initiative
is to defend people and our military forces" (p.
3). He explains how the SDI program might evolve
from the current research phase, through the
systems development phase, into the transition
phase involving incremental and sequential
deployment, to the final phase. The last is
described as "the period of time during which
deployments of highly effective multi-phased
defensive systems are completed and during which
ballistic force levels reach their negotiated
nadir. This is the president's goal" (p. 5).
Abrahamson also explains the functions of a
multilayered defense against ballistic missiles
and describes the various SDI technologies that
might be used in the different defensive layers.
Included in this discussion is the "very critical
issue" of battle management and command and
control. The SDI director closes with an upbeat
statement:

> We must have the full involvement of
> the nations's best minds and the long-
> term commitment of our people to the
> Strategic Defense Initiative. It
> represents a bold, hopeful effort to find
> a path to a safer world for ourselves and
> our children--to bring reality to the
> president's vision of a world made safe
> by rendering nuclear ballistic missiles
> "impotent and obsolete." (p. 11)

2. Adelman, Kenneth. 1985. The impact of
    space on arms control. _Defense Science
    2003+_ 4 (April/May): 41-48.

The director of the Arms Control and
Disarmament Agency argues that the prime purpose

84

of the   Soviet Union is "to abort U.S. research
on SDI while maintaining their own programs" (p.
42). He defends SDI research as being the only
research permitted under the ABM Treaty and notes
that research on SDI is a prudent hedge against
the Soviets' active defensive and research
programs. He also maintains that the Soviets may
have moved beyond their allotted ABM deployment
around Moscow toward a nationwide ABM capability
in direct violation of the ABM Treaty, adding
that they have extensive air defense and that
"they are engaged in vigorous research on lasers
and neutral particle beams for strategic
defenses" (p. 44).
Adelman claims to blunt criticism of the SDI's
negative effect on the ABM Treaty by writing:

> I believe that the main threats to that
> treaty lie elsewhere. First and foremost
> of these is the Soviets' almost certain
> violation of ABM provisions with the new
> radar under construction at Krasnoyarsk.
> This Soviet development is most
> disturbing. (p. 44)

Adelman is disappointed that the assumption
accompanying the ABM Treaty--that limitation on
defenses would lead to limitation on offensive
weapons--has not worked out. He argues that SDI
must be survivable and cost-effective, and that
even a less than leak-proof defense "could
markedly increase a potential attacker's
uncertainty about his likelihood of success.
This is the quintessence of deterrence" (p. 46).
A lengthy section of his piece is devoted to
the morality of SDI and the lack of morality of
MAD: "we cannot simply sit back and forever
assume that the only deterrent is the threat of
mutual annihilation, a markedly depressing
condition which today drives humanity toward some
inevitable psychic breakdown" (p. 48). Adelman
claims support for the morality issue by citing
the fact 1,000 clergymen have publicly endorsed
SDI with the statement "that if a non-nuclear,
genuinely defensive system is feasible, then its
deployment . . .is not only morally justifiable,
but perhaps even obligatory for the American

people and their government" (p. 48).
The author further writes:

> To the extent that defensive systems
> can actually reduce the risks of war,
> regardless of whether that war results
> from accident, miscalculation or
> deliberate design, it would be morally
> proper, if not morally imperative, to
> deploy those systems (p. 48).

Adelman provides further moral perspective by
quoting from Bishop O'Rourke of Peoria Illinois:
" 'To destroy unmanned missiles . . . far removed
from all population centers would be a vastly
superior form of defense compared to the policy
of deterrence as we know it today'" (p.48).

3.   Brown, Harold. 1986. Is SDI technically
        feasible? Foreign Affairs 64 ("America and
        the World 1985" issue): 435-454.

In this article the former secretary of defense
in the Carter administration sets forth his
assessment of various SDI technologies. He
specifically excludes an analysis of the
political desirability of SDI.
Brown estimates that around the year 2000
several types of technologies could be
technically feasible. Those nearest to
deployable status include hard-point defenses for
protection of ICBM silos, hardened and mobile
ICBMs, and certain C^3I centers from warheads in
their terminal phase of flight. Such a program
would involve hardened radars used in conjunction
with improved models of the Spartan and Sprint
ABMs developed two decades ago. As both
missiles were designed to employ nuclear
warheads, their use with conventional warheads
would require redesign and would prolong the time
needed before they are deployable.
Another potentially deployable system would
involve space-based kinetic-energy weapons. Such
a system would consist of satellites carrying
rockets to be fired at Soviet ICBMs in their
boost phase. But Brown cautions that considerable
work is required on this type of SDI program and

notes that the success of such a system would
depend not only upon American technological
success but upon the lack of Soviet
countermeasures as well.

Looking five to ten years beyond 2000, Brown
writes that more elaborate space- and ground-
based technologies could be feasible, but that
"increased uncertainty, however, naturally
attaches the further out we look" (p. 438).
Among the more likely of these technologies Brown
mentions the neutral particle beam and the
chemical laser. He notes that, in regard to
both, substantial technical problems remain to be
resolved, including for the former the need to
provide a powerful new energy source, possibly a
nuclear power plant for placement in orbit.

Further past 2000 are two lasers, the free-
electron laser and the excimer laser. About
these Brown writes, "Both are now many orders of
magnitude away from achieving the intensity
necessary for the required lethality" (p. 440).
Because of weight and energy considerations,
Brown suggests that these lasers should be
ground-based. Used in this mode, the laser beams
would be directed at mirrors on satellites and
then focused upon their targets.

Still further away in terms of the time needed
to work out a deployable system are x-ray lasers
powered by nuclear explosions and electromagnetic
railguns. Brown states that the proof of the
basic principle for a bomb-driven x-ray lasing
capability has been established, and that the
railgun technology may also have promise.

Brown observes that the costs for the software
needed to provide battle management of the
various SDI weapons could range from between $500
million and $5 billion. His view is that the
expense is less a factor than designing an
effective software system and developing the
means to find and correct errors within it. He
notes that such problems are only now being
addressed, and that considerable time will be
required to fully evaluate the state of the
technology in relation to the duties that will be
required by an SDI system.

According to Brown, all the SDI weapons will
need to be provided with early warning capability

with advanced infrared sensors carried on satellites in, near, or above geosynchronous orbit. Such satellites, he, writes would have to be protected from various Soviet efforts to suppress them.

In his assessment of various SDI weapon feasibilities, Brown writes that the post-boost and midcourse phases of the flight trajectory appear to offer the most difficulty to defensive measures. He also calls attention to the need for ensuring that catastrophic failure in one of the defensive layers does not lead to overall system failure. This goal, he suggests, will be a difficult and expensive one to achieve.

Brown offers a set of suggestions regarding the placement of priorities in the SDI program: (1) Work should commence to define the design of a ground-based terminal defense system capable of defending ICBM silos and possibly the population as well, if the latter should become feasible. Full-scale engineering development of such a defense should be deferred for several years pending the answering of two questions--whether less vulnerable ICBM basing modes can be developed, and whether mutual reductions in strategic offensive missiles can be worked out with Moscow. (2) Space-based kinetic kill weapons should be deemphasized because potential Soviet countermeasures make them seem unpromising. (3) A full-scale program is needed to develop the technology to provide surveillance warning, and tracking capability to support whatever SDI weapons technologies are built. (4) Development of a range of optical technology is needed to ensure the necessary brightness and accuracy of beam weapons. (5) The electromagnetic railgun, nuclear-pumped x-ray laser, and probably the neutral particle beam programs all belong to the preliminary technology category. (7) Directed-energy weapons such as the excimer laser and the free-electron laser should continue to receive support.

Brown concludes by writing that population defense against a responsive Soviet threat looks "poor through the year 2010 and beyond" (p. 454). Peering further into the future, Brown feels that population defense is still questionable owing to the inherent advantages of offense over defense.

4.   Douglass, Joseph, Jr., and Samuel T. Cohen.
      1985.   SDI: the   hidden   opportunity.
      Defense Science 2003+ 4 (August/September):
      5-8.

Douglas and Cohen argue that SDI is in trouble:
The Pentagon bureaucracy has opposed the concept
since its introduction because bureaucrats
correctly see the SDI costs as coming out of
their hide, so to speak, and because supporters
have promised more than they can deliver in
unattainable objectives. Thus, the authors
maintain, SDI is being unfairly judged because
its immediate role is not being adequately
explained.
    The authors explain that SDI's role now is to
defeat Soviet strategy before it can be
implemented. Their contention is that Soviet
strategy calls for a first strike designed to
destroy the majority of the U.S. nuclear forces
and so prevent the successful mounting of a well-
orchestrated second strike. According to this
logic, the minimum (and most important)
requirement for the SDI is to ensure the ability
of the United States to deny the basic Soviet war
objective, and to retain the capacity to reply to
a first strike with an organized powerful second
strike.
    The authors further note that protection
against ballistic missiles alone is not
sufficient, as U.S. retaliatory forces can be
placed in jeopardy by other types of delivery
systems such as cruise missiles and bombers.
Thus, defense against these must be developed and
deployed.
    Secondary roles for the SDI would be to help
protect strategic reserves that are not committed
immediately upon attack and to limit damage to
the United States. This last measure should
involve not only substantial meshing of the SDI
with civil defense but also a recovery program.

5.   Fletcher, James C. 1984. The technologies
      for ballistic missile defense. Issues in
      Science and Technology 1 (no. 1):15-29.

Fletcher was the leader of the study team that
produced for President Reagan the so-called

Fletcher Report on the technologies that could be moved forward to eventual SDI utilization. In this article Fletcher expands upon the study's analyses.

The author states that the conclusion of the Fletcher Report holds that despite "enormous hurdles," technological developments of the past several decades "show great promise for ballistic missile defense" against a massive Soviet attack involving thousands of ICBMs and SLBMs propelling tens of thousands of warheads. He also explains the rationale behind the layered defense-in-depth concept favored by the Fletcher Report. The idea is that a series of moderately effective defense layers can produce a very high overall system effectiveness. For example, four layers, each of which is 70 percent effective, will provide an overall effectiveness of more than 99 percent. This is more efficient in terms of economic costs than building one layer that is 99 percent effective.

Fletcher describes a hypothetical SDI system to explain how a future SDI might work. He explains that the purpose of the research suggested in the Fletcher Report is to define those technologies which must be demonstrated in the 1990s to permit a future administration to determine whether to proceed with ballistic missile defense for the twenty-first century.

The technological optimism seen in the Fletcher Report is reflected in Fletcher's article. The author writes that a complete four-phase layered system has the potential after the year 2000 "for protecting nearly all of the population perhaps even greater than 99 percent, in my opinion--against massive nuclear attacks" (p. 26).

In response to criticism of SDI concepts, Fletcher writes that his study team took into consideration such factors as Soviet countermeasures and the difficulties of developing a battle management program, and that identified obstacles seem capable of being resolved. He notes that some of those who make systems analyses suggesting SDI failure are making arbitrary assumptions of performance that could be in error. He also calls attention to the fact that the cooperation of the USSR in reducing the number of its offensive missiles will make the SDI task considerably easier.

6.   Fusion Energy Foundation Scientific Staff. 1984. Beam weapons--an alternative to nuclear destruction. Fallbrook, CA: Aero Publishers.

This book offers unabashed support for directed-energy weapons. Much of its thrust is the claim that the Soviets are substantially ahead in the military applications of various beam technologies. The unqualified statement is made that "no matter what the Russians say, within the next 10 years they will have space-based antimissile beam weapons" (p. 72). The statement is based on the allegation that the Soviets have been working on such weapons for more than twenty years and that the infrastructure of radar installations, including mobile radars, has already been constructed.

In a section entitled "Answering the Critics," the authors suggest that the critics of beam weapons should be placed in the same general category as those who used to assert that airplanes would never fly. The book contains the familiar explanations of the principles upon which the various potential weapons for SDI might be based (e.g., chemical lasers, particle beam, etc.).

7.   Graham, Lt. General Daniel O. (Ret.). 1983. We must defend America-and put an end to MADness. Chicago: Regnery Gateway, 1983.

Daniel O. Graham is a retired Army lieutenant general. His last assignment in 1976 was as director of the Defense Intelligence Agency. He too became concerned about the state of affairs regarding the strategic relationship between the United States and the USSR. In particular, General Graham was unhappy with the nuclear strategy followed throughout much of the cold war that sought to protect the United States from nuclear attack by promising an even more devastating nuclear retaliation upon the Soviet

Union--the policy known as mutual assured destruction, or MAD. In the years immediately preceeding the president's speech of March 23, 1983, General Graham personally organized a task force to investigate the possibilities for a non-nuclear ballistic missile defense (BMD). He called his organization High Frontier, Inc. The strategic logic advanced in We Must Defend America--and Put an End to MADness reflects much of the thinking that gave emphasis to, and readily accepted the thrust of, President Reagan's Star Wars speech.

General Graham proposed his High Frontier plan against a background of comparison with the unpreparedness of the English vis-a-vis Nazi Germany in the late 1930s. His tragic hero of that period was Sir Winston Churchill, whom Graham characterizes as the one politician who correctly perceived the growing danger from Germany but whose entreaties to increase military preparations went partially unheeded. Graham draws direct parallels between the time of England's blindness to threat and the United States of the present:

> We are witnessing an eerie and tragic repetition of history. The United States, today's leader of the opposition to the powerful totalitarian communist system, is following the footsteps of Great Britain, yesteryear's leader of the opposition to Nazism. The stench of appeasement, pacifism, self-flagellation, and abandonment of principle hangs heavy over our land. (p. 11)

And,

> When Churchill and the military leadership demanded repairs of Britain's defenses, Baldwin and Chamberlain countered with arguments that such action was "provocative and destabilizing," that "increased defense spending would hurt domestic social programs," and that the small British heavy bomber force was an "adequate deterrent." (p. 13)

Further,

> one need not be a historian to realize
> the disturbing similarities between pre-
> war Britain and America today. In the
> face of an even more powerful
> totalitarian state with even more clearly
> stated goals of world domination,
> American politicians and intellectuals
> pursue the same arguments and policies
> which tempted the aggressor to strike
> Britain in 1939. (pp. 15-16)

Striking the ubiquitous note found in much pro-
SDI literature, Graham castigates those who made
the decisions in the late 1960s and mid-1970s not
to build an ABM, and suggests that those
decisions be reevaluated in the light of new
technologies and other changes. Graham argues
that deserting strategic deterrence and
emphasizing "a balance of terror involving
visions of indescribable disaster for everyone,
which is all that our present sole emphasis on
offensive forces seems to offer" (p. 23), was a
serious mistake that can be rectified by
redirecting scientific talent to strategic
defense. He further argues that if the United
States were adequately defended, the dangerous
policy of MAD could be abandoned along with its
pernicious political side effects. These,
according to Graham, are the terrorization of
Americans by the consequences of MAD if the
policy of nuclear deterrence fails, and the
resultant adoption by such citizens of
disarmament programs like the Nuclear Freeze
movement, as they are led to enlist in the
pacifist Left in desperation.

Graham suggests that due to technological
advancement over the years since the ICBM threat
first became apparent, in the late 1950s, it
would have been possible to build a BMD, and he
asks why such defenses were never built. Among a
number of answers he says the root of the problem
is "adherence to bad strategy. The bad strategy
is mutual assured destruction, although
'strategy' is an unduly flattering term to apply
to this odd theory" (p. 37). Two corollaries of

the MAD policy particularly distress Graham and others. The first is that to maintain the balance of terror (MAD) necessary to maintain peace at the nuclear level, cities and populations must not be protected. This of course means that if MAD fails, populations are lost. The second unappealing corollary is that maintaining the balance of terror also requires that the strategic offensive forces remain balanced, with no advantage accruing to either side that could be turned into a first-strike temptation. Graham suggests that while an effective arms control regime might keep the appropriate balance, such a regime has not been successfully negotiated. Thus both sides, the Soviet Union far more than the United States, have resorted to piling up more offensive missiles to be assured of riding out the other sides' potential first strike. The situation is made worse, Graham emphasizes, by the fact that the Soviets are not only disregarding arms control constraints; they are also undercutting MAD by building both offensive and defensive forces for a "war-winning nuclear advantage" (p. 39).

What to do? Graham outlines four options, discards three and concludes that the fourth--strategic defense--is the proper policy for the United States. The three rejected options are to (1) sharply increase U.S. nuclear offensive forces so that a heavy Soviet first strike could be absorbed without appreciably diminishing the number of surviving weapons that could cut through Soviet defense to kill many more millions of Soviets, thus reestablishing the balance of terror; (2) place U.S. offensive forces on an "attack on warning" alert, which means that Soviet cities would be fired at should intelligence indicate a Soviet attack; (3) adopt a counterforce strategy in a preemptive mode, which would require the United States to contemplate first striking the Soviet offensive missiles and reducing the Soviet retaliatory capacity so that the United States would survive. Finally, the fourth option would be to defend the United States against strategic nuclear attack.

In arguing for strategic defense Graham states that a perfect defense is possible, but, fortunately for his case, he claims it is not necessary. What he offers is a three-layered non-nuclear, defense that takes advantage of weakness in parts of the Soviet ballistic flight path from launch to termination, thus nearly guaranteeing the survival of land-based ICBMs against a Soviet attack. This strategy, in Graham's view, would add so much uncertainty to a Soviet attack on the silos that any confidence in the efficacy of a Soviet first strike would be destroyed. Coupled with deterrence, it would also prevent attack. Graham extols the non-nuclear characteristics of his plan, which is based on kinetic kill vehicles and fast accelerating rockets with conventional explosive warheads. He supports the use of the more exotic beam weapons for later deployment if and when technology makes them appear effective.

An interesting aside is Graham's analysis of the nuclear-pumped x-ray laser as being a poor candidate for BMD because of its one shot character. It destroys itself after firing one burst of x-rays--a feature easily used to its great disadvantage by the Soviets, who could presumably send a missile to attack it, thus resulting in its self-destruction. Graham supports a vigorous civil space program. Regarding Soviet threats to the survivability of the High Frontier system, he states, "Each threat became manageable through a combination of technical or operational countermeasures" (p. 95). Concerning SDI's effect on the ABM Treaty (i.e., nullification of it), Graham states that in his opinion it is not an issue. He also brings up the matter of mutual deployment of BMD, such that neither side could realistically target the other's offensive forces in a first strike, as preparatory to reducing the number of offensive systems.

8. Gray, Colin S. 1985. SDI necessary for national security. <u>Defense Science</u> <u>2003+</u> 4 (February/March):14-19.

Gray considers the dilemma of keeping weapons out of space, but also the need to protect the

American people. He concludes that when these
two principles clash, the decision must be made
in favor of protecting the American people.
Weapons in space are preferable to a ground-based
offensive arms race and a system that cannot
stand "a single serious malfunction" (p. 14).

Gray does not believe the SDI will become a
leakproof astrodome in space protecting the
United States and its allies. Taking the long
view, and based on his belief that each weapon
system has its season, he argues that a mature
defensive transition will become an offensive
transition waiting to happen and that SDI weapons
will be useful only for a while. But he also
notes that such an observation should not be
viewed as a criticism of the SDI. The SDI will
provide for a more robust form of deterrence that
should be used to buy time so that states can
address the political problems that threaten
their security. That states may not use such
time wisely is not a fault of the SDI.

Gray further argues that development and
deployment of space weaponry is both necessary
and inevitable. He compares those who argue
otherwise with the horse cavalrymen who argued
against mechanization and the surface navy
advocates who stood against naval airpower.
Space weaponization will follow what has already
happened--namely, space militarization with U.S.
satellites for early warning, intelligence
gathering, communications, navigation, and
weather observation. These activities have given
the Soviets incentives to work toward the ability
to target U.S. military space assets.

Gray charges that the Soviets would like an
ASAT treaty that would place real constraints on
the SDI while leaving the Soviets free to cheat
on it as they do on most other treaties to which
they are signatories. In addition, he notes the
close connection between space BMD and ASATs.
Then he suggests that a reasonable man should
give strategic defense the benefit of the doubt
because "there are too many key technologies that
are already proven as least as devices, if not as
weapons systems, too many promising options for
the future, and too many severe problems of the
offensive" (p. 18). If the SDI fails it will

likely be because of government failure to
develop a policy base adequate to bear the
technical program traffic, election of the wrong
person between now and 2000, enticement by an
alluring Soviet arms control plan, or U.S.
unwillingness to put national security ahead of
the political difficulty involved in amending the
ABM Treaty. As the author wryly observes, "The
United States is always capable of snatching
policy defeat from the jaws of technical victory"
(p. 19).

Gray takes on directly the criticism of the SDI
that it will not be a perfect defense and should
therefore not be built. He argues that while
thoroughly effective defense may be the goal, it
is not a high-confidence expectation;
nevertheless, there is a moral, political,
strategic, and economic case for limiting the
threat to the United States to several hundred
nuclear weapons rather than leaving the United
States completely vulnerable to however many
weapons are currently targeted on the country. He
notes that an uncertain level of defensive
effectiveness, well short of 100 percent,
seriously erodes the confidence of Soviet
planners that they can design a rational plan of
attack. Soviet confidence would be further
decreased if U.S. defensive strategy involved
preferential defense.

In answer to the charge that the Soviets might
be provoked through fear to first strike before
SDI is in place, Gray answers that "the
possibility of a near-term nuclear ambush for a
U.S. defensive transition is wildly implausible"
(p. 19). The United States can enhance that
implausibility by carefully guarding the SDI
during the defensive transition and by
maintaining deterrence. The offensive forces
holding a deterrent threat will be assisted in
their survivability of a Soviet strike by even
leaky defensive deployments.

Gray warns of Soviet efforts to thwart the SDI
militarily, through offensive and defensive
deployments. More likely to succeed, in his view,
will be Soviet efforts to derail the SDI by
feeding to U.S. domestic critics evidence that
allegedly shows them it will fail and by offering

arms control bribes. He concludes by writing
that he has more faith in United States' mastery
of the SDI technology than in its ability to deal
with its allies, and to build and sustain the
policy commitment necessary to succeed in the SDI
mission.

9.   Gray, Colin S. 1985.   Emerging policy triad
        defense, offense & arms control. Defense
        Science 2003+ 4 (April/May):26-40.

The author is concerned about what he terms
"prudent defense planning" for the Geneva
bargaining process. He warns that a series of
related events may erode support for the
modernization of the U.S. strategic offensive
forces which he deems important for Geneva
negotiations. Erosion of support for force
modernization may come from technological success
in SDI research coupled with politically
expedient denigration of offensive forces. The
disfavor which Gray fears will befall the
modernization of offensive forces could also be
augmented by government hesitancy to proceed with
what critics might call a first-strike
capability. Further, the modernization process
could wane due to the pressure for funding to be
increasingly allocated to defensive systems.
        Countering these potentially negative trends
for offensive force modernization, Gray argues
that Washington should develop and deploy state-
of-the-art strategic offensive forces in order to
create a political climate in which Moscow will
be more likely to respond to American arms
control negotiators. Rounding out the kind of
leverage Gray would like the United States to
possess at Geneva would be action which he views
as complimentary to force modernization, such as
maintenance of the SDI research momentum.

10.   Hoffman, Fred S. 1983.   1983 summary
        report: ballistic missile defenses and
        U.S. national security. Washington, D.C.:
        Institute for Defense Analysis, October.

Following President Reagan's 1983 speech, two
government studies were undertaken to define a

long-term research and development program for ballistic missile defense. One of these studies, the Future Security Strategy Study, was designed to assess the role of defensive systems in future security strategy. The assessment was done by two teams, one an interagency group and the other composed of outside experts. The latter group was chaired by Fred S. Hoffman and its assessment is generally referred to as the Hoffman Report. It is summarized as follows.

The study team identified four major factors in support of the SDI. First, effective defensive systems will reduce reliance on morally unacceptable threats of massive destruction and can open up new avenues for arms control agreements with the Soviet Union. Second, rapidly developing new technologies present opportunities for resisting aggression and the deterrence of conflict that are more attractive than has previously been the case. Third, strategic defense offers the possibility of denying enemy attack objectives and countering the erosion in confidence in U.S. alliance guarantees resulting from the growth in Soviet military capabilities. Fourth, strategic defense is necessary as part of the United States hedge against the ominous threat that the Soviets will unilaterally deploy an SDI.

Although the study team recognized the possibility of a multilayered defense providing a "nearly leakproof defense," it felt that this objective was a distant one and thus suggested consideration of "intermediate options" first. The examples given of intermediate strategic defense include anti-tactical ballistic missile defenses for NATO; defense of selected high-priority targets in the United States, with terminal and midcourse defenses; and a limited boost phase intercept capability against the largest Soviet ICBMs. The study team also noted that the intermediate options should be accompanied by a "comprehensive review of air defense technologies, leading to the development of useful systems concepts" to counter the possible increase in the air-breathing threat (p. 3).

The study team pointed out that strategic

stability might be increased by using the SDI to
reduce the prelaunch vulnerability of U.S.
offensive forces, but that to accomplish this
goal, the defensive forces themselves would have
to be relatively invulnerable to Soviet attack.
It also expressed the guarded hope that if the
Soviets become convinced that the West has the
will to resist Moscow's goals of destabilization
and domination of other states, a regime
featuring mutual restrictions on offensive forces
and the deployment of defensive forces could
develop.

In a section of the study summary entitled
"Supporting Rationale," considerable effort was
devoted to explaining the advantages of negating
the effectiveness of a Soviet military strike
against U.S. offensive assets such as C^3I targets
and ICBM silos. The argument advanced is that
even a leaky defense of such targets could
seriously erode the confidence of Soviet
planners and thus deter attacks. Regarding the
problem of defending NATO, the study team sees
advantages for deployment of SDI components with
modest capabilities against Soviet tactical
ballistic missiles, either conventional or
nuclear-tipped. The study team's argument is
that the Soviets would be much less inclined to
attack NATO if Moscow had considerable
uncertainty about the success of a missile attack
against critical military targets in an SDI-
protected Western Europe. Further, the study
team reasoned that if an SDI could modestly
protect the means of quick reinforcement of the
NATO battle from the United States, the Soviets
would think twice about significantly raising the
ante by increasing their attack upon selected
U.S. resupply targets by a massive amount.

11. Hoffman, Fred S. 1984. Active defense and
    Western security. Paper presented at the
    26th Annual International Institute for
    Strategic Studies Conference at Avignon,
    France, September 13-16.

As noted, the author was the chair of the so-
called Hoffman Report, which was delivered to
President Reagan after the Star Wars speech. In

this paper Hoffman analyzes the United States' decision in the early 1970s to abandon active defenses against ballistic missiles. His assessment is that the decision was prompted by the existence of MAD and the belief that leaky ABM defenses were not useful.

Hoffman suggests that Soviet leaders have not subscribed to the MAD doctrine and that the United States should seek to work on the true motives of the Soviet leaders. He writes:

> Soviet leaders are most likely to consider the use of nuclear weapons if they are considering or involved in non-nuclear military operations against the general purpose forces of one or more of the major Western allies." (p. 4)

Hoffman then suggests that in Soviet eyes the success of such a venture would involve, first, destruction of the Western recourse to nuclear weapons and then the destruction of the ability of the United States and its allies to reinforce their troops engaged in a European battle. He thus reasons that denial by means of the SDI of such Soviet objectives "would contribute powerfully to deterring attacks by them" (p. 6).

Hoffman argues that preferential defense of the kinds of military targets the Soviets might want to destroy in the context of a European war could be an effective dissuader of Soviet attack, even though this strategy would not protect cities in a MAD context.

Among the problems for an SDI that Hoffman cites as the most serious is the vulnerability of SDI components to attacks against them, particularly with respect to space-based assets. He suggests that this concern must be a major part of SDI research.

Hoffman also disputes the views held by anti-SDI groups. First he notes that the fear of quick release of firing orders is much less a factor with the non-nuclear SDI than with the traditional nuclear ABMs. Next he suggests that the addition of protection to U.S. cities will not worry the Soviets. His evidence is that at those times when the United States had great

superiority over the Soviets and U.S. cities were
not so vulnerable, the Soviets seemed not to be
worrying about U.S. first strikes insofar as they
built the Berlin Wall and placed missiles in
Cuba. Hoffman also argues that the addition of
defenses to vulnerable offensive forces need not
be destabilizing.

Hoffman urges that a modest BMD would be worth
having. In particular he points out that certain
modest development might offer considerable
protection against theater ballistic missiles and
SLBMs that threaten NATO. Since the Soviets have
propounded the notion that missiles that do not
reach the United States are not strategic, it
follows that theater ballistic missile defense
would not constitute an ABM as defined in the ABM
Treaty; hence it would be legal.

Concerned about unanswered Soviet SDI activity,
Hoffman writes that "superimposed on the other
trends in the military balance, a one-sided
Soviet deployment of effective defenses could be
a disaster for the West" (p. 16).

Hoffman's analysis leads him to suggest that
the SDI is unlikely to render nuclear weapons
obsolete in the foreseeable future, but does
offer the possibility of so complicating a Soviet
planner's task as to reduce the military primacy
of the ballistic missile. He also notes that SDI
will permit a growing degree of imprecision
regarding the number of mobile ICBM deployments,
assuming the absence of reliable verification
arrangements.

12.   Jastrow, Robert. 1983. How to make
       nuclear weapons obsolete. Boston: Little,
       Brown.

Jastrow presents an elaborate discussion of the
threat to the survivability of the land and air
legs of the U.S. strategic triad. He then argues
that U.S. missile-launching submarines may be a
deterrent against attack on the U.S. cities, but
that they may not deter attack upon U.S.
strategic forces. In the rest of the book he
provides a description of the various types of
space defense weapons and how they might work
against ballistic missiles in the four phases of
ballistic missile flight.

13. ----. 1984. Reagan vs. the scientists: why the president is right about missile defense. <u>Commentary</u>, January, 23-32.

Jastrow, himself a noted scientist, responds in this article to such well-known critics of President Reagan's SDI proposal as Richard Garwin, former Secretary of Defense Robert McNamara, former National Security Advisor McGeorge Bundy, and Senator Edward Kennedy, and to such media persons as Anthony Lewis and James Reston. In particular he outlines their objections to the SDI (which concern the difficulty of effectively shooting down ICBMs and warheads) and their attachment to mutual assured destruction as a deterrent policy.

In rebuttal, Jastrow argues that two legs of the U.S. strategic triad, land-based ICBMs and intercontinental bombers, have become increasingly vulnerable to the new Soviet ICBMs. Further, he is not comfortable with a monad composed essentially of U.S. submarines carrying SLBMs. He worries about the difficulty of command and control for a far-away submerged submarine, and about the fact that until the new Trident II is deployed, SLBMs are best suited for destroying cities rather than Soviet ICBMs in their silos--and thus represent a poor response for a Soviet attack on U.S. strategic forces.

Correction of the growing vulnerability of the land-based ICBMs is the basic rationale Jastrow uses to support the SDI concept. His preference is a hard-point defense application.

Jastrow ends his article on a different note. He suggests that nuclear-tipped missiles will become less useful as advances in technology permit a conventional TNT warhead to hit within "a yard or two" of its target. Then:

> The military uses of the nuclear bomb will dwindle into nothingness. And so it may come to pass, as President Reagan suggested, that the scientists who gave us nuclear weapons will also give us "the means of rendering these weapons impotent and obsolete" (p. 32).

14.   Keyworth, George A. 1985. Security and
stability: the role for strategic defense.
Institute on Global Conflict and
Cooperation, Policy Papers, No. 1,
University of California, San Diego. (This
booklet was written while the author was
science advisor to the president, a post he
has since relinquished.)

Keyworth argues that the stability of MAD has
been gradually eroded by the thrust of technology
that has rendered two parts of the U.S. strategic
triad, bombers and land-based missiles,
increasingly vulnerable to a first strike. He
notes that the deterrent utility of the third
part of the triad, submarines, rests upon their
continued ability to remain hidden in the oceans.
    The author reports that three motivations led
to the president's speech of March 23, 1983:
the immorality of MAD, the decreasing number of
options from which future presidents could select
to maintain the survivability of U.S. deterrent
forces, and the "utter failure of the mechanisms
of arms control" (p. 2) to reduce the aggregation
of nuclear weapons. He writes that prior to 1983
President Reagan was concerned about these
problems, but that it was not until 1983 that the
technology appeared to offer a chance for
effective BMD.
    Keyworth reflects that the 1970s represented a
test of whether it is likely that offensive arms
will be reduced in the guaranteed absence of
defense (a reference to the ABM Treaty). He also
recalls the results of that test as being "most
discouraging."
    He describes the ICBM as being the first
nuclear system to be defended against with the
SDI because it is the most destablilizing given
its first-strike capability. Concerning the
Soviet ICBM force Keyworth writes that "an ICBM
arsenal this size can be structured for only one
logical purpose for the Soviets--to launch or to
threaten a preemtive strike against our own
retaliatory forces" (p. 3).
    Seeking to clear up uncertainties about what
the SDI is intended to protect, Keyworth writes:
"SDI is intended to protect populations, not just

weapons, and it's intended to protect not just the United States, but our Allies as well" (p. 4). The basis for this claim is Keyworth's optimism that the United States can devise boost phase intercept capabilities of remarkable capacity, possibly involving ground-based pulsed lasers and the use of mirrors for focusing.

He supports his claim that the SDI is not just for silo defense by quoting from a speech President Reagan gave in April 1985 before the National Space Club: "Now, this [SDI] is not, and should never be misconstrued as, just another method of protecting missile silos" (p. 7).

15. Krebs, Thomas H. 1985. Ballistic missile defense: Soviet countermeasures. Defense Science 2003+ 4 (August/September):65-75.

Krebs postulates eight Soviet countermeasure strategies to SDI: ignoring the U.S. BMD effort; reducing the U.S. BMD effort in time of war; deploying a Soviet BMD last; deploying a Soviet BMD simultaneous with the United States; deploying a Soviet BMD first; increasing other types of forces; slowing or stopping the U.S. BMD program by indirect means; and attacking the SDI as it is being deployed. Although the last prospect listed is of considerable concern to opponents of the SDI, Krebs argues that it is very unlikely because the Soviets would not run the cataclysmic risks involved in bringing it about. A reduction of SDI's importance in time of war would be difficult for several reasons.

The first use of destructive countermeasures has the singular disadvantage of giving advanced warning of an attack. Use of destructive countermeasures runs the risk, although a low one, that the U.S. has adopted a launch on warning strategy. But the most telling argument against the use of countermeasures is that in most instances they add substantial weight, cost, or accuracy penalties. The option of deploying a Soviet SDI last would probably be a choice not willingly made. Deploying Soviet SDI simultaneous with the United States would require U.S. cooperation. Construction of a Soviet SDI first would permit such a potential shortcut to the achievement of the Soviets' assumed preeminent geopolitical goal that is hard to believe they would not adopt it. Increasing other types of forces, such as cruise missiles, would depend upon U.S. anti-cruise missile activity. In a world where offensive missiles are really limited, the Soviets might increase dependency upon conventional forces, which in turn could be countered by the United States' diversion of SDI technology to this threat. Finally, slowing or stopping the U.S. BMD program by indirect means could involve either real or feigned arms control efforts.

What the Soviets actually will do could be a combination of strategies based in part upon what the United States does.

The author concludes that the United States should rapidly deploy a BMD system, air-breather defenses, and enhanced conventional forces, as it would thus be in a strong bargaining position regarding arms control.

16.   Nitze, Paul H. 1985. The objectives of arms control. Department of State Bulletin 85 (May): 57-63.

In this address, made before the International Institute for Strategic Studies in London, Ambassador Nitze reviews the development of arms control concepts from the period immediately following the nuclear bombing of Japan to 1985. Central to his discussion is the argument concerning which of two deterrence alternatives best serves the nation's interest and how various arms control measures can contribute to one alternative or the other. Nitze's preference at the beginning of the nuclear age, and currently, is that deterrence is strengthened by adding to the existence of nuclear weapons the military capability to deny an enemy a realistic hope of achieving his objectives. Nitze contrasts this view with the position that the destructiveness of nuclear weapons is such that their very presence is sufficient to deter their use by enemy states.

The president's special advisor on arms control also writes that SALTs I and II failed to provide adequate restraint on Soviet offensive nuclear force buildup, and that Moscow was not willing to comply with the SALT constraints on strategic defensive systems. These circumstances, in addition to the technical advances in BMD possibilities, set the stage for President Reagan's SDI proposals. Assuming SDI technologies are feasible and meet certain criteria, Nitze explains that the United States would begin a transition to a posture whereby greater reliance would be placed upon defensive systems, but one that for many years to come would feature strategic offensive systems. In particular, he writes that "defenses could enhance deterrence by creating excessive complications for an aggressor's planning for a possible first strike, thereby lessening the chance that he might seriously contemplate it" (p. 62).

Perhaps the most important part of Nitze's address, a point that he has made in other contexts, is the explanation of the criteria by which the Reagan administration says it will judge the feasibility of SDI technologies. As Nitze himself states, the criteria will be demanding. First, the new technologies must result in defensive systems that are "reasonably survivable." Otherwise the defenses themselves would constitute tempting targets for a Soviet first strike, thus decreasing rather than increasing, stability. Second, Nitze stated the new technologies must be "cost-effective at the margin." By that he means that it must be cheaper for the United States to build additional defenses than it is for the Soviets to add offensive capability needed to overwhelm the defense. Failure to meet this criterion would mean that the SDI might encourage an offensive systems competition rather than redirecting efforts away from offensive forces to defensive forces.

Nitze underlined the president's intention that the SDI not be used to achieve superiority and that the transition to a posture featuring both defense and offense would be balanced, with the deployment of SDI technologies being a matter for negotiation with the Soviets. Regarding SDI

negotiations, however, Nitze stated that to
support negotiation does not imply that the
Soviets would have a veto over U.S. strategic
defense programs.

Looking ahead to a world less dependent for
security upon nuclear weapons, or even to a world
in which nuclear weapons have been eliminated,
Nitze suggests that very substantial arms control
on conventional forces would be required or, in
the absence of arms control, that conventional
forces would probably need to be substantially
improved.

17.   Payne, Keith, and Colin S. Gray. 1984.
Toward ballistic missile defense. In the
nuclear reader, Charles W. Kegley, Jr.,
and Eugene R. Wittkopf, eds. New York: St.
Martin's Press.

The authors focus upon the advantages of a
transition from strategic offense to strategic
defense and how such a transition may be more
safely made. They also issue warnings regarding
Soviet advantages during the initial transition
period, given the existing Soviet infrastructure,
which supports BMD to a greater extent than do
comparable U.S. assets. To prevent the Soviets
from taking advantage of a first strike in a
crisis situation afforded by their head start on
some aspects of the SDI, the authors counsel
early deployment of the means to terminally
defend U.S. land-based missiles.

Patience spanning a number of administrations
is suggested, along with incremental building of
the SDI with each increment capable of standing
on its own merits, even if successive deployments
were to fail for political or technical reasons.
Success in the achievement of superiority of
strategic defense over offense will require
patience as well (it also seems unlikely given
the trends of the past thirty years), but the
authors remind their readers that defense has
often achieved superiority in the last 100 to
1000 years.

The authors claim a crucial distinction between
offensive and defensive types of deterrence: If
the former fails, a holocaust is virtually

ensured, whereas if the latter fails, there is a chance to avoid a holocaust.

The authors predict that NATO will not be enthusiastic about the transition to strategic defense because of concerns that the U.S. nuclear umbrella will thereby be eroded. Hence they prescribe that NATO should enhance conventional forces to allay fears and deter Soviet adventurism. Regarding the Soviet response to the transition to strategic defense, the authors also predict that Moscow will likely respond with a combination of arms control, diplomatic initiatives, and strong military programs, as suggested by past behavior.

The authors believe that this strategic transition would be compatible with arms control. For example, deep reductions in offensive missiles, which probably cannot be verified, could be tolerated in the presence of the SDI, which would compensate for all but large-scale cheating. They also see the possibility that a strategic transition will lead to the transformation of U.S.-Soviet deterrence, but they doubt it can be transcended.

18.   Teller, Edward. 1985. Science and technology in the Strategic Defense Initiative. _Defense Science 2003+_ 4 (April/May):17-24.

The author, a nuclear physicist, opposes the policy of mutual assured destruction for several reasons. It is morally bankrupt. The American people appear unhappy with the policy. And it is Teller's view that the Soviets are working on strategic defenses that might erode the value of MAD's retaliatory threat.

Teller extols the x-ray laser, which can be popped up on the receipt of warning of a Soviet attack, as an alternative to the pre-deployment of battlestation satellites, which he claims are too vulnerable.

The author decries the fact that the United States has no strategic defense at this time. As he puts it, "That we have no defense, that we have practically no attempt at defense is indeed a scandal" (p. 21). He thus urges further work

on the SDI technologies involving the protection
of ICBM silos, which may in turn suggest ways to
protect cities. Teller notes that U.S. SDI
efforts may force the Soviets to intensify their
SDI work and that such a consequence will be
useful in the sense that both nations would be
building shields rather than offensive weapons.
He writes approvingly of such a situation: "This
will bear less of a resemblance to a balance of
terror. At least there will be more balance and
less terror" (p. 24).

19.   Teller, Edward, and Carl Sagan. 1985. Pro
      and con. Discover, September, 66-74.

Teller argues that the Soviet rulers have never
accepted the policy of mutual assured
destruction. He notes that at the time the U.S.
was dismantling its ABM system, the Soviets were
constructing a defense system near Moscow.
Further evidence of Soviet rejection of MAD,
according to Teller, is the fact that the
Russians have built an extensive civil defense
system. He notes that in 1984 the Soviet Union
spent $13 per person on civil defense, whereas
the United States spent only 78 cents. Teller
also points out that some of the more ingenious
possibilities for the U.S. SDI have come from
insights gleaned by U.S. scientists from the work
of Soviet scientists, persons whose work has not
been published since 1979. Teller wonders
whether this means that the Soviets are
considerably ahead of the United States in SDI
research.
The author advances a new reason for supporting
ABMs with small nuclear warheads--namely, the
possibility that the Soviets would carry
biological agents in ICBM warheads instead of
nuclear warheads. If struck by a non-nuclear
kinetic kill vehicle, the bacteria or viruses in
a warhead would not be destroyed. But they would
be vaporized if the U.S. defensive missile
carried a small nuclear weapon. Another
advantage of using small nuclear defensive
warheads is that they might prevent the salvage-
fusing of Soviet warheads more effectively than
would be the case if non-nuclear kinetic kill
vehicles were used.

20.   Toomay, John C.   Summer 1985.   The case for
      ballistic missile defense.   <u>Daedalus</u>
      114:219-237.

Toomay is a retired Air Force major general who
was a member of the Defensive Technologies Study
Team, the so-called Fletcher Panel, gathered to
advise President Reagan on SDI.   Expressing
concern over the movement of the United States
from a position of strategic superiority to "a
declining strategic margin," the author analyzes
four types of BMD in terms of relationships with
the ABM Treaty and strategic arms control
criteria, effectiveness, effect on the Soviets,
and economic costs.
Toomay gives high marks to terminal defense for
hard-point targets, particularly that which he
calls high-leveraged defense, a combination of
preferential defense with ICBMs whose benefits
include mobility, hardness, and concealment.   He
argues that hard, mobile Midgetmen or Minutemen
moved among many silos would enhance strategic
stability by leaving U.S. cities unprotected--not
threatening Soviet cities, but greatly adding to
the survivability of U.S. land-based missiles.
Such a deployment would meet all the author's
analytic criteria, but it would require
renegotiation of the ABM Treaty to obtain
sufficient numbers of ABM terminal interceptors.
Local area defenses, those for airbases,
seaports, and some command and control centers,
do not appear practical for technical reasons and
also because preferential attack would probably
be successful.
A light area defense for the entire nation is
attractive because it would be responsive to a
number of potential attack modes (i.e., third
nations, accidents, or terrorist strikes), and
it would raise the threshold of Soviet strikes.
The claim is made that it would be cost-effective
in the context of tens of thousands of lives
saved; but the ABM Treaty would need
modification.   An advantage of a light area
defense is that it would serve as the base from
which a more robust effort could evolve as the
threat evolves.

Regarding whole-country BMD, Toomay suggests that the unsolved technical problems that undercut confidence in the ABMs of the 1970s have been replaced by order-of-magnitude improvements in "every area previously deficient." But this observation is tempered by another one: "There are still a good number of problems to be addressed."

In reply to the concern over the Soviet response to SDI, Toomay suggests that Moscow would be more likely to react strongly to a space-based BMD than to terminal defenses. The possibility of vigorous reactions would mean that the United States should consider various ways to protect SDI launch pads and build defensive satellites to protect the space assets of an SDI system.

Advantages of whole-country BMD would include the raising of the threshold for Soviet attacks and the enhancement of the uncertainty about outcomes of Soviet planners.

Toomay claims that whole-country defense would shift the strategic balance away from deterrence by MAD to respect for the other nation's defensive forces. Arms control would loom large in a whole-country defense regime in order to limit the offensive increases triggered by defensive activities.

Although a whole-country defense would erode deterrence based upon retaliatory capability, a more attractive relationship would develop in which an aggressor would be dissuaded not by fear of retaliation so much as by "recognition of futility." Moreover, large economic costs over time should be viewed in the context of what one is willing to pay in order to avert "nuclear holocaust for centuries."

Toomay defends the need to renegotiate the ABM Treaty, and possibly other treaties, by the argument that these treaties served other purposes at other times and that new negotiations are needed for these times.

Writing to opponents of SDI, Toomay states:

> Temptations are irresistible for intellectuals, who deal in words rather than hardware, to attack broad system

concepts as if they were actual system designs, and to predict confidently the outcome of decades of research. (p. 237)

21.   U.S. Department of Defense. 1984, 1985, 1986. Soviet military power. Washington, D.C.: U.S. Government Printing Office.

This annual publication was begun by the Reagan administration. Each year it contains a detailed description, assessment, and updating of Soviet military capabilities and the technical infrastructure that supports Moscow's military forces. The documents are profusely illustrated with color and black/white photographs, artists' renditions, and charts and graphs.

The issues of Soviet Military Power published since the president's Star Wars speech indicate the growing emphasis being given by the administration to the warning that the Soviets are building an SDI that, in part, justifies the current U.S. effort.

In the 1984 issue, information regarding Soviet space operations, ASATs, ABMs, and directed-energy weapons research was scattered throughout the document. In the 1985 issue an entire chapter was devoted to the topic of "Strategic Defense and Space Programs," including air defense. The following statement is made:

By the late 1980s, the Soviets could have prototypes for ground-based lasers for ballistic missile defense. Testing of the components for a large-scale deployment system could begin in the early 1990s. The many difficulties in fielding an operational system will require much development time, and initial operational deployment is not likely in this century. However, with high priority and some significant risk of failure, the Soviets could skip some testing steps and be ready to deploy a ground-based laser BMD by the early-to-mid-1990s. (p. 44)

The 1985 document also contains what has become the standard allegation regarding ABM Treaty cheating:

> The Soviet Union is violating the ABM Treaty through the siting, orientation and capability of the large phased-array, early warning and ballistic missile target-tracking radar at Krasnoyarsk. (p. 46)

The 1986 _Soviet Military Power_ issue contains a chapter entitled, "Strategic Defense and Space Operations." In it is an artist's rendition of a ground-based laser. The explanation that accompanies the pictures states:

> The USSR already has ground-based lasers. . . capable of interfering with some U.S. satellites and could have prototypes for ground-based lasers for defense against ballistic missiles by the late 1980s. (p. 41)

Further:

> In the Soviet view, the USSR could best achieve its aims in a nuclear war if it attacks first, destroying much of the US and allied capability for retaliation. Defensive measures, both active and passive, would in turn prevent those enemy forces that survived a Soviet first strike from destroying targets in the USSR. (p. 42)

22.   U.S. Department of Defense. 1985. _Report to the Congress on the Strategic Defense Initiative._ Washington, D.C.: U.S. Government Printing Office.

In this document various agencies within the Department of Defense, including the Strategic Defense Initiative Organization, provide information regarding progress on the SDI effort. Much of the report is devoted to listing the research programs which are described in general terms, together with the amount of funds allocated to each one.

The basic research programs are: surveillance, acquisition, tracking and kill assessment; directed-energy weapons technology; kinetic-energy weapons technology; systems concepts and battle management; survivability, lethality, and key technologies (which include the development of energy sources for spacecraft and logistic systems to place payloads into space); and general management support.

It is estimated that the SDI effort will cost approximately $26 billion between fiscal years 1985 and 1989. The statement is made that this amount will represent less than 2% of the entire defense budget, and less than 15% of the defense research budget, for that period. Approximately 40% of the SDI budget for FY 85 through FY 89 will be invested in one item, surveillance, acquisition, tracking and kill assessment. Money for weapons research is about equally divided between directed-energy and kinetic weapons.

The report contains a response to the fact that the Congress reduced the amount of SDI funding President Reagan had requested for FY 85:

> Reallocation difficulties were exacerbated by the fact that the FY 1985 reductions were significant (21%). The SDIO was reluctant to cut back those programs which are not only a necessary part of the SDI, but also are required for other programs (such as improved missile attack detection and warning programs). The FY 1985 reductions were clearly detrimental. (Emphasis added).

The report contains appendices which describe the consultations the United States has conducted about the SDI with its allies, how the SDI interfaces with other U.S. strategic defense activities, and the compliance of SDI research with the requirements of the ABM Treaty. This last appendix lists the various research experiments and explains how they are in compliance with the ABM Treaty. This section of the report may be of particular interest to those concerned about potential violations of the Treaty's requirements.

23. U.S. Department of Defense and Department of State. 1985. Soviet strategic defense programs. Washington, D.C.: U.S. Government Printing Office, October.

This is an unusual document jointly released by the Departments of Defense and State, with a foreword jointly signed by Secretary of Defense Caspar Weinberger and Secretary of State George Shultz. As the title suggests, this booklet details Soviet SDI type activities, including cheating on the ABM Treaty, by way of providing support of the president's SDI program. Another justification for SDI activity by the United States is the assertion that a two-decade-long buildup in Soviet strategic offensive forces is eroding the retaliatory capacity of the United States upon which deterrence rests.

The document takes special note of Soviet efforts to denounce President Reagan's SDI proposal. Reference is made to a letter critical of SDI and signed by more than 200 Soviet scientists that appeared in the New York Times. That this was a propaganda effort is suggested by the fact that a number of the signatories "have been instrumental in the development of both traditional and advanced ballistic missile defensive systems" (p. 22). This statement is followed by the names of seven prominent scientists who signed the letter with explanations of the kind of SDI type work they reportedly have done.

24. U.S. Department of Defense. 1984. The Strategic Defense Initiative defensive technologies study. Washington, D.C.: U.S. Government Printing Office, April.

Following President Reagan's 1983 speech, two government studies were undertaken to define a long-term research and development program for ballistic missile defense. One of these studies, the Defensive Technologies Study, was designed to identify the most promising approaches to development of an effective ballistic missile defense, and to sketch out a suitable research and development program. James C. Fletcher was the study team's leader and the report is frequently referred to as the Fletcher Report.

The study team identified a long-term technically feasible research and development plan for the SDI. It also proposed system componets that could provide near-term options for deployment of systems with a modest effectiveness against limited threats, as well as ideas for enhancing the defense of NATO and other allies. The study concluded that the appearance of powerful new technologies justifies a major technical effort to implement the SDI; that such an effort will require strong central management; that the most effective SDI will probably be composed of multiple layers of defense and that the survivability of each layer is crucial; and, finally, that significant demonstrations of the new technologies for a layered ballistic missile defense can be performed within the next ten years.

The study team highlighted seven key functions that would have to be performed to achieve total engagement during the four phases of a ballistic missile attack flight path. These are rapid and reliable warning of attack; efficient intercept during the boost and post-boost phases; bulk filtering of lightweight penetration aids; enduring birth-to-death tracking of all threatening objects; low-cost intercept during the midcourse phase; high endoatmospheric terminal intercept; and the battle management of all the preceding functions.

The study team identified the survivability of space-based components of the SDI as a "potentially serious problem." The most likely threats to U.S. space assets were described as direct-ascent anti-satellite weapons; ground and/or space-based lasers; orbital anti-satellites with either conventional or directed-energy weapons; space mines; and fragment clouds. The study team also identified a special space logistics set of requirements. These included development of a lift vehicle capable of carrying 100 tons; the capability to service space components; the ability to make available, on orbit, material for component shielding against attack; and the capacity to transfer objects from

one orbit to another. Also noted as being
necessary were multimegawatt sources of power.
The summary report ended thus:

> The members of the Defensive
> Technologies Study Team finished their
> work with a sense of optimism. The
> technological challenges of a strategic
> defense initiative are great but not
> insurmountable . . . . The Scientific
> community may indeed give the United
> States "the means of rendering" the
> ballistic missile threat "impotent and
> obsolete". (p. 13)

25. U.S. Department of State. 1985. Bureau of
     Public Affairs. The ABM Treaty and the SDI
     Program, Current Policy Paper No. 755.
     Washington, D.C.: U.S. Government Printing
     Office, October.

In this State Department release Paul H. Nitze,
special advisor to the president and secretary of
state on arms control matters, and Abraham D.
Sofaer, legal advisor to the Department of State,
are quoted as to the testimony they gave before
the Subcommittee on Arms Control, International
Security, and Science of the House Foreign
Affairs Committee, which bears on the so-called
broad and restrictive interpretation of the ABM
Treaty.
Nitze stated that, after extensive examination,
it is the view of the Reagan administration:

> that a broader interpretation of our
> authority than that which we have applied
> to restrict our SDI research program is
> fully justified. This is, however, a
> moot point. Our SDI research program has
> been structured and, for solid reasons,
> will continue to be conducted in
> accordance with a restrictive
> interpretation of the treaty's
> obligations. (p. 1)

The president's chief arms control advisor said
that in the administration's view, the SDI

program can answer the questions originally posed by the president about new defensive technologies "while adhering to this more restrictive interpretation" (p. 1).

Sofaer set forth the basis for both the broad interpretation and the restrictive interpretation of the ABM Treaty, before echoing Nitze's statement that:

> Notwithstanding our belief in the merits of the broader interpretation, the President has decided to pursue the SDI program as currently structured, which can be accommodated within the confines of the "restrictive" interpretation-- namely, research into, but not development or testing of, systems or components based on future technology and capable of substituting for ABM interceptors, launchers, or radars. (p. 3)

The argument about a broad or restrictive interpretation of the ABM Treaty revolves around the question of how the Treaty applies to systems based on physical principles other than those understood in 1972. Those holding to a restrictive interpretation contend that Article V (1) is clear and unambiguous and means exactly what it says--that the parties to the treaty agree "not to develop, test, or deploy ABM systems or components which are sea-based, air-based, space-based, or mobile land-based." Proponents of the restrictive view also define an ABM system according to the statement made in Article II (1), as "a system to counter strategic ballistic missiles or their elements in flight trajectory, currently consisting of" ABM interceptor missiles, ABM launchers, and ABM radars.

Those supporting the broad interpretation of the Treaty agree, like Sofaer, that the restrictive interpretation is plausible, but they suggest that it is not the only reasonable interpretation and that an even more reasonable interpretation exists. Their case is based on the contention that the reference to an ABM system does not include future technology such as the exotic systems of SDI. The broad interpretationists rely heavily on reference to Agreed Statement D, a side agreement accompanying the Treaty that states:

> In order to insure fulfillment of the obligation not to deploy ABM systems and their components except as provided in Article III of the Treaty, the Parties agree that in the event ABM systems based on other physical principles and including components capable of substituting for ABM interceptor missiles, ABM launchers, or ABM radars are created in the future, specific limitations on such systems and their components would be subject to discussion in accordance with Article XIII and agreement in accordance with Article XIV of the Treaty. (p. 2)

Arguing for a broad interpretation, Sofaer claims that since the parties felt it necessary to refer to ABM systems based on other physical principles, it follows that the phrase "ABM systems" or "components" is limited to systems and components based on 1972 technology.

Having established the fact, at least in his mind, that the Treaty language is ambiguous, Sofaer uses the accepted method of handling such a situation--that is, by researching the circumtances surrounding the drafting of the Treaty to seek guidance as to its interpretation. His findings are that the negotiation records support the proposition that the Treaty definition of "ABM system" and "components" be limited to those based on the 1972 physical principles.

If one accepts Sofaer's logic, then the requirements of Agreed Statement D for discussion regarding ABM systems of exotic character will be necessary if, and when, such exotic systems are created.

26. U.S. Department of State. 1985. The
Strategic Defense Initiative. Special
Report no. 129. Washington, D.C.: U.S.
Government Printing Office, June.

The case is made in this pamphlet that Soviet
offensive and defensive buildups are perceived in
Washington as threatening the strategic stability
based upon nuclear deterrence. Special attention
is paid to what is called the "Soviet pattern of
noncompliance with existing arms control
agreements" (p. 2) and "actions which affect our
ability to verify Soviet compliance" (p. 2). An
example of the first is the radar construction at
Krasnoyarsk, in central Siberia. An example of
the second is the use of encryption of telemetry
during testing to degrade U.S. monitoring of new
Soviet military developments.
The argument presented is that an appropriate
response to the Soviet challenge is to modernize
U.S. strategic retaliatory forces and to move
ahead with the SDI as a means of preserving
deterrence and stability. It is pointed out that
"Our allies understand the military context in
which the Strategic Defensive Initiative was
established and support the SDI research
program". (p. 3)
The document concludes with the explanation of
twelve key points in which the SDI program is
explained and defended. Much emphasis is placed
on the fact that the SDI is currently made up of
research, and that only time will tell exactly
what kind of defensive architecture will be most
appropriate to U.S. needs.

27. U.S. White House. 1985. The president's
Strategic Defense Initiative. Washington,
D.C.: U.S. Government Printing Office,
January.

This booklet begins with a two-page foreword by
President Reagan, who suggests that mutual
assured destruction based upon nuclear deterrence
originally seemed to be reasonable because of two
assumptions. One was that it appeared the
Soviets accepted the proposition that both sides
should have roughly equal forces and that neither
should seek to alter the strategic balance to

gain an advantage. The second was that technology did not provide any alternative in as much as defensive systems were impractical. The president then argues that the first assumption has been upset by the pace of Soviet strategic offensive buildup, and that the second is not valid because of newly developed technologies "which may make possible a truly effective non-nuclear defense" (p. i).

The rest of the booklet is devoted to a general explanation of the SDI proposal. In the section on arms control the statement is made that the United States "does not view defensive measures as a means of establishing military superiority" (p. 5); it then continues:

> Because we have no ambitions in this regard, deployments of defensive systems would most usefully be done in the context of a cooperative, equitable, and verifiable arms control environment that regulates the offensive and defensive developments and deployments of the United States and the Soviet Union. (p. 5)

The booklet concludes with a series of questions and answers about the SDI proposal.

28. Van Cleave, William. 1986. <u>Fortress USSR</u>. Stanford, CA.: Hoover Institution Press.

The author traces the early history of the ABM debates in the United States and concludes that arms control considerations and doctrinal preferences carried more weight in preventing ABM development than cost factors or technical uncertainty. While noting that the United States has been constrained in its ABM development by the ABM Treaty and adherence to the MAD doctrine, Van Cleave argues that the Soviet Union has not been constrained by the Treaty and that Moscow has not been interested in MAD. The consequence is that the Soviets have made decisions and initiated a program that are very different from those of the United States. He writes that if the Soviet Union continues unchecked, or if no compensation is made to Soviet ABM development, an ominous advantage will accrue to Moscow. Specifically, Van Cleave is concerned about the combination of enormous strategic offensive forces coupled with a Soviet SDI, both of which are supported by an extensive Civil Defense program. This combination gives Moscow a war-fighting capability, whereas the United States has maintained only a deterrent capacity.

By way of emphasizing his point that the United States is responding to an extensive Soviet strategic defense program, that has long been in existence rather than having initiated such a program itself, Van Cleave chooses to redesignate the SDI as SDR--which stands for strategic defense response. He lists a number of Soviet activities in the air defense area, augmented by research on the same exotic technologies being investigated in relation to the U.S. SDI, to justify his assertion about the extent and duration of Soviet strategic defense activities. One of the most serious of Van Cleave's concerns is the so-called SAM upgrade problem. His contention is that advanced Soviet surface-to-air missiles such as the SA-10 and SA-12, which are ostensibly part of an air defense system designed to shoot down bombers, are capable of being upgraded to ABM status. In this context Van Cleave quotes from the Committee on the Present Danger study to the effect that Soviet modernization and upgrading may permit Moscow to quickly "break out" from the ABM Treaty with the rapid deployment of an extensive ABM system.

Van Cleave writes that the real Star Wars effort is Russian, not American, and that the Soviet space program is predominantly military in character. He warns that Soviet propaganda and disinformation activities have concentrated on convincing the world that Moscow's space program is civilian, scientific, and peaceful--all of which he claims is false.

Van Cleave devotes an entire chapter to providing evidence in support of his charge that the Soviets are systematically violating the ABM Treaty. He cites as a particularly obvious treaty violation the Krasnoyarsk radar

installation. According to the author, this
facility is not on the periphery of the Soviet
Union to provide early warning of attack as
permitted by the Treaty but, rather, is located
in central Siberia. Moreover, it is not directed
at space in support of space activities as
contended by Moscow, but is pointed at the
horizon in a mode to provide proscribed battle
management for the defense of an ICBM field in
the facility's radar coverage.

The author also maintains that the Reagan
administration has repeatedly accused the Soviet
Union of cheating on the ABM Treaty and other
arms control agreements. But he then states that
"in what must be one of the most inconsistent
policy decisions made by any president, Reagan
announced U.S. intention to continue to abide by
the same agreements that he said the Soviets were
violating" (p. 36). After comparing Soviet
violations of the ABM Treaty with the constraints
accepted by the United States on its strategic
defense development, the author writes:

> If the administration is serious about
> strategic defenses--even about research
> and development of them, since so much
> development is constrained by the ABM
> Treaty--its only choice is to act
> decisively and declare the ABM Treaty
> void by reason of Soviet nonobservance;
> or, even more to the point, because it is
> contrary to U.S. national security
> interests. (p. 37)

Van Cleave reviews the Fletcher and Hoffman
Reports submitted to President Reagan after his
1983 speech by study teams appointed to evaluate
the SDI. Although he cautions that the
optimistic projections in the Fletcher Report may
be premature, Van Cleave argues that there is
justification, nevertheless, to conclude that
technology is shifting the offense-defense cost
ratio in favor of defense, and that space
systems will play a useful future strategic
defense role. Van Cleave worries that the
enthusiasm exhibited by some SDI supporters for
the more ambitious ABM objectives, which they

often characterize as nearly in hand, will have a negative effect on the U.S. strategic posture. His point is that such a perspective tends to depreciate the importance of continued modernization programs for the current strategic offensive forces. As he puts it, "Yet for the foreseeable future, deterrence and U.S. strategic objectives depend on having modern, robust strategic offensive forces" (p. 46.)

In contrast to those SDI advocates he describes as futurist-only-oriented, Van Cleave cites the Hoffman Report as offering more modest, and thus more readily obtainable, recommendations. In particular, he supports the objective of protecting U.S. ICBMs because "the single most pressing strategic problem that has been facing the United States is the vulnerability of the ICBM force" (p. 47). Other objectives on Van Cleave's list of strategic defense goals for the near term are: (1) defense of C^3I facilities; (2) theater or tactical ABM defenses for the European allies; and (3) light area defense of the United States, including cities, to reduce death and economic loss resulting from a Soviet attack on U.S. strategic forces.

29. Yonas, Gerold. Spring 1985. The Strategic Defense Initiative. Daedalus 114:73-90.

The author summarizes the background of SDI, in the process explaining why persons such as himself, have given support to the broad objectives that flowed from President Reagan's speech of March 23, 1983. Central to the enthusiasm for basic SDI research is a sense of frustration over the current times and the resultant search for new directions. The present situation is held to be frustrating because of such issues as the buildup of Soviet strategic forces, possible violations of the ABM Treaty, the ineffectiveness of the Treaty in leading to more comprehensive constraints on strategic forces, and the difficulty in selecting a suitable basing mode for the MX. Additional impetus for the quest to find a new direction is the presence of the Nuclear Freeze movement, which is calling for a halt to further production

and testing of nuclear weapons, and the Catholic
Bishops' Pastoral Letter on War and Peace, which
expressed deep skepticism regarding the moral
acceptability of nuclear weapons use.

These perspectives are linked to the main
conclusion of the Defensive Technologies Study
Team--that an optimistic view of new technologies
suggests that a robust BMD can be made to work
eventually, but that its ultimate effectiveness
will depend not only upon technology but also
upon the degree to which the Soviets will
cooperate on or oppose mutual defense
arrangements.

The author contends that a deficiency resulted
from the fact that conclusions of the Fletcher
Panel, upon which he served to study
technologies, were not fully integrated with
conclusions from the Miller and Hoffman panels,
and that this deficiency has been seized upon by
critics of SDI to oppose the entire concept.

4

The Case Against the
Strategic Defense Initiative

Since President Reagan delivered his speech of March 23, 1983, hundreds of articles and books have been written in opposition to the Strategic Defense Initiative concept. Other materials have also appeared that may not have been written specifically to oppose Star Wars but which nevertheless examine many of the problems that SDI would encounter and hence are useful to Star War's opponents. Both types of resources have been utilized in the writing of this chapter, and examples of both have been included in the abstracts found at the conclusion of the chapter. As a whole, this body of literature either explicitly or implicitly contains seven kinds of analyses, each of which in its way suggests substantial reasons why the Strategic Defense Initiative should not be attempted:

1. The flight trajectory of an ICBM and its payload is analyzed, and a number of serious problems that would have to be overcome are identified.

2. The various technologies under investigation by the SDI Organization are analyzed and deficiencies are described.

3. An examination of the computer and software requirements needed by an SDI to perform as a complete system during a strategic defense battle underscores a number of potentially difficult problem areas for what is called "battle management."

4. Informed speculation regarding the technological countermeasures the Soviet Union is
likely to adopt in response to the SDI suggests a
number of possibilities for disruption and defeat
of a Star Wars defense.

5. Consideration of the similarities between
Star Wars weapons technology and ASATs
(Anti-satellite Systems) points to ambiguities
regarding the success of the former if the latter
is deployed.

6. Review of potential political costs
attendant to the deployment of a Star Wars
defense system indicates possible damage to
progress in arms control, U.S. relations with the
Soviet Union, and the political relationship
between the United States and its allies.

7. Negative assessments of economic costs
associated with an SDI deployment are frequently
presented. The concern is both about direct
economic issues such as cost-effectiveness
analyses and about deleterious secondary effects
upon the economy.

Broad coverage concerning many facets of these
seven potential problem areas for the SDI is
found in several works. An SDI anthology
published in Daedalus, the Journal of the
American Academy of the Arts and Sciences,
contains articles both in support of and in
opposition to Star Wars (these materials were
published in book form in 1986 as Weapons in
Space). A 1986 collection of statements by world
leaders and eminent scholars about the SDI is
found in The Strategic Defense Initiative: Folly
or Future, edited by Edward Haley and Jack
Merrit. The Wizards of Armageddon by Fred Kaplan
provides a historical analysis of the nuclear era
by focusing upon the personalities involved in
U.S. nuclear development and includes a chapter
on the early ABM debates. Additional historical
perspective to the early ABM debates is provided
by Alexander Flax in the Spring 1985 issue of the
Daedalus issue on space weapons.

Analyses focused specifically on various technical facets of the SDI--such as the difficulties encountered by defensive efforts in different phases of the ballistic flight trajectory, the problems with developing and using the array of SDI technologies, and the problems created for the SDI by the potential of Soviet countermeasures--are found in a number of sources. In particular, see "BMD Technologies and Concepts in the 1980's," by Hans A. Bethe, Jeffery Boutwell, and Richard L. Garwin; and "Appendix A: New BMD Technologies," by Bethe and Garwin. Both appear in the Daedalus anthology.

In 1984 the Union of Concerned Scientists published a book entitled The Fallacy of Star Wars, edited by John Tirman, and in 1985 Robert Bowman wrote the book Star Wars: Defense or Death Star.

Other citations follow: Hans A. Bethe, Richard L. Garwin, Kurt Gottfried, and Henry W. Kendall, "Space-based Ballistic-Missile Defense," in the October 1984 issue of Scientific American; Coit D. Blacker, "Defending Missiles, Not People: Hard-Site Defense," in Issues in Science and Technology, Fall 1985; McGeorge Bundy, George F. Kennan, Robert S. McNamara, and Gerard Smith, "The President's Choice: Star Wars or Arms Control," in Foreign Affairs, Winter 1984-1985; Sidney D. Drell and Wolfgang Panofsky, "The Case Against Strategic Defense: Technical and Strategic Realities," in Issues in Science and Technology, Fall 1984; Richard L. Garwin and John Pike, "Space Weapons," in Bulletin of the Atomic Scientists, May 1985; William Hartung, "Star Wars Pork Barrel," in Bulletin of the Atomic Scientists, January 1986; John Kogut and Michael Weissman, "Taking the Pledge Against Star Wars," in Bulletin of Atomic Scientists, January 1986; Charles Krauthammer, "The Illusion of Star Wars," in The New Republic, May 14, 1984; Robert S. McNamara and Hans A. Bethe, "Reducing the Risk of Nuclear War," in The Atlantic Monthly, July 1985; George Rathjens and Jack Ruina, "BMD and Strategic Instability," in Daedalus, Summer 1985; and George Rathjens, "The Imperfections of 'Perfect Defense,'" in Issues in Science and Technology, Winter 1986.

PROBLEMS CAUSED BY THE BALLISTIC FLIGHT TRAJECTORY

In reviewing the arguments against the SDI concerning the problems that the defense establishment will encounter because of the characteristics of the ballistic missile flight trajectory, we will find it useful once again to break down the 30-minute flight path into its constitute phases, as was done in Chapters 2 and 3. These are the boost phase, post-boost phase, midcourse phase, and terminal phase.

The Boost Phase

SDI opponents point out that while Soviet missiles are particularly vulnerable during the boost phase, they are also in close proximity to the Soviet Union, where the operation of U.S. defensive systems, carried on satellites, are in turn the most vulnerable to Soviet countermeasures. In addition, several of the most spectacular of the exotic SDI technologies such as neutral particle beams and nuclear-pumped x-ray lasers, do not operate effectively in the lower portions of the atmosphere, where the boost phase takes place. Further, anti-SDI writers note that four to five minutes, on the other side of the world, where Soviet countermeasures might be particularly effective, is not much time to detect, track, and attack Soviet missiles.

The Post-Boost Phase

If a ballistic missile can propel the bus and its load of warheads and decoys from the boost phase, where it is especially vulnerable, into the post-boost phase, an impressive advantage has been gained over the defense. Those opposed to SDI suggest that an unmanageable load may thus be placed upon the subsequent defensive effort to coordinate the tracking and targeting of thousands of objects by the remaining layers of defense. The initial reasons are that (1) the target is now much smaller than the entire missile vehicle was during the boost phase; (2) the large and easily identified flame is gone;

and (3) the bus is traveling at a much higher speed than did the missile that carried it. Further, and more important, during the post-boost phase the bus is releasing warheads and decoys that are very difficult to distinguish from one another. As it is unlikely that the United States will have the capability to destroy more than 100,000 objects in twenty minutes, it is imperative that the strategic defense be able to conduct what is known as birth-to-death tracking. This concept involves both the differentiation of warheads from decoys at the moment each exit from the bus and the maintenance of the distinction between the two types of objects until the warheads have been killed or neutralized. Currently, research is being conducted on the possibility that slight differences in temperature and energy between warheads and decoys might serve as the means to distinguish between the two. At the same time, this could be quite difficult to accomplish.

The disadvantages for the defense during the post-boost phase are somewhat offset by the fact that the bus is out of the earth's atmosphere and is therefore subject to the full range of defensive weapon technologies, some of which, as pointed out previously, do not work effectively, or at all, in the dense atmosphere below.

The Midcourse Phase

SDI critics view this segment of the ballistic flight path as being particularly difficult for a defensive system to handle. Their basic perspective is that prospects for successful midcourse defense appear to be slight because of the tens of thousands of warheads and decoys released during the post-boost phase, all of which will be presented at a time of the attacker's choosing.

According to Bethe et al. (1985), "every missile that survived boost phase would become a complex 'threat cloud' by the time it reached midcourse" (p. 42). The defensive battle management system would have to find all the objects in the threat cloud, distinguish the warheads from the thousands of decoys, track the targets, order attacks, assess the resultant damage, and attack again, and again, if necessary. These activities would have to be accomplished within twenty minutes. Another difficulty faced by midcourse defense efforts is that in this phase warheads and decoys are traveling in excess of 16,000 miles an hour. The former, which are hardened against the stresses of atmospheric reentry, are therefore partially resistant to destructive technologies aimed against them.

The Terminal Phase

The fourth and final segment of a warhead's flight is generally thought by those opposing the SDI to hold more promise for defensive success than the other phases. A common view is that even though the time frame is less than two minutes, the fact that the decoys have been filtered out by the atmosphere will enable technology based upon the developments of the 1960s and 1970s to enjoy some success in a certain context. That situation is the defense of hardened targets such as underground missile silos and command bunkers. SDI critics do not expect that terminal defense will be successful in defending cities, where the leakage of one warhead through the defense would be catastrophic for the target area. Recognition of the marked difference in the probable success in defending hard-site targets and cities has produced a second perspective of Star Wars that focuses on the merits of defending hard-site targets rather than cities.

It has been charged that hard-site defense advocates have discarded President Reagan's perfect defensive shield in favor of partial defenses that enhance nuclear deterrence instead of replacing it. Adding perspective to the view that the only Star Wars defense likely to be even modestly successful involves the protection of hard-site targets is this statement by former Secretary of Defense Robert McNamara and Hans Bethe (July 1985):

> Virtually everyone in the administration now agrees that a leakproof defense of

population is not in the cards for decades,
if ever. Therefore, while the President
and the Secretary of Defense adhere to
their original proposal, the technicians
and others working on the SDI program are
producing less radical rationales that blur
crucial distinctions between hard-point
defense, which is technically feasible, and
comprehensive defense, which is not. These
ever-shifting and intermingled rationales
for Star Wars call for careful scrutiny.
(p. 46)

Ruina (1986) asserts that "neither a compelling
technical nor strategic case can be made for
hard-site ballistic missile defenses" (p. 129).
And he argues that "although the Strategic
Defense Initiative promises new technologies,
these are not likely to have much effect on hard-
site ballistic missile defense capabilities in
this century, if ever" (p. 129).

Critics also suggest that vulnerable land-based
ICBMs could be protected without terminal
defenses if they are made mobile (as in the
proposed Midgetman missile) or by using various
types of deceptive basing modes. Some propose
doing away with land-based ICBMs altogether and
relying upon less vulnerable submarine-based
ballistic missiles instead. Both Blacker (Fall
1985) and Ruina (1986) contend that deployment of
major hard-site defense will violate the ABM
Treaty, which limits the United States and USSR
to one emplacement of 100 ABM missiles each
(Ruina, p. 133; Blacker, p.43).

SDI TECHNOLOGIES CURRENTLY UNDER EXAMINATION

Those opposing the SDI have made various
criticisms of the exotic technologies being
investigated by the Department of Defense, and
much of their case rests upon pessimistic
assumptions about these technologies, as
suggested below.

Kinetic Kill Vehicles

Every SDI technology has certain inherent liabilities. In the case of electromagnetic railguns, problems arise from the tremendous velocity of the projectile. The first is that at desired speeds the projectile seriously damages, and at times even destroys, the railgun from which it is fired. The second problem is that guidance devices in the projectile currently have difficulty withstanding the acceleration forces sustained by the projectile. A third problem is that the passage of the projectile through the atmosphere, if it should be used there, causes a heat buildup from friction that might distort the heat-sensing guidance mechanism. Further, it appears that large quantities of electricity will be required for successful railgun operation, which might prove to be a problem if the railgun is carried aboard a satellite.

SDI critics note that the demonstration of a successful kill in the artificial context of the Homing Overlay Experiment does not mean that the concept can be made effective in the face of substantial Soviet countermeasures. These critics point out that in a real attack situation, the defense would be responding to thousands of potentially hostile objects, not just one. SDI opponents also point out that while kinetic kill rockets could theoretically be fired from satellites at Soviet ICBMs, there is a catch to this potential SDI system: The satellites carrying the rockets would be vulnerable to Soviet countermeasures, meaning that such a rocket defense would be unreliable.

Of the various kinetic kill possibilities, the swarm jet may hold the greatest potential for effective use, and that would be in the terminal phase of an attack. As the incoming warheads could be salvage-fused to explode when attacked, however, a swarm jet defense would need to intercept them far from soft targets such as cities. On the other hand, the use of swarm jet defense could be restricted to the defense of hard-site targets.

Lasers

As the Union of Concerned Scientists has pointed out, a serious problem with the use of lasers as SDI weapons is that the earth is round, whereas laser beams travel in a straight line. This means that in order to attack Soviet ICBMs directly in their most vulnerable phase, as they rise from lift-off on the other side of the world, U.S. lasers must be carried in satellites, that operate over the Soviet Union. As will be noted later, the use of satellites to carry SDI weapons is fraught with problems stemming from the use of countermeasures against them.

Because of weight and energy considerations, some laser weapons would probably need to be ground-based rather than satellite-based. As their beams cannot be bent over the North Pole to focus on Soviet ICBMs, other means of utilizing them would be required. The means proposed by SDI proponents is to relay the beams from earth lasers up and over the North Pole by using a series of mirrors carried on satellites. Opponents of the SDI note that to be effective, the laser mirrors must be polished with extremely fine surfaces and be made of materials that can withstand the laser beam's intensity; in addition, the satellites carrying the mirrors must be invulnerable to destruction or degradation by the Soviet Union.

SDI opponents also argue that while substantial technical problems remain to be worked out, the nuclear-pumped x-ray laser is facing serious political problems as well. Their point is that the Reagan administration, having noted with satisfaction that other SDI weapons concepts are non-nuclear, is finding it difficult to justify the use of nuclear weapons in a plan billed as being directed toward the goal of rendering nuclear weapons impotent and obsolete.

Critics of the SDI point to still other disadvantages of the nuclear-pumped x-ray laser. One is the obvious problem with a weapon that destroys itself after it is used once. Furthermore, as x-ray laser beams are not effective in the atmosphere, this system could probably be used only against targets in space, which means that it could not be employed against ballistic missiles in the particularly vulnerable boost phase. Another potential problem with the nuclear-pumped x-ray laser is that the effects of its use might adversely affect other parts of an SDI system, such as communication and radar observation components.

Particle Beams

SDI opponents note that neutral particle beams are subject to bending in the atmosphere. Thus, like nuclear-pumped x-ray lasers, they are best utilized above the atmosphere in satellites, against Soviet warheads and decoys in part of the post-boost phase and all of the midcourse phase of the ballistic flight path. The critics point out that in these two phases the Soviet warheads and decoys enjoy substantial advantages vis-a-vis defensive efforts.

A potential problem with particle beams is that instead of destroying a warhead, they could interfere with its internal mechanism. Thus it may not be immediately apparent as to which warheads have had their electronic "brains" scrambled. This situation could be unacceptable in a time-sensitive situation where it is imperative to distinguish immediately which targets have been disabled so the attack can be refocused on still-dangerous warheads.

Yet another potential problem with neutral particle beam weapons is the question of whether they and their energy source can be built for easy packaging aboard satellites, where the beam accelerators would have to function without benefit of periodic maintenance.

Nuclear Armed ABMs and Underground Nuclear Detonations

The late 1960s and 1970s witnessed substantial political opposition to the deployment of nuclear-tipped ABMs in the United States. Aside from the emotional aspect of preparing to use nuclear weapons above one's country, SDI

opponents point to the collateral physical damage
that could result from such usage.
Underground nuclear detonations type of defense
against ballistic missile attack carries the
potential for harm both to the military forces
they are meant to protect and to the general
civilian population. The primary concern noted
by SDI opponents is the radioactive fallout such
a defensive posture would create.

A CURIOUS POTENTIAL PROBLEM

In one of the New York Times articles cited in
Chapter 2, Philip M. Boffey (March 7, 1985)
points to an unusual possible problem with
certain SDI technologies--they could become too
powerful! For example, critics note that if
lasers or kinetic kill vehicles, capable of
operating from satellites downward through the
atmosphere, could be upgraded to permit them to
attack ICBM silos, a new first-strike capability
would have been created. The strategic
implications of a first strike that could be
carried out at the speed of light would be
profoundly destabilizing.
Boffey reports that, to date, most commentators
on the subject believe the degree of hardness
found in missile silos would preclude the direct
use of SDI weapons against them. As Robert
Bowman points out, however, lasers, in theory,
could be used to incinerate cities and might even
lead to "laser winter," which would result from
decreases in incident sunlight for a prolonged
period of time due to smoke from burning cities.
A more plausible offensive role for SDI
technologies according to SDI critics would be as
a backup to a U.S. first strike against the
Soviet Union. In this scenario the United States
would seek to destroy a major portion of the
Soviet land-based strategic nuclear forces with a
first strike delivered by ICBMs and SLBMs, as
well as a quantity of Soviet SLBM submarines by
means of U.S. anti-submarine warfare units. The
Soviet bombers and ballistic missiles that
survived might then be fired in a ragged and
uncoordinated retaliatory counterattack, but they

would pose much easier targets for SDI technologies because missile numbers would already have been dramatically reduced.

It can be argued that such a scenario might make nuclear war acceptable because the gains would not be as easily nullified by the threat of Soviet retaliatory strikes. It should be pointed out that this possibility was addressed by President Reagan in his Star Wars speech, with the subsequent denial that such a policy would be adopted by the United States. Nevertheless, one of the widespread concerns about SDI is that the Soviets will view it as provocative and hostile in intent and that Moscow will therefore react strongly to it, in unpredictable ways that could be deleterious to U.S. interests.

PROBLEMS WITH THE BATTLE MANAGEMENT OF THE SDI

Because of the enormous amount of complex data that must be processed within a time frame calculated in minutes, human minds are inadequate for the real-time battle management of an SDI system. Therefore, a significant facet of any potential SDI will be the integration of C^3I and SATKA into the overall system. The reader may recall that the symbol C^3I stands for command, control, communications, and intelligence. These are electronically propagated functions necessary for the overall operation of the various components constituting an SDI. The acronym SATKA stands for surveillance (of Soviet ballistic missile deployments), acquisition (of ballistic missiles and their payloads that have been launched), tracking (of the missiles and payloads), and kill assessment (of the various targets). Much of the case against Star Wars stems from analyses suggesting that neither the computer hardware nor the software designed to direct the computers will be adequate for the stresses of managing an SDI system during a space battle.

Command, Control, Communications and Intelligence

In an article on command and control of nuclear forces, Ashton Carter (January 1985) notes that:

> weaponry tends to dominate discussions of nuclear war. Missiles and bombers, throw weights and flight times, and the elaborate counting rules of arms control agreements provide the grist of public debate. . . . Weapons and strategic doctrine are meaningless, however, unless the superpowers also have the means to know what is happening in the chaos or crisis of war, to provide for decisions by legitimate authorities and to have orders carried out precisely and faithfully. (p. 32)

In the last few years, defense specialists have begun to analyze U.S. nuclear forces as an integrated system that includes organizations, satellites, sensors, computers, communication links, people, and the weapons themselves. Analysts have identified major weaknesses in existing command, control, and communication systems, and suggest that the addition of strategic defenses will greatly complicate existing problems. Of particular concern is the perceived need for SDI battle management computer capacity of unprecedented size and complexity.

In discussions of the systems currently managing U.S. offensive nuclear forces, several problem areas have been identified: time constraints that require automatic system responses; ambiguous political control over the nuclear forces; the vulnerability of system components to sabotage and nuclear attack; and the need for modernization and even redesign of existing systems. For these reasons, some SDI critics consider command, control, and communication in regard to an SDI to be the weakest link in the entire strategic defense proposal.

Paul Bracken (1983), Ashton Carter (January 1985), and Daniel Ford (1985) discuss the generic characteristics and weaknesses of command, control, and communications; their work thus provides a background critique to potential C^3I problems. Charles Zraket (Spring 1985) considers the range of SDI systems issues from strategy to software. Herbert Lin (July and December 1985) and Ware Myers (February 1986) focus upon the prospects of developing an adequate battle management software.

Computers and Software

The C^3I system for a comprehensive ballistic missile defense must be capable of flawlessly receiving and acting upon information pertaining to thousands of missile launches, tens of thousands of warheads, and a hundred thousand decoys, all within thirty minutes. As Herbert Lin (December 1985) points out, because the system must be highly automated there would be virtually no time for human intervention to correct unexpected failures. For the most part the execution of a computer program would replace human decisionmaking once the BMD system was engaged (pp. 44-53). Ware Myers (February 1986) notes that in a report by the SDI Organization panel on battle management, it was conceded that software errors are unavoidable in all systems of useful complexity (pp. 31-46). In ordinary software development, such errors are identified during testing and operations of the system. Star Wars critics state that as SDI battle management software can never be fully tested, critical "bugs" that could lead to catastrophic failure will remain unidentified.

Lin (December 1985) describes the normal iterative process of identifying and correcting program errors that took place during operational testing of the U.S. Aegis air-defense system. He comments that:

> unlike the performance of Aegis, the performance of a comprehensive ballistic-missile defense against a large-scale attack will not improve with experience. Because large-scale empirical testing is impossible, the first such test for a

comprehensive BMD system would be an actual
large-scale attack on the U.S. (p. 15)

According to Lin, battle management software
can be tested only in computerized simulations of
real conditions, with no guarantee that all
contingencies have been anticipated or accurately
represented.

Programming errors increase in proportion to
program size, and current estimates of the size
of SDI software range from 10 to 30 million lines
of coded computer instructions (Myers, p. 31).
SDI advocates suggest that new software
development tools, such as expert systems and
artificial intelligence, may make strategic
defense battle management a reality. The authors
cited here, however, contend that such tools,
though helpful in some cases, will not yield
substantial breakthroughs. In particular, they
will be of no help in initial program design, one
of the more daunting tasks facing SDI software
engineers.

To many strategic defense critics, the
likelihood of producing reliable battle
management software seems remote. For example,
software expert Frederick Brooks is quoted as
having stated that "the question before us is not
whether we want to build such a thing, but if we
wanted to build it, can we build the software
part of it?" (Myers, p. 36) At this juncture in
the SDI debate, many critics and advocates alike
would agree with Charles Zraket that "our ability
to build thoroughly reliable and high-performance
command-and-control software could be the
greatest challenge to achieving effective BMD"
(Zraket, p. 121). David Parnus (1985), a
professor of computer science, created a stir
when he resigned from an SDI advisory panel.
Parnus gave as the reason for his resignation his
belief that reliable software cannot be produced
for an SDI system because it cannot be adequately
tested. Part of the testing problem, according
to Parnus, is that Soviet strategy and tactics
cannot be accurately simulated.

C³I and SATKA Vulnerabilities

In addition to formidable software requirements, the C³I and SATKA components of an SDI
system share a potentially critical weakness.
The question is whether the most exposed of the
battle management components, such as
surveillance, tracking, and communication
satellites, can function in an environment that
will probably feature determined Soviet efforts
to ruin and degrade them. For example, it has
long been known that a phenomenon called
electromagnetic pulse (EMP), which is produced by
nuclear detonations, can either completely black
out electronic links or sufficiently scramble
them so as to cause severe retardation of their
effectiveness. Further, it is likely that the
Soviets would, in the event of war, directly
attack all of the battle management satellites
and other components of the C³I and SATKA systems
that were within reach. Moreover, as Ashton
Carter (January 1985) has noted, the strategy of
deterrence assumes that authorities and systems
would survive long enough to respond to an attack
with an appropriate retaliatory strike (p. 32).
Daniel Ford (1985) and Paul Bracken (1983)
worry about current and future C³I systems. In
particular, they contend that (1) the U.S.
officials who will most probably be authorized to
order nuclear attack are concentrated in a few
easily targeted locations; (2) space-and ground-
based sensors, and communication links are all
equally vulnerable and would likely be knocked
out in a "decapitation" attack along with
national leaders; and (3) in the event of an
attack, control over nuclear weapons would
quickly devolve to local military commanders, who
would be unable to assess or control the progress
of the war.
Bracken further argues that the U.S. and Soviet
systems are tightly coupled in real time, thus
raising the possibility that mutually reinforcing
alert procedures could lead to war during a
crisis. Integration of computerized warning and
intelligence systems with the nuclear forces
themselves reduces reaction time and increases
potential for automated initiation and control of

nuclear war. As many critics of SDI have emphasized, such automated control is a requirement for SDI systems.

In the conclusion of his book, Command and Control of Nuclear Forces, Bracken comments:

> If we follow a logic that emphasizes the process of how nuclear forces go on alert, how situations are assessed in wartime, and how command and control ties all of these pieces together, we can focus our attention on questions that cannot be answered with "technical fixes." Technical fixes have their place, but they belong in a more supporting role. The problems that do come to center stage are those of organizational design for life in a world in which immensely dangerous arsenals form the backdrop for the routine daily business of diplomacy. At any moment these forces can be triggered onto alert, and decades of sleepy, unexamined confidence that "it can't happen here" would disappear. (p. 239)

SOVIET COUNTERMEASURES TO THE SDI

A common technique in national security planning exercises is to "put on your Red hat"-- that is, to think like a Soviet strategic planner and so discern what Moscow might do in response to this or that U.S. initiative. The technique has been widely applied by SDI critics, with the result that a number of Soviet countermeasures have been identified. In various ways, these could seriously erode the effectiveness of SDI weapons technologies and their command and control systems. In fact, General Secretary Gorbachev has promised to develop such countermeasures should the United States build an SDI.

Opponents of the SDI frequently cite the potential Soviet countermeasures as one of their fundamental arguments against the U.S. deployment of strategic defenses--the belief that the SDI simply will not work in the face of determined Soviet efforts to degrade and overwhelm it.

A typical means of analyzing Soviet countermeasures is to follow the same pattern used in describing the flight trajectory of a ballistic missile and its payload--that is, to focus the analysis upon the four phases of the thirty-minute flight. Particularly useful in making such an analysis are <u>Ballistic Missile Defense Technologies</u>, cited in Chapter 2; the Bethe, Boutwell, and Garwin article (Spring 1985) and the Bethe and Garwin article in the <u>Daedalus</u> anthology, and the articles that appeared in the <u>New York Times</u> and the <u>Christian Science Monitor</u> series, also cited in Chapter 2.

Soviet Countermeasures in the Boost Phase

If the Soviets could reduce their boost phase from the current approximate 300 seconds for the SS18 ICBMs to something equivalent to the U.S. MX--180 seconds--SDI weapons would have considerably less time to mount an attack during this critical first phase. Further, if the booster rockets' burn-out time could be reduced to occur entirely within the atmosphere, weapons technologies such as the x-ray laser and neutral particle beam could not be used against the Soviet missiles in their most vulnerable period. Another countermeasure in the boost phase would be for the Soviets to fire simultaneously their loaded ICBMs and their retired ICBMs, the latter carry no payload but would nevertheless appear to U.S. sensors as the real thing.

Additional countermeasures in the boost phase include rotating the missiles so that a laser beam could not dwell for a lethal period on the vehicles. Reflective or ablative materials could be used to coat the missiles. These would either reflect the laser beam or evaporate when heated by it and so dispense the heat, thus protecting the ICBM.

Soviet Countermeasures in the Post-Boost Phase

Both buses and warheads could be hardened against the effects of lasers and particle beams.

The "birth" of decoys and warheads could be hidden from prying sensor "eyes" by umbrella-like devices, thus thwarting the discrimination necessary for birth-to-death tracking of the objects expelled by the buses.

Soviet Countermeasures in the Midcourse Phase

In this environment a number of countermeasures might be employed--reflective and ablative coating; rotation; use of smoke and aerosols to mask the warheads; and deployment of a variety of decoys such as mylar balloons and heavier dummy warheads.

Soviet Countermeasures in the Terminal Phase

Early detonation or salvage fusing of the Soviet warheads would create nuclear explosion effects that could degrade the radars that track inbound warheads and disrupt the electronic components of C^3I. In addition, the use of MaRVs (Maneuverable Reentry Vehicles) in the terminal phase might enable the warheads to use extensive evasive action, zigging and zagging on the way to their targets.

Soviet Countermeasures Against the Entire SDI System

One straightforward countermeasure to degrade the entire SDI system would be for the Soviets to simply increase the number of their ballistic missiles. This in turn would increase the numbers of everything else involved in the thirty-minute flight trajectory--buses, warheads, dummy warheads, decoys. Another form of this response would be to increase the number of warheads carried on each ICBM. The Soviets could use what is known as preferential offense; a concept that involves targeting a greater number of warheads on a preferred target, thus making its destruction more likely. Nuclear explosions along the thirty-minute flight trajectory could be employed to degrade and black out electronic links. Yet another Soviet countermeasure for use against an entire SDI system would be to fire SLBMs from points near the U.S. coastlines in a depressed trajectory. Missiles and payloads fired in this mode would have reduced flight times and would spend more time in the atmosphere, where some SDI technologies are much less effective.

All SDI satellites, whether C^3I and SATKA, or those carrying defensive weapons, could be attacked directly. Opponents of the SDI repeatedly emphasize that satellites are much easier to destroy than their warhead prey. Satellite locations are predictable; they depend upon fragile electronic components to function; and they are vulnerable to various forms of attack (Drell et al., 1984, p. 49; and Bethe et al., October 1984, p. 47).

The Air-breather Countermeasure

Another way in which the Soviet Union might respond to a deployed SDI would be to increase its investment in nonballistic missile delivery systems and so maintain Moscow's capability to deter a U.S. nuclear attack with the threat of retaliation. Such systems are called air-breathers because they operate only within the atmosphere. Examples would be cruise missiles and low-flying jet bombers, both of which could be configured in ways to reduce their detection by radar. This kind of response to a U.S. SDI would take advantage of the fact that the United States has allowed its defenses against air-breathers to deteriorate owing to the decreasing Soviet bomber threat in the recent past. Cognizant of this possibility, Secretary of Defense Caspar Weinberger has noted that in order to complement the SDI deployment, the United States may find it necessary to rebuild and expand its defensive capability against the air-breathing threat.

The Soviet SDI/ASAT Countermeasure

The Soviet Union could build upon the ABM system already deployed near Moscow, its tested ASAT system, and the research on laser and particle beam weapons that the Department of Defense claims has been conducted, to produce its own SDI, coupled with an ASAT capability. SDI opponents claim that this is exactly what will happen should Washington deploy its SDI, or an ASATs. They also maintain that the consequence of a Soviet SDI/ASAT deployment would be extremely negative to U.S. interests. The argument is that Moscow would then have the capacity either to destroy the U.S. SDI in a precursor strike to a nuclear attack on the United States, or to destroy the U.S. SDI as part of a Soviet retaliatory blow should Washington initiate a nuclear attack upon the Soviet Union.

A bleak outcome is predicted by SDI opponents for the scenario in which both the United States and the Soviet Union engage in an SDI/ASAT competition--namely, that the U.S. SDI will be answered in kind by the Soviet Union. Then both nations would be strongly motivated to protect their eroding deterrence capabilities by increasing their offensive forces vis-a-vis the other's defenses. Thus two simultaneous arms races would occur--an offensive one and a defensive one--whereas today there is only the former.

Such a dual arms race would also mean, according to those opposed to SDI, that large new sums would be spent on defensive systems, and additional monies would be spent on offensive systems, with no correlative increase in the security of either the United States or the Soviet Union. This would be true because the offense would continue to be dominant, as Bernard Brodie suggested would be the case at the beginning of the nuclear age.

Expanding upon Brodie's observations, Robert McNamara and Hans Bethe (July 1985) wrote as follows:

> There is no evidence that any combination of the "defensive technologies" now on the

> most visionary of horizons can undo the
> revolution wrought by the invention of
> nuclear explosives. "War" is only one of
> the concepts whose meanings were changed
> forever at Hiroshima. "Defense" is another.
> (p. 45)

This statement defines the fundamental concept
underlying all the technical criticism of
President Reagan's Star Wars program. In an 1984
article reviewing the case against strategic
defenses, physicists Sydney Drell and Wolfgang
Panofsky elaborate:

> In considering defenses against nuclear
> weapons, one must recognize that the
> enormous increase in the explosive power of
> nuclear bombs had wrought a fundamental
> discontinuity in the relative effectiveness
> of offensive and defensive measures. We
> must now recognize that a single relatively
> small nuclear bomb is a weapon of mass
> destruction. A modern nuclear warhead
> weighing perhaps 100 pounds can pack an
> explosive power equivalent to 100 kilotons
> or 200 million pounds of a "conventional"
> explosive such as TNT. . . . Given the
> staggering destructive potential of nuclear
> bombs, effective defenses must meet a much
> higher standard of performance today than at
> any other time in the history of warfare.
> (p. 45)

In "The Illusion of Star Wars," Charles
Krauthammer (May 1984) illuminates the
distinction between offensive and defensive
dominance:

> Leverage means that whatever defense can
> do, offense can do better, and cheaper. The
> clincher, though, . . . is that the offense
> does not have to do it nearly so well to
> prevail. The demands for success of offense
> and defense are wholly disproportionate. An
> American defense that is 99 percent
> effective would still allow a hundred
> nuclear weapons to land on American soil.

That is a failure. A Soviet offense that is 5 percent successful could, if targeted at cities, kill half the U.S. population instantly. That is success. The principle at work here is the concentration of awesome offensive power in a tiny volume, a property of nuclear weaponry that has transformed the balance of offense and defense. Defense may yet one day come up with an answer, but today, and for as far as the eye can see, no one has any idea what that is. (p. 16)

SDI critics note that the Fletcher panel, a group of experts brought together to advise the government on SDI, defined an extraordinary standard of performance for defensive success. The panel suggested that a multilayered defense in which the tiers destroyed 99.9 percent of incoming warheads would meet the performance requirements necessary to protect the American society. It has been reported, however, that the panel--which was otherwise sanguine about the SDI--concluded in the classified version of its report that such near-perfect performance was "not technically credible" (Hafner, p. 95).

As such perfect protection against nuclear weapon attack is seen as impossible by SDI opponents, they _reluctantly_ _maintain_ that U.S. security must continue to rest upon the strategy of deterring an attack by the threat of unacceptable retaliation. This posture is based squarely upon the concept that offense is dominant; and in no way does it indicate moral approval of the policy of mutual assured destruction.

The Macro Soviet Countermeasure--A First Strike

The maximum response the Soviet Union could make to a U.S. SDI deployment would be to deliver a nuclear first strike against U.S. offensive forces. The logic for such a claim is that Moscow cannot permit the United States to couple an SDI to its existing strategic offensive forces. This is the case because, in Soviet eyes, such a combination would be life-threatening to the Soviet Union. The scenario Moscow would fear, it is asserted, is that with an SDI to blunt a Soviet retaliatory strike, the United States would be much less restrained in launching a first strike that would disarm the Soviet Union and leave it helpless to U.S. demands.

The technical case against Star Wars is summed up in the following quotation from a Winter 1984/85 article in Foreign Affairs by McGeorge Bundy, former presidential national security advisor; George F. Kennan, dean of American Kremlinologists; Robert S. Mcnamara, former secretary of defense; and Gerard Smith, former chief of the U.S. SALT I delegation: "We believe the President's initiative to be a classic case of good intentions that will have bad results because they do not respect reality". (p. 264)

SDI AND ASATs--THE PROBLEM OF STRATEGIC OVERLAP

Both the United States and the Soviet Union have tested anti-satellite systems. In the Soviet case a killer satellite was launched and then maneuvered in the course of several orbits about the earth to a position sufficiently close to the target satellite that an explosion destroyed it. The U.S. ASAT consists of a rocket carried aloft by an F-15 jet fighter plane. After release from the plane, the rocket carries still higher a Miniature Homing Vehicle. The latter then homes in on the target satellite and destroys it.

There are other potential ASAT technologies. One frequently mentioned is the space mine-- basically a satellite carrying a conventional or nuclear explosive. It would be launched so as to trail its quarry within lethal range. A space mine could be detonated either on command or when it was being attacked or disturbed in some way. Killer satellites could be equipped with radio-frequency devices that produce beams of electromagnetic radiation. At lower power settings these devices could jam communication and radar systems. At higher power levels they could burn out an enemy satellites' electronic equipment.

Some of the most lethal ASATs would be certain SDI weapons, such as lasers and particle-beam weapons designed to attack warheads in the midcourse phase of their flight trajectory. Analysts agree that a satellite in a low earth orbit is very similar to a warhead in the midcourse phase, but with one qualification: Satellites are generally viewed as more easily destroyed than warheads.

There are several reasons for this perspective. An SDI weapon capable of disabling or destroying anything as hard, small, and elusive as a missile warhead should have an even greater kill capacity against a satellite. A comparison of warheads to satellites will lend credence to this observation. Satellites are generally larger than warheads (one version is the size of an eighteen-wheel, semi-trailer truck), thus offering a more easily detectable target. Satellites are not hardened to the extent that a warhead is, and they typically travel in readily observed and monitored orbits around the earth. Furthermore, there are many fewer satellites than there would be warheads in a massive attack, and satellites are not convoyed by thousands of decoys and dummies. Satellites operate above the atmosphere, where some SDI technologies are at their most lethal capacity.

Peter Didisheim, in a monograph published by the Union of Concerned Scientists, notes that at least one SDI weapon could be used against satellites positioned as high as the 22,300-mile geosynchronous early warning zones:

> The ASAT-BMD overlap extends to satellites in geosynchronous orbits as well. For example, a boost-phase defense system using ground-based lasers and orbiting mirrors could be used to attack spacecraft in low and high orbits. (Papers on Strategic Defense: The ASAT/SDI Link, p. 3)

Of course, satellites can be hardened, made maneuverable, and convoyed by decoys and even by defensive satellites. The latter are called DSATs and would probably be armed with beam weapons or kinetic kill weapons to protect themselves and the escorted satellite from enemy satellites. Nevertheless, the predominant opinion among both proponents and opponents of SDI is that satellites will remain easier targets for many of the SDI technologies than will warheads.

Ashton Carter, in "The Relationship of ASAT and BMD Systems" (1985); Herbert York, in "Nuclear Deterrence and the Military Uses of Space" (1985); and Didisheim provide background information on the military missions of "space-based assets" and suggest thereby why such satellites would be tempting targets for a nation with an ASAT system. York, a former presidential science advisor, explains that some satellites may become targets because they "will soon be supplying essential data to war-fighting systems in real time" (p. 22). Presumably satellites carrying SDI weapons, observation and tracking capabilities, and mirrors for laser aiming would become even more attractive targets insofar as their operation could place a nation in peril. So it is that Ashton Carter (1985) writes:

> Potent ASATs would drive BMD deployment from space, and that means other military support missions heretofore conducted from space would have to find more survivable backups. In such a world, space would be ASAT dominated, and strategic warfare would remain offense dominated. (p. 187)

The complex relationship and potential overlap between SDI and ASATs remain unresolved as of 1986. The following quotation from an Office of Technology Assessment report (1985) explains the situation:

> Since the debate over ballistic missile defense involves a fundamental reassessment of this country's strategic policy, decisionmakers are reluctant to proceed with ASAT weapon development, deployment, or arms control decisions that may tie their hands

with respect to future technologies or that
may commit them irrevocably to a course with
unforeseen consequences. Some people
believe that ASAT weapon development
programs will be used to accomplish BMD
research, thereby avoiding the strictures of
the ABM Treaty and the scrutiny of Congress.
Others believe that ASAT arms control
restrictions would impede future BMD
research and development programs. Given
these opposing viewpoints, the decision to
go forward with or, alternatively, to
restrict ASAT development must be made in
the broader context of this country's
reassessment of its strategic posture and
the military utility of space. (Anti
Satellite Weapons, Countermeasures, and Arms
Control, p. 26)

POTENTIAL POLITICAL COSTS OF THE SDI

Critics of the SDI argue that strategic defense
technologies offer few security benefits for the
future while creating many serious political
problems for the present. Potential political
casualties include the relatively stable
strategic balance between the United States and
the USSR; the existing network of arms control
agreements and procedures; political
relationships between Washington and Moscow; U.S.
relations with the NATO Alliance; and the
domestic consensus on current national security
research and procurement expenditures.

SDI and the Strategic Balance

A great deal of attention has been devoted to the
argument that a perfect defense against nuclear
ballistic missiles cannot be achieved. Charles
Zraket (Spring 1985) comments that assessment of
missile defense:

should begin with the premise that a perfect
defense against all nuclear threats is
feasible neither technically nor

economically, at least not in the foreseeable future. On this there now seems to be general agreement throughout the defense community. (p. 109)

Therefore, he argues, analysis of strategic purposes must recognize that "security will continue to rest upon a combination of offensive and defensive forces" (p. 109). Such a combination of offenses and defenses bears no resemblance to the world freed of nuclear weapons that was described by President Reagan in his 1983 speech.

According to those opposed to SDI, combining strategic defenses with existing offensive arsenals will have detrimental consequences, such as:

1. renewal of the offensive arms race, now constrained to some extent by the "gentlemen's agreement" embodied in the SALT II accord, which has not been ratified by the Senate but which the Reagan administration tentatively recognizes and abides by, although with increasingly critical evaluation;

2. augmentation of the potential advantages of a first strike by improving an attacker's ability to cope with a "ragged" and uncoordinated retaliation.

According to Charles Glaser (March 1985) and Donald Hafner (May 1985), this destabilizing situation is likely to prevail during the development, deployment, and operation of defensive systems. They suggest that the transition period during which defenses are being deployed but strategic offensive forces are still very much in evidence will be an especially dangerous time. The reason for this is that the temptation to use offensive ICBMs before they can be destroyed by defenses may be a powerful inducement to strike first.

Glaser suggests that any perfect defense will be perfect only temporarily, owing to the advantages that accrue to the side that can penetrate them. Hence there is no reason to think that development of defenses will halt technological innovation, and alternating periods of offensive and defensive dominance will thus ensue.

Negative Effects of the SDI upon Arms Control

How will the SDI affect arms control efforts? Among the analysts attempting to answer this question are Longstreth, Pike, and Rhinelander, in _The Impact of U.S. and Soviet Ballistic Missile Defense Programs on the ABM Treaty_ (1985); Alan Sherr, in _Legal Issues of the "Star Wars" Defense Program_ (1984); and Chayes, Chayes, and Spitzer, in "Space Weapons: The Legal Context" (1985). These authors summarize the ABM Treaty history, provisions, and current challenges. Carter (Spring 1985), Gottfried and Lebow (1985), and Peter Didisheim (1986) focus on the link between anti-satellite weapons and the ABM Treaty. They and others point to the following negative impacts of SDI on the arms control process:

1. Limiting defenses is a precondition to limiting offensive nuclear arms. But neither superpower has been willing to limit its offenses if defenses could render them useless.

2. The SDI violates the fundamental principle underlying the Anti-Ballistic Missile Treaty, the cornerstone of the existing arms control regime.

3. Tests of SDI components scheduled for the late 1980s will violate several explicit ABM Treaty conditions.

4. Strained interpretations of the ABM Treaty undermine confidence in U.S. commitments to limit nuclear weapons.

5. Bypassing agreed procedures for dealing with compliance issues weakens the Standing Consultative Commission, a long-standing forum for effective U.S.-Soviet cooperation.

6. Attempts to circumvent the ABM Treaty by
testing prohibited devices in the guise of anti-
satellite weapons encourage the Soviets to test
the limits of the Treaty.

The pessimistic view of the SDI's impact upon
arms control held by opponents to SDI is summed
up by Alan Sheer (1983):

> The impact of the Strategic Defense
> Initiative will be felt across the spectrum
> of arms control agreements--the foundations
> of which are the SALT Treaties limiting
> defensive and offensive strategic nuclear
> arms. . . . The almost certain effect of an
> all-out defensive effort will be, in
> addition to a responsive defensive effort,
> an all-out _offensive_ effort. Any
> constraints imposed by the SALT agreements
> will be swept away. The prospects for
> limiting offensive weapons in future
> negotiations, not to mention freezing or
> reducing those armaments, will evaporate.
> The costs will be truly staggering. (p. 11)

Of particular concern to opponents of the SDI
is the impact it will have upon the ABM Treaty.
Rhinelander writes that the Strategic Defense
Initiative, introduced by President Reagan and
funded at unprecedented levels, "raises
fundamental compliance issues with the ABM
treaty, as such, [and] its high level support
signals a monumental change in the U.S.
commitment to arms control" (in Sheer, p. vii).
And Chayes, Chayes, and Spitzer (1985) write:

> The fundamental strategic assumption
> underlying the ABM treaty is that the
> security of the United States is best
> guaranteed by a relationship of mutual
> deterrence between itself and the Soviet
> Union, and that the stability of this
> relationship would be threatened by the
> deployment of defensive systems that might
> call into question either side's retaliatory
> capability. To this end, the basic
> provisions of the treaty sharply curtail for

the indefinite future the development of such systems, permitting only token deployment at a single site. (p. 194)

R. Jeffery Smith (November 1985), writes that the testing of potential BMD elements in the ASAT mode suggests a U.S. intention to break out of the ABM Treaty. Further, recent administration reinterpretation of critical ABM Treaty provisions raises new doubts about the survival of the ABM agreement. The administration's current view is that exotic defense weaponry is not included in treaty prohibitions against strategic defenses. (p. 644)

The provisions of the ABM Treaty are summarized by Longstreth et al. (1985) as follows:

As amended by the 1974 Protocol, the ABM Treaty limits the U.S. and the U.S.S.R. to one ABM site of 100 interceptors and 100 launchers either around the national capital or an intercontinental ballistic missile field. The Treaty also places strict limits on the number of ABM radars at the permitted ABM site. It allows research on all types of ABM systems and components. Advanced development, testing, and deployment of certain types of ABM systems and their components are banned. . . . Article V(1): bans the development, testing, or deployment of ABM systems which are sea-based, air-based, space-based, mobile land-based, or not of a permanent fixed type. . . . Article VI(a) bans giving non-ABM systems ABM capabilities, or testing such non-ABM systems "in an ABM" mode. . . . Agreed Statement D: establishes that future ABM systems based on other physical principles will be subject to discussion. (pp. 5-7)

Currently at issue between the Reagan administration and opponents of the SDI are the following arguments: that development and testing of space-based ABM systems and components are permitted; that certain projects are adjuncts rather than <u>components</u> of ABM systems, and are therefore permitted; that exotic ABM space weaponry is not prohibited; and that ABM components may be developed if initially intended for use in anti-satellite systems (Sheer, p. ix). The authors cited herein describe these arguments as "ingenuous" and "specious," and as "strained legalisms," and they maintain that the arguments fail to disguise the administration's intention to break its solemn obligations under the Treaty.

Chayes et al. note that the Standing Consultative Commission (SCC), composed of Soviet and U.S. delegates, is "an important innovation in the area of compliance" and, as such, is endangered by the administration's resort to rhetoric rather than to established procedures in handling Treaty compliance issues. The SCC was designed to clarify questionable actions on both sides, and it is "not well-suited to deal with the accusations and confrontations." According to these authors, the SCC record shows that complaints about compliance from both the United States and the Soviet Union were resolved satisfactorily between 1972 and 1980. Since that time the claim has been made that the Commission was politicized by the Reagan administration (p. 210).

The SDI and Political Relationships Between Washington and Moscow

In "The Strategic Defense Initiative and the Soviet Union" (Fall 1985), David Holloway comments:

> None of the important questions that have been raised about the technical and operational feasibility of the SDI, or about its effect on U.S. security, the risk of nuclear war, and the prospects for arms control, can be answered without some consideration of the Soviet leaders' view of President Reagan's initiative and of their likely response. (p. 257)

Other views on the Soviet response to the SDI
are offered by Bundy, Kennan, McNamara, and Smith
in "The President's Choice: Star Wars or Arms
Control (1984)" and by Jerry Hough in "Soviet
Interpretation and Response" (1985).

These commentators agree that the Soviets
interpret the SDI as a U.S. drive to achieve
nuclear superiority at the expense of Soviet
deterrent forces. In the Soviet view, SDI
proposals signal U.S. offensive ambitions.
Moscow fears a first strike by the U.S. strategic
forces, followed by defensive interception of a
weakened Soviet retaliation.

Donald Hafner (Spring 1985) notes that the
Fletcher panel concluded that no defensive system
can protect United States unless the Soviet Union
cooperates in reducing offensive arsenals. And
Hough et al. (1985) comment:

> SDI absolutely destroys any Soviet
> incentive to accept any reduction in the
> number of offensive missiles or warheads. .
> . . Why should the Soviet Union increase the
> effectiveness of US space defense and
> simplify the task of US planners by reducing
> the number of Soviet rockets to be shot down
> in case of war? (p.7)

SDI opponents generally believe that instead of
cooperating with the United States in reducing
offensive forces the Soviets will respond to a
U.S. SDI by increasing their strategic offensive
forces. Bundy et al. (Winter 1984/85) reflect
the consensus on the likely Soviet response to
SDI:

> In this real world it is preposterous to
> suppose that Star Wars can produce anything
> but the most determined Soviet effort to
> make it fruitless. Dr. James Fletcher. . .
> has testified that "the ultimate utility. .
> ..of this system will depend not only on
> the technology itself, but on the extent to
> which the Soviet Union agrees to mutual
> defense arrangements and offense
> limitations." The plain implication is that
> the Soviet Union can reduce the "utility" of

> Star Wars by refusing just such concessions.
> That is what we would do, and that is what
> they will do. (p. 272)

Holloway (Summer 1985) suggests that the USSR
will respond to the SDI with military efforts to
defeat strategic defenses, including offensive
force buildup, development of ASATs with direct
attack capability, and the deployment of its own
BMD systems. He also notes that the Soviet
leadership is committed to the effort of limiting
the SDI at the strategic bargaining table (p.
270).

Bundy et al. point to a central problem
perceived by SDI opponents in President Reagan's
conception of the SDI:

> The President seems unaware of the
> difficulty of making the Soviet Union accept
> his vision, and he has repeatedly proposed a
> solution that combines surface plausibility
> and intrinsic absurdity in a way that tells
> a lot about what is wrong with Star Wars
> itself. Mr. Reagan says we should give the
> Russians the secret of defense, once we find
> it, in return for their agreement to get rid
> of nuclear weapons.. . . In the real world
> any defensive system will be an imperfect
> complex of technological and operational
> capabilities, full understanding of which
> would at once enable any adversary to
> improve his own methods of penetration. To
> share this kind of secret is to destroy its
> own effectiveness. Mr. Reagan's solution is
> as unreal as his original dream, and it
> rests on the same failure of understanding.
> (p. 272-273)

According to Hough et al. (1985), the key
factor in the Soviet emphasis on the SDI is
domestic political considerations. In his view,
the U.S. strategic defense program conveniently
offers a long-term threat that will require
Soviet expenditure in high technology. He
comments that:

> the domestic message is quite clear-cut,
> and is drummed in incessantly: U.S.
> technological advantage threatens national
> defense. The implicit message is also
> clear-cut: the Soviet Union must catch up
> in technology. (p. 11)

Few of these commentators see much hope for
success in the current strategic arms talks.
Soviet and U.S. objectives appear to be very far
apart, and the existing circumstances may serve
Soviet domestic policy needs as well as offer
propaganda benefits in the West.

SDI Impacts upon U.S.-Allied Relations

According to Christoph Bertram (Summer 1985),
most Europeans regard any major change in the
structure of nuclear forces as either
destabilizing, irrelevant, or both. They dismiss
as inherently implausible the vision that new
efforts in space might rid the world of the
threat of nuclear devastation (p. 283).
   Bertram, John Newhouse, and Stanley Sloan
assess the SDI from the European perspective.
Newhouse (1985) reports on the reaction in
European capitals to the announcement of the
Strategic Defense Initiative and subsequent
events throughout 1984. Bertram and Sloan (1984)
focus on the expected impacts of the SDI on NATO
Alliance relations, emphasizing strategic
considerations. Sloan's analysis is tied to the
1979 NATO decision to deploy new intermediate-
range nuclear forces in Europe, and he suggests
that Star Wars may have a similar divisive effect
on European and Alliance politics. These authors
highlight the following aspects of the European
reaction to the SDI:

1. The SDI shift in strategy from deterrence
to defense undercuts the philosophical foundation
of the NATO Alliance.

2. Modernization of European and NATO nuclear
forces to enhance deterrence carries heavy

political costs now that President Reagan claims that deterrence is immoral and that offensive nuclear forces will become obsolete.

3. Proximity to the Soviet Union intensifies European interest in arms control and detente. The NATO allies are concerned about SDI effects on East-West relations.

4. In the European view, security problems are best solved by political rather than technological approaches. This perspective is reflected in the NATO policy of linking arms control negotiations to weapons deployments.

5. The Europeans have their own space interests that may be adversely affected by Star Wars.

6. Europeans fear that the SDI will elicit Soviet deployment of a similar ballistic missile defense, which will effectively disarm the independent nuclear forces of France and Great Britain.

Europeans feel that their security rests on the threat of mutual assured destruction, and upon U.S. willingness to respond to a Soviet attack against Western Europe with strategic weapons. However, the SDI now implies a U.S. determination to "escape from the risk of conflict in Europe" (Bertram, p. 294). Europeans are concerned with the United States' inability to come to terms with its vulnerability to nuclear attack. If the United States moves to erect a defensive shield over itself, the implication will be that Washington is seeking a way out of sharing the fate of Europe in a nuclear war. Hence the SDI is seen as a reversal of the very principle upon which the North Atlantic Treaty Organization is founded. According to Bertram, the U.S. offer to erect a similar shield over Europe does not mitigate the concern. It is the intent to decouple U.S. and European security that constitutes the threat; Europeans have little confidence that defensive shields can actually be built.

Bertram, Newhouse, and Sloan note that NATO relations were strained by the deployment of Pershing II and ground-launched cruise missiles mandated by the Intermediate Nuclear Force (INF) decision of 1979. The aim of those deployments was to enhance deterrence by strengthening the link between a Soviet attack on Western Europe and U.S. strategic retaliation; however, installation of missiles in NATO countries was achieved at considerable internal and external political cost. The SDI program seems to question the value of those deployments; it also weakens the case of the Europeans who supported installation of U.S. weapons. John Newhouse (1985) quotes a French diplomat: "We cannot all go to the ends of the earth persuading Europeans that they should accept deployment of missiles, and then call them immoral and about to become obsolete. This is a great contradiction" (p. 38). Newhouse also notes that British Prime Minister Thatcher has committed 10 billion pounds sterling to the purchase of new U.S. Trident nuclear submarines equipped with D-5 missiles. Thus an effort to make nuclear weapons obsolete will be difficult for her government to support.

In discussions with President Reagan at Camp David in 1984, Mrs. Thatcher outlined four points that define the conditions for European participation in the SDI with the United States:

1. Disavowal of Western intentions to achieve strategic superiority;

2. Potential deployment of SDI-related systems, which will be a matter for negotiation;

3. The goal of the SDI to enhance rather than undercut deterrence;

4. The efforts that must be made to reduce offensive arms at the Geneva talks on arms control.

Bertram notes that European leaders have "muted" their criticism of the SDI. The reason for this may be that NATO governments want to take part in SDI research in hopes of reaping

research advantages and commercial benefits.
Such participation does not, however, indicate
support of SDI political or strategic objectives;
with the exception of France, the allies are
simply not willing to confront a popular U.S.
president on a program to which he is obviously
so committed.   Newhouse (1985) writes that the
allies are waiting and hoping that the SDI "won't
outlast the Reagan Presidency" (p. 54).

ECONOMIC CONSEQUENCES OF THE SDI

   The Star Wars proposal has revived economic
arguments about the comparative costs of offense-
and defense-dominant strategies and their
correlative weapons systems. SDI critics charge
that (1) deploying comprehensive strategic
defenses will cost as much as $1 trillion without
improving U.S. security; (2) costs to the Soviets
of defeating strategic defenses will be substantially lower than costs of implementing defenses
will be for the United States; (3) the expenditure of $60 billion on SDI research and develop-
ment is not justified; and (4) the emphasis of
the Department of Defense and the Reagan
administration on Star Wars will deflect needed
resources from more deserving military programs.
   Charles Zraket (1985) issues the reminder that
funding for modernization and improvement of the
readiness for strategic offensive forces may be
more important than the SDI. Yet, "building such
a system would dominate the defense and space
activities of the United States for decades and
would require extraordinary organizational and
funding support" (p. 125).
   Economic costs are discussed as an ancillary
issue by many of those opposed to Star Wars.
Technical arguments include estimates of the
costs to transport fuel for lasers into orbit and
to power ground-based lasers. Defense analysts
compare potential costs of various offense- and
defense-dominant strategies, while other
commentators note European fears that SDI
priorities may reduce U.S. resource commitments
to NATO.

In "Defending Missiles, Not People: Hard-Site Defense" (1985), Coit Blacker describes several methods of determining ballistic missile defense costs, including forecasting and aggregating total system costs, calculating the cost to an attacker of overcoming a defense, and assessing incremental costs (p. 36). In regard to the last point, it should be noted that when costs were calculated for U.S. strategic defense projects in the late 1960s, the cost of an additional defensive unit was substantially higher than that of adding an offensive weapon to defeat it. Some critics, and also some advocates, of the SDI have suggested that costs cannot now be reliably estimated for the SDI, which is a program of unknown complexity and duration. However, Rathjens and Ruina (Summer 1985) analyze various levels of defense and conclude that the cost-effectiveness advantage of offensive forces is likely to prevail; they also suggest that cost-exchange ratios appear to favor terminal defense of hard-point targets, if defenses are deployed to exact the greatest expenditure of the adversary's offensive forces (p. 248).

In a March 1986 paper in _Science_, George Field and David Spergel calculate cost-exchange ratios for orbiting platforms carrying infrared laser weapons. Using the cost to orbit the Hubble Space Telescope as a basis for their calculations, and adopting lower limits to the costs of defense and upper limits to the costs of offense, these authors conclude that:

> If our estimates and methods are confirmed, a space-based laser BMD system would not be able to maintain its effectiveness against the offense at less cost than it would take to proliferate the missiles to overcome it. It is therefore not likely that such a system would satisfy the president's requirement...for an effective system. (p. 1392)

Writing in the January 1986 _Bulletin of the Atomic Scientists_, William Hartung sounds a warning regarding SDI funding that is similar to the broader warning about the Military-Industrial

Complex issued by President Eisenhower in his farewell address. Hartung voices several concerns. One is that the government tends to seek technical information from defense corporations that is then used to help make decisions about the procurement of major weapons. Often these are the same businesses that are given the contracts to produce the weapons--a potential conflict-of-interest situation according to Hartung. He also suggests that pressures are mounting on members of the Congress to fund SDI research owing to the influence of defense corporation political action committees (PACs). In addition, Hartung is worried about two potential problem areas he sees in regard to SDI research funding on university campuses. One is the creation of yet another constituency that will support SDI because of the money involved. The other is the legitimacy that may accrue to SDI due to the stature of scientists whose time has been bought by government funding (p. 20).

Also writing in the January 1986 Bulletin of the Atomic Scientists, John Kogut and Michael Weissman recount their efforts to organize scientists and engineers to refuse SDI research monies. Motivated by their opposition to Star Wars, and by the kinds of concerns mentioned by Hartung, the two University of Illinois physicists drafted an anti-SDI pledge in the spring of 1985. They describe a similar pledge that was drawn up by scientists at Cornell University. A copy of the Illinois-Cornell combined pledge is reproduced in the abstract of this article.

SUMMARY

In his analysis of hard-site defenses, Coit Blacker comments that strategic defense issues are numerous, complex, and impossible to treat individually (p. 40). A review of the arguments criticizing the Strategic Defense Initiative bears out this observation. Contributing to the difficulty in assessing the SDI is the apparent administration advocacy of two different strategic defense programs. There is President Reagan's plan to protect the American population by replacing the immoral policy of mutual assured destruction with what could be called mutual assured defense; and there is the program to defend hardened military targets with defenses primarily deployed against the terminal phase of ballistic flight.

Most SDI critics agree that the individual components of a multitiered defense system can eventually be demonstrated successfully. They are also united in rejecting claims that the system as a whole can meet the president's requirement of rendering nuclear weapons impotent and obsolete. This view is reinforced by the nearly universal belief among the critics that the Soviets will vigorously react to a SDI by emphasizing an array of countermeasures that are less expensive to deploy than additional defensive units deployed by the United States.

Opinions on the contribution of hard-site defense to nuclear stability are divided. Some SDI opponents suggest that deterrence will be strengthened by protecting land-based ICBMs. Others believe that the Minuteman and MX vulnerabilities can be reduced in less destablizing ways. To most SDI critics the preservation of the ABM Treaty is of paramount importance. They believe that the Treaty should not be compromised with deployment of hard-site defenses.

The development of anti-satellite weaponry is considered by opponents of strategic defense to be extremely destabilizing. Thus, encouragement of such development under the SDI stimulates additional criticism of the president's program.

The debate on the merits of the SDI is broadening as specialists analyze strategic defense economics, foreign policy implications, software requirements, and command and control issues, in addition to the traditional debates over offense and defense dominance. Although the effect of the SDI on domestic politics has not yet been widely covered in the journal literature, discussion of what amounts to an update of President Eisenhower's warning about the Military-Industrial Complex is emerging, as

is commentary on the professional opposition to
the SDI research program on university campuses
and elsewhere.

ABSTRACTS

1. Bertram, Christoph. Summer 1985. Strategic defense and the Western alliance. Daedalus 114:279-296.

Bertram analyzes the potential impacts of the SDI on NATO and concludes that a U.S. effort to deploy strategic defenses will undermine the philosophy binding the Western alliance and introduce into the European-American relationship a deep rift that could permanently break up the alliance. In describing European attitudes on deterrence, Bertram notes the conviction that deterrence is essential to the security of Europe, the vested interest of NATO countries in arms control, and their interest in protecting investments in scientific and commercial uses of space. European reaction to U.S. defense programs focuses fears that a leaky defense will be destabilizing, that strategic defenses will decouple U.S. and European security, that the SDI will undercut support for INF deployment, and that defense priorities will reduce the resources available for NATO needs. Bertram notes that the foundation of the Alliance and Western European security is U.S. willingness to share vulnerability to Soviet attack. The allies view the SDI as another indication that the United States wishes to escape from the risk of European conflict, shifting from coalition policies to a strategy of going it alone.

2. Bethe, Hans, A., Jeffery Boutwell, Richard L. Garwin. Spring 1985. BMD technologies and concepts in the 1980s. Daedalus 114:53-70.

This article appears in the two-volume issue of Daedalus that is entirely devoted to the subject of weapons in space. Bethe, Boutwell, and Garwin could have written in the most esoteric scientific style about this subject. They did not, however, and therein is found much of the utility of the piece. Without "talking down" to

their readers, the trio straightforwardly
examines the task faced by the United States in
defending against MIRVed Soviet ballistic
missiles. The authors also discuss various
countermeasures that the Soviets may adopt to
confuse, overwhelm, and destroy U.S. defensive
systems, as well as the matter of expenditures
for strategic defense in the context of cost-
effectiveness.

The authors' discussion of the major new BMD
weapons technologies being considered by the
government (lasers, particle beams, and kinetic-
energy weapons) parallels the four environments,
or phases of ballistic missile flight path
against which the defensive systems will have to
operate. These are the boost phase, the post-
boost phase, the midcourse phase, and the
terminal phase. This discussion is followed by
an examination of the means to deploy various BMD
systems and command and control functions
required for successful battle management.

The explanation of potential Soviet
countermeasures to U.S. BMD is divided into three
categories of Soviet responses: passive, active,
and threatening. Passive measures are
exemplified by decoys that do not attack the
defensive systems; active measures are described
as devices such as space mines that could destroy
U.S. systems; and threatening measures are
methods such as adding additional warheads to
overwhelm the defenses.

In the cost-effectiveness section of the
article, the authors point out that if a
negative cost-exchange ratio exists (i.e., if it
is cheaper for the offense to enhance its
capabilities than for the defense to negate such
improvements), a strong case will likely be made
against defensive deployment. Further, the
authors note that an expensive BMD could cause
opportunity cost problems. They mention that if
strategic defense is even marginally cost-
effective, the cost to deploy and maintain the
system could require funds needed to modernize
conventional forces and to develop other
legitimate military programs.

The authors conclude that "despite remarkable
advances since the 1960s in BMD related
technologies, there are major uncertainties

surrounding the ultimate feasibility of deploying and maintaining strategic defenses against ballistic missiles" (p. 70)

3.   Bethe, Hans A., and Richard L. Garwin. Spring 1985. Appendix A: new BMD technologies. Daedalus 114:331-368.

This is another article in the two-volume issue of Daedalus on space weapons. The focus is the relatively new category of potential BMD weapons--directed-energy weapons--for which the kill mechanism is a concentrated beam either of light or of particles that travel at essentially the speed of light (186,000 miles per second). In either case the directed-energy weapons would have a substantial advantage over defensive missiles propelled by chemical means, which would be extremely slow by comparison; however, in the authors' view these extraordinarily fast weapons are plagued by numerous propagation and deployment problems not easily solved.

In comparison with the article by Bethe, Boutwell, and Garwin, this article was written at a higher level of technical sophistication, with a sprinkling of calculations appearing throughout the text. The authors focus much of their attention on the various basing modes designed to enhance the effectiveness of lasers and particle beam weapons, taking into consideration the strengths and weaknesses of these weapons and how the former can be countered by the Soviets and the latter exploited. Highlights of this discussion are the absentee problem for satellites carrying lasers in low earth orbit, the weight and energy characteristics of excimer lasers, which suggest the prospects of ground deployment with space-based mirror delivery, the pop-up deployment of nuclear-powered x-ray lasers, and the propagation of neutral hydrogen particle beams.

The authors also examine kinetic-energy weapons such as rocket-propelled missiles, objects propelled by electromagnetic railguns, and swarm jets. They then briefly mention the use of buried nuclear detonations that would send a column of earth skyward to intercept descending warheads, shortly prior to impact.

The authors' summary evaluation is that space-based BMD is not very promising against the strong offensive threat posed by the Soviet Union, particularly the threat to soft targets such as cities and unique targets such as command and control centers against which large numbers of RVs can be shot. In regard to the proposed layered defensive system contemplated by SDI planners, the authors note that if one layer fails, the burden on successive layers becomes great. They add that post-boost and midcourse defense depend upon "birth-to-death" tracking of warheads and that this tracking depends upon the operation of a number of space assets not likely to survive Soviet efforts directed at their destruction and degradation.

An endoatmospheric terminal defense for hardened ICBM silos, using kinetic kill vehicles and possibly the buried nuclear detonation procedure, is deemed by the authors most likely to succeed.

Last, the authors state their belief that the natural reaction of the Soviet Union to a U.S. BMD system would be for Moscow to increase its offensive capability, thus intensifying the arms race with the result that the United States would be less secure rather than more so.

4.   Bethe, Hans A., Richard L. Garwin, Kurt Gottfried, and Henry W. Kendall. 1984. Space-based ballistic missile defense. Scientific American", October, 39-49.

The authors summarize the technical and political arguments against the SDI and describe BMD technology, with an emphasis on boost phase interception and potential countermeasures. They also review the history of the U.S. BMD debate and identify the parameters of current SDI criticism, including implications for command and control, strategy, the ABM Treaty, and ASATs. The authors conclude that the SDI's questionable operational performance, vulnerability to countermeasures, and potential use in an ASAT capacity will damage U.S. security. The authors recommend both continued BMD research at traditional levels of expenditure within ABM Treaty constraints, and negotiation of a bilateral ban on the testing and use of space weapons.

5.   Blacker, Coit D. 1985. Defending missiles, not people: hard-site defense. Issues in Science and Technology 2:30-44.

Coit Blacker notes the divergence in the SDI debate between the president's request for "physical protection of the U.S. homeland, including population and industry" and the alternative SDI rationale for hard-site ballistic missile defense offered by many administration officials. He suggests that policymakers must determine whether we have the technology to defend specific assets, whether we can afford defense systems, and how hard-site defense will affect the strategic balance. Blacker describes the criteria for assessing effectiveness of hard-site BMD and summarizes arguments about the need for such defenses, methods of determining system costs, effects on strategic stability, and implications for arms control. He states that the goal of his discussion is to examine issues rather than to make recommendations, and concludes that the potential negative consequences of the SDI are important enough to warrant intensive, prolonged, and serious study.

6.   Boutwell, Jeffrey, and F. A. Long. Summer 1985. The SDI and U.S. security. Daedalus 114:315-329.

Boutwell and Long summarize the arguments of SDI supporters and opponents, then discuss the political appeal of strategic defense, the political risks of the SDI, and the effect of the SDI on mutual security. They note that the prospect of "saving lives rather than avenging them" is appealing, as is the potential use of the SDI to gain leverage in the Geneva arms talks. The authors suggest that presentation of the SDI solely as a means of enhancing deterrence may not have succeeded in gaining the necessary

domestic political support. They also point out
that projected tests of BMD components may
compromise the viability of the ABM Treaty in
1987, and that senior administration officials
are openly critical of both the Treaty and SALT
limitations. The authors recommend restraint of
SDI funding, updating and improvement of the ABM
Treaty, and negotiation of an anti-satellite
weapon test ban.

7.   Bowman, Robert. 1985.   Star Wars:
     defense or death star. Potomac, MD:
     Institute for Space and Security Studies.

   In this book the author discusses and
criticizes Star Wars technology from a military
perspective. Bowman, a retired USAF lieutenant
colonel, is the former director of Advanced Space
Programs Development for what is now the Air
Force Space Division. He supervised many
programs that are now part of the SDI. His
narrative is readable and provides interesting
technical details. First he discusses background
on space technology and national security; then
he reviews the Star Wars technology, including
boost-phase intercept, candidate kill mechanisms,
and countermeasures. In a chapter on BMD
strategy and objectives he evaluates the systems
requirements and technical challenges of four
potential levels of BMD: BMD as a replacement
for deterrence; BMD used to limit damage, BMD as
first-strike support, and BMD as enhancement for
deterrence. His discussion of Star Wars and arms
control includes sections on Soviet treaty
compliance, legal aspects of weapons in space,
the ASAT-BMD Treaty link, and the prospects for
ASAT negotiations. In the final chapters he
considers the potential benefits of U.S.-Soviet
cooperation in space as well as alternate futures
including the "Death Star" (SDI) and "Friendship"
alternatives. The latter aims for maintenance of
deterrence, recognition of mutuality, enhancement
of stability, reduction of threat, provision of
security, diversion of resources, growth of
interdependence, diminishment of differences,
establishment of law, and development of
friendship.

8.   Bracken, Paul. 1983. The command and control of nuclear forces. New Haven: Yale University Press.

According to Bracken, the most likely cause of World War III will be the escalation of crisis into major confrontation, and ultimately into war. the author supports this argument with thoroughly detailed analysis and discussion of nuclear forces, warning and intelligence, war plans, problems of assessment, special problems of war in Europe, and command and control. Major themes include (1) the need to examine organizational structures within the institutions created to control nuclear weapons, rather than focusing solely on the technology of command and control; (2) the "tight coupling" of warning systems and weapons that has resulted from the need to analyze the continuous flow of real-time warning and intelligence information; (3) the barriers to maintaining political control in a strategic war which are now seemingly insurmountable; and (4) current war-fighting plans based on unrealistic peacetime conditions. Bracken recommends an incremental arms-control approach to strengthening national security. Nuclear "rules of the road" focusing on operational issues should be established to govern operation of forces and alerts. For example, short flight-time weapons capable of decapitation attack, such as Pershing 2 missiles and Soviet SLBMs, should be banned; unilateral declaration of no first strikes against national command authorities should be accompanied by arms-control talks; and operational aspects of arms control, such as war termination and crisis defusing, should be emphasized.

9.   Bundy, McGeorge, George F. Kennan, Robert S. McNamara, and Gerard Smith. Winter 1984/85. The president's choice: Star Wars or arms control. Foreign Affairs 63:264-278

This paper by prominent American statesmen is notable for its discussion of the political implications of the SDI. The authors suggest that the fundamental flaw in the Star Wars proposal is that its goals cannot be achieved; they then discuss the SDI problems of destructiveness of nuclear weapons, "impotence" of second-strike forces, inability to test SDI systems, limited human control, vulnerability of space-based components, and potential penetration by aircraft. In discussing the SDI as a program for terminal defenses of military targets, the authors contend that such a program would destroy the ABM Treaty, accelerate the arms race, and stimulate offensive and defensive weapons systems in the USSR. In their analysis of likely Soviet responses to the SDI, they emphasize the offensive aspect of Star Wars and maintain that the USSR will not permit U.S. defense to degrade the value of their deterrent forces. In addition, they maintain that the SDI poses a serious threat to the ABM Treaty. Finally, the authors conclude that the Treaty must be defended in Congress and that Congress must prevent "overcommitment of financial and scientific recourses to totally unproven schemes overflowing with unknowns."

10.   Carter, Ashton B. 1984. _Directed-energy missile defense in space_. Cambridge, MA: Massachusetts Institute of Technology, Report no. PB84-210111, April.

This document is an introduction to the technical aspects of directed-energy destruction of Soviet ballistic missiles during the initial, or boost, phase of their approximately thirty-minute flight path from launch site to impact in the United States. This is the phase during which a number of ballistic missile characteristics are present that give certain advantage to the defense.
Carter arrives at nine "Principal Judgments and Observations":

1. The prospect that SDI technolgies will provide a perfect or near-perfect defense of society from Soviet nuclear attack is so remote that it should not serve as the basis of public expectation or national policy about BMD.

2. The wisdom of deploying less-than-perfect BMD is controversial.

3. The strategic goal of President Reagan's SDI is not clear.

4. As of 1984 directed-energy weapons and other devices for boost phase intercept of ICBMs have not yet been built, even in the laboratory.

5. New BMD technologies that perform well in controlled conditions may not be effective given Soviet countermeasures. New BMD technologies do not by themselves mean new BMD capabilities, unless they can be effective in the face of Soviet countermeasures.

6. Directed-energy weapons will be developed for purposes other than BMD.

7. For modest defensive goals, traditional re-entry phase defenses and/or more advanced midcourse defenses might be sufficient.

8. Deployment of missile defense based on new technologies is forbidden by the ABM Treaty.

9. There is a close connection between advanced BMD concepts and future ASAT systems.

11.   Carter, Ashton B. 1985.   The command and control of nuclear war. Scientific American, January, 32-39.

   Carter provides an overview of command, control and intelligence (C^3I) issues. Although he does not discuss the SDI, his description of the basic elements and shortcomings in the U.S. C^3I system provides an important assist to understanding the SDI debate. Carter points out that nuclear weapons are meaningless without a means of control; he then discusses the four components of the U.S. C^3I system, describing the weaknesses of each with respect to command posts, sensors, communication links, and procedures. Carter suggests that the potential vulnerabilities of the C^3I system may prevent the United States from carrying out "the most rudimentary aspect of its nuclear deterrent policy: to discern the nature of an attack by the USSR and to retaliate according to a prearranged plan" (p. 38). The author recommends improving both technical and procedural elements of the U.S. C^3I system.

12. Carter, Ashton B. 1985. The relationship of ASAT and BMD systems. Daedalus, 114:171-188.

Carter distinguishes between the ASAT and BMD roles of proposed Star Wars weapons and suggests that they should be treated separately in public policy decisions. He also describes existing U.S. and Soviet systems and discusses the ASAT potential of SDI weaponry as well as the BMD potential of current ASAT weapons. He analyzes four scenarios in which arms-control limits on BMD and ASAT systems could be combined: (1) no ASAT Treaty; (2) ASAT Treaty and ABM Treaty; (3) ASAT Treaty but no ABM Treaty; and (4) no arms control. He concludes that developing a policy to manage the BMD/ASAT overlap will not be possible until the fundamentally different security concerns of each mission are considered separately.

13. Chayes, Abram, Antonia Handler Chayes, and Eliot Spitzer. Summer 1985. Space weapons: the legal context. Daedalus 114:193-218.

The authors examine the legal regime governing the uses of space for ballistic missile defense and anti-satellite weapons, including the Outer Space and Anti-Ballistic Missile Treaties, and issues of ABM Treaty interpretation and compliance. They point out that the ABM Treaty is the "only permanent and legally operative bilateral arms-control agreement in effect between the two superpowers." The fundamental strategic assumption underlying the ABM Treaty—that is, maintenance of peace through nuclear deterrence—would be threatened by deployment of strategic defenses as described by the president. The authors also suggest that the abrogation of the ABM Treaty would call into question the future of negotiated arms control. The administration's legal defense of the SDI rests on its status as an R&D activity, which is not prohibited by the Treaty. The authors claim that the Reagan administration is attempting to exploit ambiguities in the Treaty that relate to distinguishing between research and development, defining system "components" and "adjuncts," and developing and testing dual-purpose weapons systems such as ASATs and anti-tactical ballistic missiles. They further charge that the Standing Consultative Commission established by the ABM Treaty is threatened by the politicization of the process to examine treaty compliance. The authors recommend clarification of ABM Treaty provisions and negotiation of a bilateral treaty defining the limits of ASAT activities.

14. Cunningham, Ann Marie, and Mariana Fitzpatrick. 1983. Future fire-weapons for the apocalypse. New York: Warner Books. See Chapters 5, 6, and 7.

This book contains a straightforward critique and, to some extent, an expose of that part of the U.S. military establishment which has created and is responsible now for nuclear weapons, and which may create in the future and be responsible for operating space weapons. It also constitutes a primer of advanced weapons technology written from the political perspective that advanced weaponry, exacerbated by fear of "the Soviet threat," is getting out of hand, and that an informed electorate should thus impose constraints on the future growth of sophisticated military technology. In Chapters 5 and 6 the authors present easy-to-read descriptions of lasers and particle beams and their possible military applications. In Chapter 7 they suggest potential military missions for the space shuttle and discuss how killer satellites might be employed.

15. Didisheim, Peter. Winter/Spring 1986. The
     ASAT/SDI link: papers on strategic
     defense. Cambridge, MA: Union of Concerned
     Scientists.

     In this paper the author analyzes the complex
relationship between ballistic missile defense
(BMD) and anti-satellite (ASAT) weapons
development. He also surveys the research efforts
involved in the Strategic Defense Initiative
program and finds that many of the SDI projects
would result in potent ASATs long before they
would yield any form of BMD capability. In
addition, he discusses the effects of the SDI on
ASAT arms control, the relationship of ASAT
development to the ABM Treaty, and the
vulnerability of space-based defenses to ASAT
attack. He concludes that advanced ASAT
development should be prevented through (1) a
restructuring of the SDI away from advanced
engineering development toward fundamental
laboatory research; (2) a shift in focus of the
program from space-based defense toward ground-
based BMD research; and (3) the prompt
negotiation of an ASAT Limitation Treaty.

16. Drell, Sidney D., Philip J. Farley, and
     David Holloway. 1985. The Reagan Strategic
     Defense Initiative: a technical,
     political, and arms control assessment.
     Cambridge, MA: Ballinger.

     In a brief introduction the authors summarize
the ABM debate of the late 1960s and describe the
goals of the president's initiative. They then
analyze the SDI in terms of the ABM Treaty and
the U.S.-Soviet strategic relationship, strategic
defense technology and its implications for the
U.S.-Soviet strategic relationship, and
enhancement of stability and arms control
prospects under ABM limitations. Conclusions and
recommendations follow. The appendices contain
the conclusion of President Reagan's speech of
March 23, 1983; excerpts from General Secretary
Andropov's speech on March 27, 1983; Richard De
Lauer's statement on the SDI; the text of the ABM

Treaty; and a brief review of Chinese and
Japanese assessments of the SDI, by John Lewis.
In the assessment of SDI implications the authors
emphasize Soviet reactions and likely responses,
which would include countermeasure development,
direct attack on defenses, increasing offensive
forces, deploying ballistic missile defenses, and
refusal to limit offenses. They discuss SDI
impacts on the ABM, with emphasis on the U.S.-
Soviet agreement on nuclear stability that
underlies the Treaty. The authors conclude that
the SDI faces several operational problems, that
no foreseeable technology is likely to change the
offense-defense equation to favor defense, and
that pursuit of ABM will undermine deterrence and
strategic stability. They recommend limiting the
SDI to research, with deliberate deferment of
engineering development; annual funding levels of
about $2 billion; formation of a non-partisan
SDI advisory and monitoring panel; initiation of
voluntary, regular consultation on SDI and
related matters in the Standing Consultative
Commission; consultation with our major allies
and other interested countries; and, finally,
recognition that the absence of Soviet ABMs is of
greater value than a partially effective U.S.
defense, and that strategic modernization and
related arms control measures are more promising
for timely improvement of U.S. deterrent posture
than ABM plans or deployment.

17. Drell, Sidney D., and Wolfgang K. H.
Panofsky. 1984. The case against
strategic defense: technical and strategic
realities. Issues in Science and
Technology, 1 (no. 1): 45-65.

   This paper contains a discussion of the
strategic and technical implications of the SDI.
First, the authors examine the causes of "offense
dominance"; then they evaluate the arguments
supporting the SDI--that nuclear weapons would be
rendered obsolete, deterrence would be enhanced,
the offensive deterrent would be protected, and
the United States would be keeping pace with
Soviet technology. The technical potential of
SDI defense concepts is examined in some detail,
with attention to space-based interceptors,

boost phase interception, midcourse intercept,
and terminal defenses. The authors also discuss
the effects of the SDI on the ABM Treaty and arms
control. They conclude that there is "no
practical prospect whatsoever of constructing a
strategic defense . . . that can enhance deterrence, much less render nuclear weapons impotent
and obsolete," in the absence of drastic
reductions in nuclear arms. Furthermore, the SDI
faces severe operational problems, will decrease
crisis stability, endanger existing treaties, and
act as an incentive for increased arms
competition. They suggest that the U.S. continue
limited BMD research in new technologies, comply
fully with the ABM treaty, and insist that the
USSR strictly adhere to the treaty as well.

18.   Field, George, and David Spergel. 1986.
       Cost of space-based laser ballistic missile
       defense. Science, March 21, 1387-1393.

The authors set for themselves the task of
working out a method to estimate the cost-
exchange ratio for a space-based missile defense
system of satellites carrying infrared lasers
which is intended to destroy Soviet ICBMs. Since
each laser beam must dwell for a certain amount
of time on a missile in order to destroy it, each
laser is limited as to the number of missiles it
can destroy in a given period of time. In the
offense/defense competition postulated by the
authors, a possible Soviet countermeasure would
be to launch additional missiles to swamp the
capacity of the lasers to destroy them. In turn,
a possible U.S. response would be to deploy
additional laser satellites, and so regain the
advantage.
Field and Spergel use the costs for the Hubble
Space Telescope as a point of departure for
developing their procedure for determining the
cost to destroy an additional missile compared
with the cost for the Soviets to deploy an
additional missile. A disadvantage for some
readers who attempt to follow the calculations
which are used is that they will not be readily
comprehended by some.
The authors conclude that:

> If our estimates and methods are
> confirmed, a space-based laser BMD system
> would not be able to maintain its
> effectiveness against the offense at less
> cost than it would take to proliferate
> the missiles to overcome it. It is
> therefore not likely that such a system
> would satisfy the president's
> requirements . . . for an effective sys-
> tem. (p. 1392)

19. Flax, Alexander. Spring 1985. Ballistic
missile defense: concepts and history.
<u>Daedalus</u> 114:33-51.

This article appears in the two-volume issue of
<u>Daedalus</u> on weapons in space. The author reaches
back to the 1960s and 1970s to reconstruct for
his readers early debates over ABM. He points
out that with two exceptions much of the
technical thought of that time is reflected in
contemporary discussion. The exceptions are that
during the 1960-1970 phase, ABMs were nuclear
whereas the current SDI is not, and the
directed-energy weapon concepts today have much
more political and technical support than they
did twenty years ago.

Then, as now, a very serious problem was the
array of countermeasures that it was presumed the
Soviets would take in response to U.S. defensive
systems, including multiple warheads to penetrate
defenses, decoys and chaff to confuse radar, and
various forms of electronic jamming and spoofing,
and maneuvering warheads to defeat low-altitude
defenses. Further, there is today much technical
evidence that the SDI will prove more effective
in protecting hardened ICBM silos than soft
cities. This view is similar to the technical
analysis that led in 1975 to the decision to
deploy the ABMs allotted to the United States
under the ABM Treaty for the ICBM field at Grand
Forks, North Dakota. Finally, what was often
seen as an unfavorable cost-exchange ratio for
ballistic missile defense two decades ago still
burdens the proponents of the SDI today.

20. Ford, Daniel. 1985. The button: the Pentagon's strategic command and control system. New York: Simon and Schuster.

Ford reports on the operational weaknesses of the U.S. system for command and control of its nuclear forces and discusses the first-strike strategy supported by C[3]I systems. He also describes the condition of command and control systems at the moment of a hypothetical "H-Hour" attack by the USSR. He probes existing early warning, telecommunications, and computing systems as well as procedures for relaying orders and simulating nuclear war conditions. Ford contends that the existing C[3]I system could not ride out a nuclear attack to deliver a successful second strike, even though ordering retaliation is the basic requirement of U.S. deterrence policy. He maintains that deficiencies in the existing system stem from the fact that the actual U.S. war-fighting plan is based on taking the offensive rather than waiting for a chance to retaliate. Such a first-strike policy could be carried out with the command and control systems the United States now has. Although Ford mentions the SDI only in passing, his evaluation of C[3]I and nuclear strategy and his portraits of those in command of nuclear forces provide background against which arguments supporting and opposing the SDI can be examined.

21. Garwin, Richard, and John Pike. 1984. Space weapons. Bulletin of the Atomic Scientists 40 (May): 48-49.

Garwin and Pike summarize the developments in U.S. and Soviet space weaponry and discuss the interactions between ASAT and BMD technologies. They conclude that the national interest will be best served by banning ASATs and other weapons in space, and that such a ban could be negotiated quickly. In addition to reviewing the history of space weapon development, Garwin and Pike describe current U.S. and Soviet ASATs, noting that the Soviet device may presently threaten satellites in low-earth orbit, although its testing record is lackluster. Garwin and Pike contend the U.S. Air-Launched Miniature Homing Vehicle carried on an F-15 aircraft "constitutes an order of magnitude improvement" over the Soviet system, and state that advanced ASATs are being studied by both sides. The authors describe the destabilizing aspects of ASAT development. They also explain the SDI BMD weapons and discuss the technical basis of space weapon vulnerability. They recommend immediate negotiation of a ban on space weapons, though not on all military activities in space, and suggest that a draft ASAT treaty proposed by the USSR in 1983 could be used as a basis for negotiation.

22.   Glaser, Charles. Fall 1984. Why even good defenses can be bad. International Security 9:92-123.

Glaser examines the likelihood of improving security through bilateral deployment of strategic defenses and elimination of retaliatory forces. He assumes that highly effective defenses are available and that they would be deployed by both the United States and USSR. U.S. ability to avoid nuclear war is discussed in terms of deterring premeditated Soviet attack, maintaining nuclear crisis stability, and achieving robustness of the U.S. deterrent relative to changes in Soviet forces. This analysis considers the probability of nuclear war occurrence and the damage that would result. Glaser concludes that even perfect defenses are not clearly preferable to the current balance of assured destruction forces and that embarking on area-BMD deployment will degrade nuclear crisis stability.

23.   Gottfried, Kurt, and Richard Lebow. Spring 1985. Antisatellite weapons: weighing the risks. Daedalus 114:147-169.

This paper concentrates on the relative risks and benefits of military use of ASAT weapons, with an ancillary discussion of the link between ASATs and ballistic missile defenses. The authors describe current and prospective ASAT technology, satellite protection, scenarios for military use of ASATs, and ASAT arms control. They note that the growing military importance of satellites makes them increasingly attractive as targets. The marginal military utility of current U.S. and Soviet low-altitude ASATs is unlikely to offset the hazards associated with their deployment; ASATs are more likely to transform crisis into war and to enlarge war than to assist a military mission or enhance deterrence. Gottfried and Lebow conclude that an ASAT test ban should be negotiated, satellites should be protected against attack, and that Anti-Ballistic Missile Treaty goals should be reinforced through a comprhensive ban on testing of space weapons.

24. Hafner, Donald L. Spring 1985. Assessing the president's vision: the Fletcher, Miller, and Hoffman panels. Daedalus 114:91-106.

Hafner contends that the report from the secretary of defense on the SDI study panels incorrectly fosters an impression of agreement among the panels, the president's vision, and the SDI program; he also notes that two of the advisory groups offered contradictory advice (the findings of the Miller panel were not reported). Hafner discusses the Fletcher and Hoffman panel reports, then examines security and strategy "in a world of perfect defenses." He concludes that the panels' reports reflect a basic skepticism about the assumptions underlying strategic defenses rather than an endorsement of Reagan's vision. The Fletcher panel found that the technical feasibility of advanced BMD is far from certain and would depend on effective arms controls. The Hoffman panel suggested plans for enhancing deterrence rather than rendering nuclear weapons obsolete. Hafner maintains that the current debate on strategic defenses would be clearer if the issues raised by the study teams had been debated and integrated into strategic defense policy; instead, it appears that the government is recommending both a nuclear-free world and "buttressed deterrence." He suggests that partial defenses may "find new life" as a compromise between no defenses at all and Reagan's perfect defenses.

25. Hartung, William. 1986. Star Wars pork barrel. Bulletin of the Atomic Scientists 42 (January): 20-24.

Hartung argues that the Reagan administration has not fared well in debates about the technology and strategy of Star Wars. Nevertheless, an extensive network of support for the president's ballistic missile defense program has been laid in terms of current and potential funding. The author worries that the economic and political base thus built will make it difficult to defeat SDI on its military and strategic merits. These he finds to be few in number.

Combining his own observations with the studies of others, Hartung outlines a dilemma in Star Wars planning as well as in that for other major defense systems. The dilemma is that, by necessity, information from contractors must be utilized in studies of new weapons systems, but such information may understandably tend to favor the building of more weapons than are actually required. He suggests that to offset contractor influence, objective technical assessment must be obtained from sources not associated with the major defense corporations.

Hartung suggests that pressures will mount on members of Congress to support SDI research, and later development, as the political action committees (PACs) representing the largest defense contractors attempt to affect key SDI votes. The statistics used by the author indicate that defense contractor PAC funds may already be influencing how selected members of the Congress vote. He warns that as other major weapons programs are completed, there will be increased pressure to use SDI funding to compensate for the resulting losses in revenue.

Looking ahead, Hartung notes that SDI contracts for research will become important sources for funding in universities. He also voices concern over two potential problems associated with SDI funding for college faculty and graduate students. One is the creation of another constituency that supports SDI because of the money involved. The other is the legitimacy that may accrue to SDI as a function of the stature of scientists whose time has been bought by government funding.

26.   Holloway, David. Summer 1985. The Strategic Defense Initiative and the Soviet Union. Daedalus 114:257-278.

Holloway reviews the roles of deterrence and defense in Soviet policy and the history of Soviet BMD activities. The USSR reduced its emphasis on strategic defense when it achieved rough parity with U.S. nuclear forces, and agreed to a maintenance of the balance in the SALT and ABM treaties. The Soviets' assessment of the SDI reflects their perceptions that the SDI is designed to disarm their retaliatory forces, that the United States is aiming for first-strike capability, and that the United States broke the agreement regarding offense and defense interaction. The official Soviet report on SDI feasibility is skeptical about escaping from deterrence but finds the SDI threatening and likely to erode crisis stability. According to Holloway, the likely Soviet military response will be to render the SDI ineffective by increasing offensive forces, deploying countermeasures and ASATs, and deploying their own BMD. Although the USSR aims to restrict the SDI via arms control, the different outlooks of the United States and the Soviet Union make agreement on the arms control unlikely.

27.   Hough, Jerry F., Stanley R. Sloan, Paul C. Warnke, and David Linebaugh. 1985. Arms control and the Strategic Defense Initiative: three perspectives, Occasional Paper 36. Muscatine, IA: Stanley Foundation, October.

In the three articles included in this paper, the authors discuss the SDI from the perspectives of Soviet reaction, effects on NATO, and prospects for arms control. In "Soviet Interpretation and Response," Jerry Hough contends that the SDI is the centerpiece of Soviet strategic arms control diplomacy for two reasons: The Soviets perceive U.S. defenses as a threat to deterrence, and, more important, the SDI serves Gorbachev's needs in instituting domestic economic reform. Stanley Sloan considers the implications of the SDI for NATO solidarity in "A New Dilemma for NATO." He discusses the SDI in light of the European experience with the INF deployment decision of 1979, and concludes that President Reagan's program may lead to a crisis in transatlantic relations. His suggestions include negotiating an ASAT ban, modifying the ABM Treaty to permit land-based terminal defenses, and including Europe in defense R&D. In "Breaking the Deadlock," Paul Warnke and David Linebaugh propose that arms race problems cannot be solved unilaterally by the United States. They recommend three steps to restore order and direction to the U.S. strategic program and revive stalled negotiations: curb defense systems; reduce nuclear warheads; and ban MIRVed missiles, sea-launched cruise missiles, and anti-satellite weapons.

28. Kogut, John, and Michael Weissman. 1986. Taking the pledge against Star Wars. Bulletin of the Atomic Scientists 42 (January):27-30.

The authors are organizers of the opposition to an effort by the SDI Organization to solicit academic scientists to work on SDI research. The immediate spark for their efforts among fellow physicists at the University of Illinois was a solicitation letter from James Ionson, director of the SDI Organization's office of Innovative Science and Technology.

In response to the SDI Organization letter inviting scientists to participate in Star Wars research, the authors drafted a pledge for circulation among scientists stating opposition to Star Wars work. A similar pledge was written by scientists at Cornell.

The authors claim that as of January 1, 1986,

2,100 science and engineering faculty members and senior researchers as well as 1,600 graduate students and junior research staff have signed the pledge, a copy of which follows:

ANTI-SDI PLEDGE

We, the undersigned scientists and engineers, believe that the Strategic Defense Initiative (SDI) program (commonly known as Star Wars) is ill-conceived and dangerous. Anti-ballistic-missile defense of sufficient reliability to defend the population of the United States against a Soviet attack is not technically feasible. A system of more limited capability will only serve to escalate the nuclear arms race by encouraging the development of both additional offensive overkill and an all-out competition in anti-ballistic-missile weapons. The program will jeopardize existing arms control agreements and make arms control negotiation even more difficult than it is at present. The program is a step toward the type of weapons and strategy likely to trigger a nuclear holocaust. For these reasons, we believe that the SDI program represents, not an advance toward genuine security, but rather a major step backwards.

Accordingly, as working scientists and engineers, we pledge neither to solicit nor accept SDI funds, and we encourage others to join us in this refusal. We hope together to persuade the public and Congress not to support this deeply misguided and dangerous program. (p. 28)

29. Krauthammer, Charles. 1984. The illusion of Star Wars: the worst offense is a bad defense. New Republic, May 14, 13-17.

In his short essay, Krauthammer asks if it is possible to repeal deterrence and replace it with a "technical miracle." His answer includes brief, nontechnical descriptions of multilayered

entakeage and boost phase interception, and details
on the extreme vulnerability of space-based
weapons proposed by Edward Teller and George
Keyworth. The author also discusses several
general considerations that make the successful
defense of the United States extremely unlikely,
including the "absurd" complexity of the defense
system, and the ease with which nuclear offensive
forces can overwhelm defenses. Krauthammer
contends that leaky defenses are destabilizing,
encourage a Soviet first strike, undermine arms
control, and prevent agreement on an anti-
satellite weapons treaty. In addition, Star Wars
defenses may lead to war before they are
operational, as the USSR could be tempted to
attack elements of the system during deployment.
Krauthammer suggests that the real reason for
pushing Star Wars is to evoke public support for
an arms race in an area where the United States
is technologically superior, and that the only
alternative to "automaticity in the nuclear
world" is the deliberate, unsatisfying path of
arms control.

30.   Lin, Herbert. 1985. The development of
       software for ballistic-missile defense.
       Scientific American, December, 46-53.

   In his analysis of SDI software development,
Herbert Lin discusses three questions: What is
the nature of a BMD system?   What are the
obstacles to BMD software development?   Can
these obstacles be circumvented?   He then
describes the process of software development,
and identifies problem areas for SDI such as the
need to predict all possible contingencies, avoid
design errors, detect and correct errors, and
assess the trustworthiness of the software.   Lin
illustrates his arguments with examples of
software development problems encountered in such
large-scale programs as the World-Wide Military
Command and Control Program, the Gemini Space
Program, NORAD, and the Aegis Air Defense system.
He also notes that the general technique for
correcting software errors depends on finding
them during operational use of the system, an

option not available to SDI software developers.
He concludes that "no software-engineering
technology can be anticipated that will support
the goal of a comprehensive ballistic-missile
defense" (p. 53).

31.   Longsteth, Thomas K., John Pike, and John
        B. Rhinelander. 1985.   The impact of U.S.
        and Soviet ballistic missile defense
        programs on the ABM Treaty. Washington,
        D.C.: National Campaign to Save the ABM
        Treaty, March.

First, the authors review the history of
ballistic missile defense, the evolution of the
1972 Anti-Ballistic Missile Treaty, and the
provisions of that treaty. Then, they describe
and evaluate U.S. and Soviet missile defense
programs. The authors also discuss treaty
definition issues, gray area weapons
developments, U.S. and Soviet compliance
questions and the impact of the SDI on alliance
relations and other treaties. They conclude with
recommendations for strengthening the ABM Treaty,
negotiating an ASAT treaty, mitigating SDI treaty
challenges in the long term, and improving U.S.-
Soviet policy processes. The authors argue that
the ABM Treaty banning nationwide defenses
against ballistic missile attack has enhanced
national security, but is now severely threatened
by the Reagan administration's SDI program.
Development of BMD components could violate the
Treaty long before deployment decisions are made;
also of concern are testing devices ostensibly
designed for purposes such as anti-satellite
warfare in a BMD role. The crucial near-term
issue is whether the United States should engage
in research leading to advanced development of
space-based BMD systems; such advanced
development is prohibited by the Treaty.
Reassessment of treaty provisions must include
the recognition that constraints and freedom of
action will apply equally to both the United
States and the USSR. Established procedures for
resolving compliance questions should be
followed, and formal amendment of the Treaty

should be minimized as a means of clarifying treaty provisions.

32.   McNamara, Robert S., and Hans A. Bethe. 1985. Reducing the risk of nuclear war. Atlantic, July 43-51.

McNamara and Bethe examine the nuclear predicament in light of current war-fighting plans and Star Wars programs for perfect or partial defenses. They recommend a different strategy to reduce the risk of nuclear destruction and suggest how the Geneva negotiations can lay the foundation for security. According to these authors, the president's Star Wars vision has been replaced by "Star Wars II"-- that is, by plans for partial defenses of population or terminal defenses of military targets. They suggest that these alternatives would decrease nuclear stability, demonstrate a provocative first-strike strategy on the part of the United States, and endanger rather than enhance arms control. McNamara and Bethe recommend an alternative vision of the twenty-first century based on a restructuring of nuclear forces to reduce the risk of war. They outline the steps necessary to achieve the ultimate goal of mutual deterrence at the lowest nuclear force levels consistent with stability. They suggest that Ambassador Paul Nitze's criteria of defense-force survivability and cost-effectiveness be combined with commitment to the ABM Treaty as a basis for negotiating deep force reductions in Geneva. In conclusion, the authors list various themes by which the negotiations should be guided, including the danger of efforts to achieve superiority, the need to reverse first-strike postures, and the fallacy of believing that threatening technologies cannot be stopped.

33.   Myers, Ware. 1986. The Star Wars software debate. Bulletin of the Atomic Scientists 42 (February):31-36.

Ware Myers reviews the issues in the emerging debate over the prospects for developing SDI battle management software. His article focuses on the findings of the SDI Organization Panel on

Computing in Support of Battle Management and on criticisms of SDI software development offered by David Parnas, a former member of the SDI Organization Panel. Myers identifies the fundamental issue in the software debate as "the number of errors remaining in any deployed SDI software despite intense efforts to remove them" (p. 31). He lists the SDI Organization Panel criteria for minimizing SDI software errors and articulates the critics' case against the likelihood of developing a reliable system. His discussion includes assessment of new programming technologies and languages, project management, and testing procedures. He emphasizes the need for real-time system operation and long-term software maintenance to correct errors.

34. Newhouse, John. 1985. The diplomatic round: test. New Yorker, July 22, 37-54.

In this journalistic account, Newhouse describes the diplomatic reaction in Europe to President Reagan's Star Wars speech and related events that occurred up to and during the NATO foreign ministers' meeting in June 1985. There is a strong consensus in Europe that ABM Treaty and SALT I compliance must be preserved and that the SDI will lessen European security. Newhouse notes that the INF talks have divided Europe on the question of installing new missiles, he also discusses European consternation with the new U.S. emphasis on the immorality of such weapons. He suggests that Europeans are interested in potential SDI high-tech commercial spin-offs, although they are concerned that European companies will not be full research participants in highly sensitive projects, that the field testing of SDI technology could jeopardize the ABM Treaty and arms control, and that the U.S. research project may lure valuable European scientists and engineers overseas. Newhouse further suggests that Prime Minister Thatcher's "Four Points"--that Western intentions to achieve strategic superiority must be disavowed, SDI deployment must be negotiable, deterrence must be enhanced rather than undercut, and the Geneva arms talks must be supported--will limit European participation in the SDI. According to Newhouse, Europeans are hoping that the SDI will not outlast the Reagan administration.

35. Office of Technology Assessment. <u>Anti-satellite</u> <u>weapons,</u> <u>countermeasures,</u> <u>and</u> <u>arms</u> <u>control.</u> Washington, D.C.: U.S. Government Printing Office, September, 1985. This is a smaller companion piece to <u>Ballistic</u> <u>Missile</u> <u>Defense</u> <u>Technologies,</u> with which it was simultaneously issued.

The United States has tested an ASAT in the form of a rocket carried to altitude on an F-15 aircraft that, after release, carried still higher a Miniature Homing Vehicle, which in turn successfully impacted and destroyed a used U.S. satellite. The United States has not tested the SDI system however; in fact, Washington has yet to determine whether the SDI is technically feasible. Nonetheless, by far the junior effort under the Reagan administration is ASATs, with SDI generating the preponderance of strategic and political debate and receiving the bulk of the funding. An effort is made in the document to explain why this situation exists. As the explanation is complicated, a direct quotation is reproduced here:

> Since the debate over ballistic missile defense involves a fundamental reassessment of this country's strategic policy, decisionmakers are reluctant to proceed with ASAT weapon development, deployment, or arms control decisions that may commit them irrevocably to a course with unforeseen consequences. Some people believe that ASAT weapon development programs will be used to accomplish BMD research, thereby avoiding the strictures of the ABM Treaty and the scrutiny of Congress. Others believe that ASAT arms control restrictions would impede future BMD research and development programs. Given these opposing viewpoints, the ASAT development must be made in the broader context of

this country's reassessment of its
strategic posture and the military
utility of space. (p. 26)

Compounding the problem is the difficulty
involved in distinguising a BMD weapon technology
that would fit into SDI from an ASAT technology.
After reviewing technologies suitable for
incorporation in various ASATs and analyzing what
ASATs thus equipped could accomplish, the authors
conclude that even a limited BMD system would
probably be a very good ASAT system.

The document contains a chapter on ASAT arms
control history, including an evaluation of ASAT
arms control options as well as a chapter in
which seven ASAT regimes are analyzed, ranging
from one featuring existing constraints to one
featuring a space-based BMD.

36. Parnus, David Large. 1985. Why star wars
software won't work. Harper's. March 17-
18.

Parnus, a professor of computer science at the
University of Victoria, Canada, created a stir
when he resigned from an SDI advisory panel in
the summer of 1985. In this adaptation from the
testimony he presented later before a Senate
Armed Services subcommittee, he sets forth the
reasons for his resignation. First, Parnus
believes that the kind of system being considered
by the Pentagon cannot be trusted; second, he
maintains that investment in such an
untrustworthy system would be counter to the
nation's best interest. He specifically states
that his opposition to the SDI is technical, not
political. In fact, he writes that he knows of
no political reason to oppose a shield to protect
against nuclear attack; rather, the problem he
sees is that such an objective is scientifically
unlikely.

Parnus bases his case against the SDI upon
several propositions. One is that although
adequate software can be written for complex
computer functions, its reliability is a product
of extensive field testing and evaluation.
According to Parnus, such testing opportunities

will not be available for an SDI system; nor will
it be possible to accurately simulate the Soviet
strategy and tactics against which an SDI would
be expected to operate.

Parnus is skeptical about the assumption that
the reliability problems he foresees with SDI
software can be solved by seeking scientific
breakthroughs or utilizing powerful new
approaches such as artificial intelligence.
Further, Parnus doubts the claims of some that
SDI money will significnatly advance the state of
the art in computer science. He warns against
unfounded expectations for SDI-funded computer
science research by quoting from an unidentified
scientist, "Overfunded research is like heroin:
it leads to addiction, weakens the mind, and
furthers prostitution" (p. 18).

37.   Rathjens, George.   1984.   The Strategic
      Defense Initiative: the imperfections of
      "perfect defense", Environment, June, 6-16.

Rathjens' paper is an overview of arguments
against strategic defenses. After tracing the
course of nuclear weapon development and "offense
dominance," the author gives a simplified
description of ballistic missile technology and
discusses the advantages and disadvantages of
terminal defenses, boost phase intercept, and
midcourse engagement. Rathjens notes that
deployment of strategic defenses would lead to
arms competition and crisis instability. He
expresses concern over the fact that the
president failed to seek competent technical
advice before announcing his strategic defense
plans and that virtually no one in the technical
community believes that the president's
objectives are realistic, although the SDI is
being used as a justification for partial
defenses. The author recommends that agreement
on program objectives should be reached before
the project goes further, that the public should
be given a realistic assessment of SDI prospects,
and that the technical advisory process in
government should be restructured.

38.   Rathjens, George, and Jack Ruina. Summer
      1985.   BMD and strategic instability.
      Daedalus 114:239-255.

   Rathjens and Ruina analyze the technology and
cost-effectiveness of perfect and near-perfect
defenses; discuss offense dominance; and evaluate
the defense of military targets and protection
against unauthorized, accidental, or third
country attack. They note that estimates of
cost-exchange ratios are based on overestimates
of one's own capabilities but also that ratios
highly favorable to offense or defense reflect
offense- or defense-dominant strategy, whereas a
ratio near unity may indicate an arms race.
After discussing the political effects of the
SDI, the authors conclude that there is virtually
no possibility of achieving even a very good
defense of populations and industry. Pursuit of
defenses, however, will likely lead to an
offensive arms race, Soviet deployment of BMD,
insurmountable obstacles to arms control, and
destruction of the ABM Treaty. Of concern are
the "political-psychological" consequences of
Star Wars on the American public and elites, and
on Allied and Soviet leaders. The appeal of
rendering nuclear weapons obsolete rests on
technical rather than political solutions,
weakens U.S. commitment to the security of its
allies, and signals American interest in trading
arms control for military opportunity.

39.   Ruina, Jack. 1986. Perspectives on hard-
      site defense. Issues in Science and
      Technology 2 (no. 2):128-133.

   In his review of strategic defense development,
Ruina concludes that neither a persuasive
technical nor strategic case can be made in favor
of hard-site ballistic missile defense. Although
SDI research could theoretically help hard-site
defense, little useful technological progress has
been made. Boost phase systems are in the
viewgraph engineering phase; midcourse defenses
have not yet--and may never become--feasible,
survivable, or cost-effective; and the costs of
terminal defense are high. Ruina argues that
hard-site defenses are not necessary to enhance

U.S. retaliatory capability, given that ICBM
vulnerability will be mitigated by Trident II
deployment. He recommends continued adherence to
the ABM Treaty while pursuing hard-site defense
R&D to maintain the option to deploy, although
such deployment would carry very high costs and
risks.

40.   Sherr, Alan B. 1984. Legal issues of the
      "Star Wars" defense program. Boston:
      Lawyers' Alliance for Nuclear Arms Control,
      June.

In his brief Alan Sherr describes the impact of
the SDI on the ABM Treaty, on other arms control
agreements and future negotiations, and on the
legal process itself. Following upon his
interpretation of the ABM Treaty, the author
concludes that development, testing, and
deployment of space-based BMD weapons should be
banned; that restrictions on space-based systems
or components apply to new technologies developed
under the SDI; that there is no legal or factual
basis for the argument that certain projects are
adjuncts rather than components of defense
systems and should thus be permitted; and that
development of BMD-capable weapons should be
prohibited even if such systems are initially
intended for use in ASAT systems. Sherr also
argues that the SDI threatens other arms control
agreements and would preclude reaching agreement
on an ASAT or Comprehensive Test Ban. He
suggests that the legal process is damaged when
it bypasses established grievance procedures, and
he recommends a bilateral moratorium on ASAT
testing, resumption of ASAT ban negotiations, and
vigorous pursuit of compliance questions through
the Standing Consultative Commission.

41.   Smith, R. Jeffrey. 1985. Reagan
      reinterprets the ABM Treaty, Science,
      November 8, 644.

In this brief news report, Smith describes the
Reagan administration's reinterpretation of the
ABM Treaty, which holds that the development and

testing of exotic weaponry for use in BMD systems are not prohibited.

42.   Tirman, John, ed. 1984. The fallacy of Star Wars. New York: Random House.

This book is a comprehensive introduction to Star Wars issues, based upon studies conducted by the Union of Concerned Scientists. The authors devote eight chapters to a detailed overview of proposed strategic defense technologies and the final seven chapters to a discussion of anti-satellite weapons, including descriptions of existing U.S. and Soviet systems and treaties limiting ASATs. Contained in the appendices are the text of the ABM Treaty, a proposed Union of Concerned Scientists (UCS) ASAT Treaty, and records from UCS testimony on ASAT before the U.S. Senate Foreign Relations Committee in 1983. In the first section of the volume the authors chronicle the ABM debate that evolved in parallel with the U.S. ABM program, from the Army Nike Zeus and Nike X through the Sentinel and Safeguard programs. The authors also discuss the strategic, political, and technical aspects of the debate, including the ABM Treaty, MIRVs, MAD, flexible response, and war-fighting strategies. The first section concludes with a description of the politics and aims of the SDI program and a brief review of ASAT issues and history. In the second section, the authors examine SDI BMD systems "in light of scientific facts and principles that will govern their performance," with an emphasis on boost phase intercept. In addition, the authors discuss low-earth and geostationary orbiting battle stations armed with x-ray and chemical lasers, kinetic kill weapons, "pop-up" x-ray laser interceptors, and ground-based lasers. Passive, active, and threatening countermeasures are described in detail, as are the requirements and operations of midcourse and terminal defenses; the topics include battle management, and weapons. The technical section concludes with chapters on defense system problems and political and strategic implications, including SDI effects on Soviet strategic planning, crisis stability, deterrence, the ABM Treaty, and NATO. In a final section on ASAT weapons the authors review current issues, existing U.S. and Soviet systems, proposed U.S. and Soviet ASAT treaties, and the ABM Treaty-ASAT link. ASAT technology is explained, verifications problems are discussed, and Reagan administration policies are analyzed. This book is a very readable treatment of virtually the entire range of technical and political SDI issues by persons who oppose President Reagan's proposal.

43.   U.S. Congress. House. Committee on Foreign Affairs. Subcommittee on International Security and Scientific Affairs. Hearings on Arms Control in Outer Space. 98th Congress, November 10, 1983; April 10, May 2, and July 26, 1984.

In this single volume one may find prepared statements by proponents and opponents taken from their testimony for and against SDI before members of Congress. Speaking for the Reagan administration was Lt. General James A. Abrahamson, director of the SDI Organization; and Kenneth L. Adelman, Director of the U.S. Arms Control and Disarmament Agency. Speaking generally against Star Wars was Richard L. Garwin. Another opponent was Kurt Gottfried, a member of the Board of Directors of the Union of Concerned Scientists. Gerard Smith, formerly the chief of the U.S. SALT delegations testified as to the harm to the ABM Treaty in particular and to arms control in general--a harm that he sees as having resulted from ABM research beyond that needed to hedge against a Soviet breakout from the Treaty. Finally, Dean Rusk, former secretary of state in the Carter administration, cautioned:

> that we should not go down the path to the utilization of outer space for weapons purposes without the most serious, persistent and honest effort to work out international arrangements which will preserve outer space as a great sphere of peaceful activities on the part of the human race. (p. 185)

More spritely in format than the prepared
statements are the question-and-answer sessions
involving members of the committee and various
witnesses. At times these sessions became rather
comical. For example, there was the following
exchange between the Committee Chair, Congressman
Dante B. Fascell, D., Florida, Congressman Gerry
E. Studds, D. Massachusetts, and Kenneth Adelman:

   Chairman Fascell. But I want to do
something that is useful. Now, for me, I
am for the development of a radiological
pill that we could take every day and we
wouldn't have to worry about the thermal
blast, you see. It would be a hell of a
lot cheaper. Mr. Studds.

   Mr. Studds. My first mistake, Mr.
Chairman, was leaving the salt air of
Cape Cod this morning. (Laughter)
It is amazing how quickly the mind can be
totally fuddled and turned upside down by
a return of a matter of hours to this
city. There is lunacy in the land. I
don't know about you, but I cannot for
the life of me explain to my constituency
conversations like this which we go
through day after day and week after
week. Mr. Adelman, This is what, the
fourth year--the administration is
nearing the completion of its first term
in office. As you look back on that
first term--or almost all of that first
term now--what would you say were the
four or five accomplishments in the area
of arms control of which this
administration is most proud?

   Mr. Adelman. No. 1 is that we followed
through in a very competent manner and
with the European allies in a very
competent manner on a very tough situation: the 1979 decision in NATO for the
deployment of intermediate-range forces,
if arms control is not going to be
successful. I think---

Mr Studds. So your first thing of which you are most proud is the deployment of additional weapons?

Mr. Adelman. No; that is not what I said, Congressman. What I said was--

Mr. Studds. I could have sworn that is what you said. (p. 86)

44. York, Herbert F. Spring 1985. Nuclear deterrence and the military uses of space. <u>Daedalus</u> 114:17-31.

York reviews the history of military uses of space, noting that SDI technologies are the logical results of decades of military R&D, even though SDI strategy is a radical departure from the past. He describes military space programs from 1946 to the present and contends that U.S. space programs have always been driven by military rather than civilian or scientific needs. Recent technological developments have blurred the distinction between the passive-sensing and data-collection activities of military satellites on the one hand, and active war-fighting capability on the other; and new satellite systems will supply information to war-fighting systems in real time. York discusses the effects of ASAT and space-based defense development on military uses of space, noting that the SDI intends to change the balance between technical and political solutions to problems of international stability and world peace. He recommends restricting ASATs to protect the deterrence role of satellites. York notes that experts on both sides of the strategic defense debate agree that perfect defenses cannot be achieved now; the SDI argument concerns the future course of technology.

45. Zraket, Charles A. Spring 1985. Strategic defense: a system perspective. <u>Daedalus</u> 114:109-123.

Zraket discusses strategic defenses in terms of the role they would play in the overall U.S.

strategic <u>system</u>, rather than focusing on defensive weapons alone. His systems view of the SDI covers the strategic purposes of defense, defense priorities, offense/defense interactions, deployment of U.S. defenses, command and control of strategic defenses, birth-to-death tracking, software design and development, defense system activation and suspension, and system maintenance, testing, and exercising. Zraket emphasizes the importance of defining the purposes of strategic systems, including deterrent and defensive weapons. He believes that pursuit of BMD will lead to a mixture of offensive and defensive systems, and notes that it is not clear that such a mix would be of greater deterrent value than current offensive forces alone. Operational interactions between offensive and defensive forces are not well understood; further research is needed to assess the costs and dynamics of strategic stability associated with BMD systems. Finally, Zraket notes that development of BMD systems would dominate U.S. defense and space activities for decades, requiring extraordinary organizational, funding, and public support.

5

Future Prospects

The first three years following President Reagan's Star Wars address have been characterized by considerable activity on the part of SDI supporters, and the opponents. Both groups have pulled old arguments from past strategic defense debates and melded these with new perspectives to fit their purposes. Despite the plethora of pro and con argumentation, however, the nation has not come to any final decisions on the subject of the SDI, nor is it likely to do so for some time.

For the foreseeable future, then, the basic perspectives set forth in Chapters 3 and 4 will be argued, refined, and possibly modified in response to technical successes--as well as failures--and to political, and economic developments here and abroad. Thus the SDI debate will be dynamic, not static. As the evolution of the SDI debate continues, the reader may wish to monitor the development of certain perspectives that are discernible in the current literature--perspectives that are likely to increase in importance in the next few years. Six of these are briefly described below.

SDI I and SDI II

Much of the SDI analysis in the next few years is likely to focus upon the continued evolution of strategic defense in ways that could lead to two versions, SDI I and SDI II. The former will

represent President Reagan's original vision--
that it might be possible to protect the entire
United States, including population centers, from
nuclear weapons delivered by ballistic missiles.
The latter would involve a much more modest
activity, seeking to provide enough protection to
ICBM silos and some command centers to make a
Soviet first-strike disarming attack more
unattractive than currently is the case, thereby
enhancing deterrence. Both options will have
their advocates.

The comparative analysis of the SDI I and II
parameters will probably include questions such
as these: Will the advantages of protecting ICBM
silos and command centers be worth the cost in
potential political damage to the ABM Treaty?
Alternatively, can the ABM Treaty be modified to
accommodate hard-site defenses without doing
undue harm to arms control prospects with Moscow?
And, finally, would a unilateral U.S. SDI II be
perceived by the Soviet Union as a destabilizing
subterfuge employed by Washington to cover the
acquisition of an SDI I capability?

Is Technology Replacing Politics?

As the SDI moves through its fourth year,
possibly appearing to some that it has acquired a
life of its own, this question is likely to
become increasingly salient: Is the SDI an ill-
founded effort to replace politics with high
technology? Put another way, those who favor
arms control and diplomatic solutions for U.S.-
Soviet differences may be expected to argue that
the SDI is a bad technological fix for problems
that are political in character. Their point
will be that problems that are intrinsically
political are most appropriately resolved by
using political processes.

The SDI II--Midgetman Dilemma

Should SDI II and the Midgetman ICBM move
simultaneously toward technical practicality, it
is quite possible that the two systems and their

supporting rationales will collide. The latter is a prototype ICBM designed to be protected from a Soviet first-strike disarming attack by mobile basing. The missile's mobility would result from its relatively small size, approximately 38,000 pounds and a single warhead.

The convergence of technical feasibility for SDI II and the Midgetman will create a dilemma for strategic planners. It is that the deployment of Midgetman will remove one of the primary arguments currently being made in support of SDI II, the need to protect ICBMs from Soviet ballistic missile attack, as a means to maintain deterrence. If some command centers are also made increasingly mobile, and therefore more survivable, the contemporary rationale for SDI II will be further eroded. Should the nation move toward SDI II deployment, in the presence of Midgetman deployment, a heated objection will be raised. That is, an SDI II deployment not justified as protection for ICBMs will be perceived in Moscow as a United States effort to achieve strategic advantage that will require potentially dangerous Soviet responses.

The SDI and Soviet Decline

Those who believe the Soviet Union is entering a period of decline will increasingly be required to wrestle with the question of how the SDI relates to their perspective. For example, some will argue that as the Soviet Union falls further behind the politically vibrant and technologically exuberant West, Moscow will become more paranoid, unpredictable, and dangerous. Those making this kind of observation may favor the SDI as providing the necessary hedge against hostile and irrational Soviet behavior in the area of nuclear weapons. Conversely, others may be expected to argue that a declining Soviet Union will be made more paranoid and potentially dangerous should the United States deploy an SDI that could appear to be particularly threatening in the context of Soviet weaknesses.

Arms Control Bargaining with the SDI

Should the Strategic Defense Initiative be used
as an arms control bargaining chip? This
question may come to dominate the discussion of
the SDI for the next several years. There are
several reasons. One is that the SDI has caught
the attention of the Soviet rulers, and it may
constitute much of the motivation for arms
control proposals that the Kremlin has tied in
various ways to the United States'limitation of
its SDI program.

Exactly why the Soviets are so interested in
striking a bargain to constrain SDI development
is not known. Their eagerness may have resulted
from the Soviet fear that U.S. technological
superiority will enable Washington to deploy an
SDI that would place the USSR in substantial
peril. Alternatively, the Soviets may be deeply
concerned that they will be unable in an economic
sense to match the United States should a
sustained SDI competition develop. Or it could
be that Moscow is worried about the possibility
that the enormous technical and fiscal effort
proposed for the SDI program will lead American
scientists to make weapons discoveries more
threatening even than any SDI component under
examination.

Another reason the SDI bargaining chip question
will remain so important is the likelihood that
as Mr. Reagan passes the midpoint of his second,
and last, four-year term, invidious comparisons
with another hardline, conservative, anti-
communist, and Republican president will be made.
That former president is Richard Nixon. During
his Watergate-shortened tenure, he engaged in
more cold war negotiations with Communist nations
than any other chief executive. Nixon's
bargaining included the ABM Treaty and the
executive agreement to limit nuclear weapons
delivery systems, collectively termed SALT I; the
negotiated withdrawal of U.S. forces from South
Vietnam; and the beginning of normalized
relations with the Communist Chinese.

Many gave Nixon high marks for these foreign
policy initiatives obtained by a person perceived
at home and in Moscow as being "tough on

Communism." Such a president had considerable opportunity to wheel and deal with the Russians because he was viewed by Americans as one who could be trusted not to give too much away at the bargaining table, and because he was seen by the Soviets as a negotiator to be respected. Today President Reagan is clearly thought of by his countrymen, and by the Soviets, as a tough anti-Communist. Thus it will be natural for some to suggest that he should utilize his special advantages, enhanced by the presence of the SDI, to negotiate a safer world, and in the process earn himself a place beside Nixon in history's judgment of great presidents in the foreign policy context.

The other side of the developing argument about the utility of bargaining with the SDI is the perspective that the president should resolutely pursue SDI development. The rationale is that the chance to convert the nuclear relationship with Moscow from one based upon an offensive threat to one characterized by defensive capability is extraordinarily meritorious. This view is furthered by the argument that the SDI is so important it should not be diluted by secondary arms control considerations; nor should it be placed in jeopardy by Soviet duplicity.

If the SDI program is not bargained away in return for Soviet arms control concessions, or constrained by some other arms control agreement, the momentum of effort will be substantially greater by early 1989. That is the year in which the next U.S. president will be inaugurated. In the absence of arms control, that new president will inherit an SDI that will then have been in existence nearly six years. In the interim it may be expected that the SDI program will have spawned a powerful set of constituents among the aerospace and related high-technology sectors of the U.S. economy. The supporters will include many among the management, labor force, and stockholders of those companies doing SDI business. Persons in the congressional and executive branches of the federal government, and in academia, will also support the SDI program. While many will be sincere in their belief that the SDI is in the nation's interest, it is possible that others may support it for narrow and selfish reasons more contributory to their personal welfare than to that of the nation. The same mixed kinds of SDI support will be found by the next president among U.S. allies.

So it is that the man who originally proposed the SDI is probably the one president who is uniquely qualified to trade it in for substantial arms control agreements, including sound verification, with the Soviet Union.

Vulnerability of Space-based SDI Components

Much of the SDI literature, both pro and con, makes the point that space-based SDI components will be vulnerable to hostile Soviet action. Just how hostile Moscow may be in response to SDI satellite deployment is suggested by past Soviet reactions to aircraft overflights of the USSR. Most notable among such incidents are the downing of an American Air Force B-47, the successful anti-aircraft missile attack upon the U-2 spy plane piloted by Francis Gary Powers, and the more recent destruction of the Korean Air Lines commercial jet with the loss of all passengers and crew.

It can be argued that these, and other overflights which triggered violent Soviet responses, were less provocative than would be the case with the positioning of SDI satellites. Further, the Soviet willingness to take lethal action against aircraft carrying human beings indicates Moscow may be even more willing to attack unmanned satellites which are perceived as posing a direct threat to the USSR.

Should the United States move toward the technical capability of placing initial SDI components in space, political judgments, and legal evaluations, about the appropriate response to potentially hostile Soviet action against the satellites will warrant increasing attention.

6

Selected Bibliography

The ABM Treaty and the SDI program. 1985.
   Department of State Bulletin 85 (December):
   37-40.

Able, J. 1985. On Star Wars. Bulletin of the
   Atomic Scientists 41 (August):61.

Abrahamson, Lt. General James A., 1984.
   Comments on directed-energy missile defense in
   space. Washington, D.C.: U.S. Department of
   Defense, May 8.

---. 1984. The Strategic Defense Initiative.
   Defense 84 August, 3-11.

Abrahamson, Lt. General James A., and
   Carl Sagan. 1985. Weapons in space: a Star
   Wars debate. Futurist 19 (October):
   15-18.

Abrahamson emphasized SDI research aspects. 1985.
   Aviation Week and Space Technology, September
   23, 18.

Abrahamson sees surge in space defense work.
   1985. Aviation Week and Space Technology,
   November 25, 16.

Ackley, Richard T. 1984. Star Wars: a necessary
   strategy. National Defense 69 (October):30.

Adam, J. A. 1985. Technology '85: aerospace and military. IEEE Spectrum 22 (January):85-88.

---. 1985. What's in a name -- SDI or Star Wars? IEEE Spectrum 22 (September):46.

Adam, J. A., and Mark A. Fischetti. 1985. Star Wars -- SDI: the grand experiment. IEEE Spectrum 22 (September):33-64.

Adams, G. 1985. Star Wars -- a dangerous chimera. Dissent 32 (no. 3): 261-265.

Adelman, Kenneth. 1985. The impact of space on arms control. Defense Science 2003+ 4 (April/May):41-48.

---. 1985. SDI: setting the record straight. Department of State Bulletin 85 (October):42-45.

---. 1986. Making arms control work. Department of State Bulletin 86 (January):39-42.

Adler, Jerry, and Gerald L. Lubenow. 1985. The star warriors. Newsweek, June 17, 34-35.

Against the militarization of outer space; Konstantin Cherneko replies to the appeal of American scientists. 1984. Soviet Life, July, 18.

Agencies plan nuclear power demonstration in 1990's. 1985. Aviation Week and Space Technology, September 9, 29.

Agnew, H. M. 1985. Ballistic missile defense. Issues in Science and Technology 1 (no. 2):4-6.

Akhromeyev, S. 1985. The ABM Treaty is an obstacle in the way of the strategic arms race. Current Digest of Soviet Press, June 26, 1-4.

---. 1985. Washington's assertions and the real facts: Akhromeyev: ABM pact bans Star Wars. Current Digest of Soviet Press, November 13, 7.

Alexander, Charles P. 1985. The Star Wars
  sweepstake; amid a swirl of controversy,
  companies and schools vie for defense dollars.
  Time, October 7, 49-52.

Allen, L., and N. Dombey. 1985. X-ray lasers to
  shoot holes in the test-ban treaty? New
  Scientist 107 (no. 1474):30-33.

Alpern, David M. 1984. Eyes on the skies; the
  terms of arms control have shifted, and weapons
  deployed in space are now the new nuclear
  frontier. Newsweek, December 31, 32-34.

Americans back Reagan on Star Wars. 1985. Gallup
  Report, March, 12-16.

Amiel, Barbara. 1985. An answer to the
  government. Macleans, June 10, 9.

Andersen, Kurt. 1983. A step closer to Star
  Wars: can a U.S.-Soviet space weapons race be
  slowed down in time? Time, December 12, 28-30.

----. 1985. The ABM treaty is an obstacle in the
  way of the strategic arms race. Current Digest
  of Soviet Press, June 26, 1-4.

Anderson, I. 1985. Academics vow to boycott
  computer for Star Wars. New Scientist 106
  (no. 1454):6.

Angell, J. E. 1983. United States Air Force
  perspective of space operations. In Computers
  in Aerospace Conference, 4th, Hartford, CT,
  October 24-26, 1983, Collection of Technical
  Papers (A84-10001 01-59). New York: American
  Institute of Aeronautics and Astronautics, pp.
  263-267.

Arbess, Daniel. 1985. Star Wars and outer space
  law. Bulletin of the Atomic Scientists 41
  (October):19-23.

Arkin, William M. 1986. Of drugs and Star Wars.
  Bulletin of the Atomic Scientists 42
  (February):4-5.

Arms-control impediment. 1986. *America*, February 8, 83.

Army to flight test nonnuclear ABM. 1983. *Aviation Week and Space Technology*, January 24, 30-31.

Atlantic Assembly refuses to support U.S. plan to develop BMD system. 1984. *Aviation Week and Space Technology*, November 19, 26-27.

Atlantic rift over Star Wars widens. 1985. *New Scientist* 105 (no. 1448):5.

Augarten, Stan. 1986. Can computers be failsafe? *PC*, January 14, 97, 101.

Avduyevskiy, V.S. 1984. US said to seek military advantage in space. *Space*, May 1985, 94-100. Translated into English from *Zemlya i Vselennaya* (Moscow) 5 (September-October 1984): 6-11. Arlington, VA: Joint Publications Research Service.

Babic, Manojlo. 1985. Space weapons in superpower strategy. *Review of International Affairs* 36 (March):10-13.

Baker, D. 1985. Star Wars. Paper presented at the British Association for the Advancement of Science Annual Meeting, Glasgow, Scotland, August 26-30, 1985.

Baker, Russell. 1985. Star Wars mania. *New York Times Magazine*, December 29, 10.

Ball, George W. 1985. The war for Star Wars. *New York Review of Books*, April 11, 38-44.

Ballistic missile defense. 1984. In *Fiscal year 1985 arms control impact statement*. Washington, D.C.: U.S. Government Printing Office, pp. 197-315.

Ballistic missile defense. 1984. *Issues in Science and Technology* 1 (no. 1):13-14.

Ballistic missile defense. 1985. *Harvard International Review* 7 (January/February):4-23.

Ballistic missile defense systems under scrutiny.
1984. Physics Today, June, 53-54.

Ballistic missile defense-United States under
pressure from Europe to share data. 1985.
Nature 316 (no. 6031):755.

Banks, Howard. 1984. It can be done. Forbes,
July 16, 30-32.

Barney, Clifford. 1985. DARPA eyes 100-MIPS GaAs
chip for Star Wars. ElectronicsWeek, May 20,
22-23.

Barrett, Paul M. 1986. Star warriors.
Washington Monthly 17 (January):50-52.

Barry, John M. 1984. Reagan bets on Star Wars.
Dun's Business Month, June, 38-42.

Bateman, M. 1985. Ballistic missile defense
control system requirements. Paper presented
at the AIAA/SAE/ASME/ASEE 21st Joint Propulsion
Conference, Monterey, CA, July 8-11, 1985.

Beardsley, T. 1985. Weapons in space--Soviet alarm
about Star Wars. Nature 313 (no. 5999):170.

----. 1985. More for Star Wars. Nature 313
(no. 6002):420.

----. 1985. Star Wars--quarrel over congressional
study. Nature 314 (no. 6006):7.

----. 1985. Strategic Defense Initiative--Star
Wars criticized by OTA report. Nature 317
(no. 6035):276.

----. 1985. SDI--Star Wars critics criticized.
Nature 318 (no. 6041):3.

Beckwith, David. 1985. High hopes, low expectations: a Time poll finds the U.S. eager for
summit progress but wary. Time, November 25,
32-33.

Behind Reagan's Star Wars strategy. 1983. US
News and World Report, April 4, 288-290.

Bellany, Ian, and Coit D. Blacker, eds. 1983.
Antiballistic missile defense in the 1980s.
Totowa, NJ: F. Cass Company.

Benson, J.T. 1976. Lab for development and
evaluation of ballistic missile defense
software quality enhancement techniques. In
Proceedings, 2nd International Conference on
Software Engineering A764129, San Francisco,
CA, October 13-15, 1976. New York: Association
for Computing Machinery.

Bernstein, Peter W. 1985. Star Wars dollars:
defense contractors line up early to get in on
a coming space-age bonanza. Fortune, April 15,
120-121.

Bertram, Christoph. 1985. Reagan's dream: a
vision that impedes an arms truce? World Press
Review, March, 37.

---. Summer 1985. Strategic defense and the
Western alliance. Daedalus 114:279-296.

Best, Derek. 1983. Star Wars. Omni,
February, 28-29.

Bethe, Hans. 1984. Exchange on laser ABM--
laser space weaponry. Laser Focus 20
(no. 8):16.

---. 1985. Why Star Wars is dangerous and won't
work. (excerpt from the Wall Street Journal,
January 2, 1985). New York Review of Books,
February 14, 26.

Bethe, Hans, Jeffrey Boutwell, and Richard L.
Garwin. Spring 1985. BMD technologies and
concepts in the 1980s. Daedalus 114:53-70.

Bethe, Hans, and Richard L. Garwin. Spring
1985. Appendix A: new BMD technologies.
Daedalus 114:331-368.

Bethe, Hans A., Richard L. Garwin, Kurt
Gottfried, and Henry W. Kendall. 1984. Space-
based ballistic missile defense. Scientific
American, October, 39-49.

Bialer, Seweryn. 1985. How Geneva talks look
through Soviet eyes. US News and World Report,
November 18, 34-35.

Biddle, Wayne. 1985. Weapons in space - the
controversy over Star Wars. Star Wars
technology: it's more than a fantasy.
New York Times, March 5.

The big "if" for arms control: will the Russians
bend? 1984. Business Week, November 19, 41.

Bilski, Andy. 1985. Setting up for a summit.
Macleans, November 11, 40-41.

Birch, S. 1985. Few hopes pinned on Star Wars
deal in the UK. Engineer 260 (no. 6727):15.

Birch, S., and P. Hill. 1985. UK firms aim at
Star Wars 1 billion pounds bonanza. Engineer
260 (no. 6742):14-15.

Bird, Kai, and Max Holland. 1985. United States:
Star Wars logic. Nation, June 1, 664-665.

----. 1986. Strategic superiority initiative.
Nation, February 1, 104.

Birthday blowout. 1985. Scientific American,
July, 58.

Bjornen, E. 1978. How you gonna get them off the
farm, after they've seen "Star Wars?" In
Proceedings, Volume 36 of the American Astro-
nautical Society Advances in Astronautical
Science Series, January 1978. San Diego,
CA: American Astronautical Society.

Black, Edwin F. Summer 1984. Assured mutual
survival: the ABM solution. Journal of Social,
Political and Economic Studies 9:141-143.

Blacker, Coit D. 1984. The United States and
the Soviet Union. Current History, October,
309-313.

---. 1985. Defending missiles, not people: hard-
site defense. Issues in Science and Technology
2:30-44.

Blakely, C. 1977. PEPE applications to a
ballistic missile defense problem. Presented
to the International Conference on Parallel
Processing A773141, Bellaire, Michigan,
August 23-26, 1977.

Boffey, Philip M. 1985. Weapons in space - the
controversy over Star Wars. Dark side of Star
Wars: system could also attack. New York
Times, March 7.

---. 1985. Weapons in space - the controversy
over Star Wars. Star Wars and mankind:
consequences for future. New York Times,
March 8.

Bon, J. J. 1985. Arms control and the President's
Strategic Defense Initiative. Air Command and
Staff College, Maxwell Air Force Base, Alabama,
April. Report No.: AD-A156334; ACSC-85-0240.

Bosma, John T., and Richard Whelan, eds. 1985.
Guide to the Strategic Defense Initiative.
Arlington, VA: Pasha Publications.

Bothwell, Anthony P.X. 1985. Teller looks to the
future; Star Wars for peace. National Review,
August 9, 33-34.

Boutwell, Jeffrey, and F. A. Long. Summer 1985.
The SDI and U.S. security. Daedalus 114:315-
329.

Boutwell, Jeffrey, and Richard A. Scribner. 1985.
The Strategic Defense Initiative: some arms
control implications. AAAS Publication no. 85-
9. Washington, D.C.: American Association for
the Advancement of Science, May.

Bova, Ben. 1984. Star Wars defense. New Republic,
June 18, 4.

---. 1984. Freedom from fear. Analog, November, 6-10.

---. 1984. Assured survival: putting the Star Wars defense in perspective. Boston: Houghton Miflin.

---. 1984. Star Wars. Sciences 24 (no. 4):2.

Bowman, Robert M. 1983. The fruits of space exploration - cornucopia or Armageddon? Presented at the 34th International Astronautical Congress, Budapest, Hungary, October 10-15, 1983. International Astronautical Federation, October, Report no. IAF PAPER 83-244.

---. 1985. Star Wars: defense or death star. Potomac, MD: Institute for Space and Security Studies.

---. 1986. Star Wars: a defense insider's case against the Strategic Defense Initiative. Los Angeles: J.P. Tarcher.

Bracken, Paul. 1983. The command and control of nuclear forces. New Haven: Yale University Press.

Brauch, Hans G., ed. 1986. From "Star Wars" to Strategic Defense Initiative: European perceptions and assessments. New York: St. Martin.

Britain opens the door to Star Wars. 1985. New Scientist 108 (no. 1486):11.

Britain ponders invitation to Star Wars. 1985. New Scientist 108 (no. 1481):17.

Britain signs MOU to participate in SDI. 1985. Aviation Week and Space Technology, December 16, 12.

British center will monitor SDI participation by U.K. 1985. Aviation Week and Space Technology, December 23, 59.

Broad, William J. 1985. Weapons in space - the
controversy over Star Wars. Reagan's Star Wars
bid: many ideas converging. New York Times,
March 4.

---. 1985. The secret behind Star Wars. New York
Times Magazine, August 11, 32-41.

---. 1985. Star warriors: a visit to the eerie
world of Lawrence Livermore's weapons
designers. Science Digest, September, 36-40.

---. 1985. Weapons in space. Science showmanship:
a deep Star Wars rift. New York Times,
December 16.

---. 1985 Star Warriors New York: Simon and
Schuster.

Brown, David A. 1985. British, U.S. defense
secretaries reach SDI accord. Aviation Week
and Space Technology, November 4, 26-27.

---. 1985. European, U.S. industrial efforts
seen as complementary. Aviation Week and Space
Technology, November 18, 115-116.

---. 1985. European industry begins to seek U.S.
SDI contracts. Aviation Week and Space
Technology, December 16, 12-15.

Brown, Harold. 1986. Is SDI technically
feasible? Foreign Affairs 64 ("America and the
World" 1985 issue):435-454.

Brown, Harrison. 1985. Star Wars once funny, now
frightening. Bulletin of the Atomic Scientists
(May) 41:3.

Browne, Malcolm W. 1985. Star Wars payoff.
Reader's Digest, August, 154.

Bryden, James F. 1984. The emerging BMD debate:
deja vu or not? Air University Review 36
(November-December):42-51.

Brzezinski, Zbigniew. 1985. How to break the
arms control impasse; a Star Wars solution.
New Republic, July 8, 16-18.

Brzezinski, Zbigniew, Robert Jastrow, and Max M. Kampelman. 1985. Defense in space is not "Star Wars." New York Times Magazine, January 27, 28-32.

Brzoska, M. 1985. SIPRI Conference on Space Weapons and International Security, Stockholm, Sweden, July 5-7, 1985. In Environmental Conservation 12 (no. 3):283.

Buckley, William F., Jr. 1985. Empty thought from our scientists. National Review, August 23, 55.

----. 1985. Self-delusion scientific-style. National Review, January 11, 62.

Budiansky, S. 1984. United States space weapons - ASAT deal in Congress. Nature 310 (no. 5974):173.

----. 1984. Star Wars - strategic weaknesses made plain. Nature 310 (no. 5978):530.

----. 1984. Star Wars killings. Nature 312 (no. 5989):8.

----. 1985. Star Wars - true cost still growing. Nature 313 (no. 6004):614.

----. 1985. Star Wars - DOD makes a monkey of anti-missile treaty. Nature 315 (no. 6014):3.

----. 1985. Caltech at war on Star Wars. Nature 315 (no. 6017):266.

Bulkeley, R. 1985. Soviets and Star Wars. Bulletin of the Atomic Scientists 41 (September):53.

Bundy, McGeorge. 1984. Ballistic missile defense. New York Times Book Review, March 11, 15.

Bundy, McGeorge, George F. Kennan, Robert S. McNamara, and Gerard Smith. Winter 1984/85 The president's choice: Star Wars or arms control. Foreign Affairs 63:264-278.

Burrows, William E. Spring 1984. Ballistic missile defense: the illusion of security. Foreign Affairs 62:843-856.

----. 1984. Skywalking with Reagan: the Pentagon, with an arsenal of lasers and killer satellites, stakes out its territory in space. Harpers, January, 50-56.

Bussard, Robert W. Summer 1984. Freedom, safety, and survival in the nuclear age. Journal of Social, Political and Economic Studies 9:164-79.

Butler, A.J. 1983. Peaceful use and self defense in outer space. In Air Force Academy Proceedings of the 1983 Symposium on Military Space Communications and Operations, Report no. AD-P002155, pp. 87-92.

Campbell, Duncan. 1985. Ascension island to be test area for Star Wars? New Statesman, May 31, 5.

Can Reagan's Star Wars plan really work? 1983. US News and World Report, April 11, 24-25.

Capture the flag, Star Wars style. 1985. Changing Times, September, 26.

Carey, P. 1985. Risks of automation with military systems. Databus (Netherlands), February, 8-11.

Carlos De Asis, Luiz. 1985. The call to arms; the imminence of space rivalry. World Press Review, March, 36-37.

Carnesale, A. 1983. On limiting technology by negotiated agreement. Proceedings of a short course on physics, technology and the nuclear arms race, April 17, 1983, Baltimore, MD. AIP Conference Proceedings No. 104, 230-38. Cambridge, MA: John F. Kennedy School of Government, Harvard University.

---. 1985 Special supplement: the Strategic Defense Initiative. In 1985-1986 American defense annual. George E. Hudson, and Joseph Krunzel, eds. Lexington, MA: Lexington.

Carter, Ashton B. 1984. Directed-energy missile defense in space. Cambridge, MA: Massachusetts Institute of Technology, Report no. PB84-210111, April.

---. Spring 1985. The relationship of ASAT and BMD systems. Daedalus 114:171-188.

---. 1985. The command and control of nuclear war. Scientific American, January, 32-39.

Carter, Ashton B., and David N. Schwartz, eds. 1984. Ballistic missile defense. Washington, D.C.: Brookings Institution.

Champion, Brian. 1985. Advanced weapons systems: an annotated bibliography of the Cruise missile, MX missile, laser and space weapons, and stealth technology. New York: Garland Publishing.

Chapline, G. 1984. Exchange on laser ABM - laser space weaponry. Laser Focus 20 (no. 8):16.

---. 1985. In defense of SDI. Defense Science 2003+ 4 (August/September):12-20.

Chayes, Abram, Antonia Handler Chayes, and Eliot Spitzer. Summer 1985. Space weapons: the legal context. Daedalus 114:193-218.

Chaze, William L. 1985. Reagan draws the line. US News and World Report, September 30, 24-29.

---. 1985. Tuning up for summit. US News and World Report, October 7, 22-23.

Chernenko, Konstantin. 1985. Space: Konstantin Chernenko: excerpts from speeches, replies and interviews. Soviet Life, April, 16-17.

Chesshyre, Robert. 1985. The Star Wars stampede. World Press Review, August, 40.

Chown, M. 1985. Doubts surround Strathclyde mirror for space weapons. New Scientist 107 (no. 1472):19.

Church, George J. 1984. Cautious talk about talks; Moscow offers a September parley; the U.S. says O.K., but... Time, July 9, 17.

----. 1985. Wagons hitched to Star Wars; despite qualms, the NATO allies consider participating. Time, May 27, 26-27.

----. 1985. Exploring the high-tech frontier; even the proponents admit that Star Wars is a tall, and perhaps impossible, order. Time, March 11, 20-23.

----. 1985. Only a step, but an encouraging one; the superpowers set more talks, though space weapons could be an obstacle. Time, January 21, 26-28.

Cimbala, Stephen J., ed. 1986. The Strategic Defense Initiative: technology, strategy, and politics. Boulder, CO: Westview Press.

Clark, Evert, Dave Griffiths, and Alan Hall. 1985. Why Reagan's Star Wars strategy isn't pie in the sky. Business Week, March 18, 132-133.

Clarke, A. C. 1983. War and peace in the space age. Spaceflight, February, 50-53.

Clausen, Peter A. Spring 1985. SDI in search of a mission. World Policy Journal 2:249-69.

Cochran, J. O. 1984. Combat-capable space system for tactical support. In AGARD Space System Applications to Tactical Operations. Symposium held in Hampton, VA, October 17-21, 1984. Neuilly-Sur-Seine, France: Advisory Group for Aerospace Research and Development. Report no. AGARD-CP-344, October.

Cockburn, Alexander. 1986. Star Wars in the eyes. Nation, January 18, 52.

----. 1986. The story of a test ban. Nation, January 18, 38.

Codevilla, Angelo. Winter 1984. Understanding ballistic missile defense. Journal of Contemporary Studies 7:19-35.

Cohen, Samuel T. Fall 1983. Whatever happened to the Nixon Doctrine? Policy Review (no. 26):88-92.

Coleman, Herbert J. 1986. SDI subcontracting opens door for small business research. Aviation Week and Space Technology, January 27, 20-21.

Colloquium on the Law of Outer Space, 25th, Paris, France, September 27-October 2, 1982, Proceedings. 1983. New York: American Institute of Aeronautics and Astronautics.

Colloquium on the Law of Outer Space, 26th, Budapest, Hungary, October 10-15, 1983, Proceedings. 1984. New York: American Institute of Aeronautics and Astronautics.

Colloquium on the Law of Outer Space, 27th, Lausanne, Switzerland, October 7-13, 1984, Proceedings. 1985. New York: American Institute of Aeronautics and Astronautics.

Committee approves 1986 appropriations. 1985. Aviation Week and Space Technology, November 11, 27.

Congressional critics question British involvement with SDI. 1985. Aviation Week and Space Technology, December 16, 15.

Connolly, Ray. 1984. General Abe's approach to space defense. ElectronicsWeek, August 20, 54.

----. 1984. Why Star Wars won't fly. Electronics, May 17, 66.

Cook, C. W. 1983. National security implications of a U.S. space station. In Space Station:

policy, planning and utilization; Proceedings
of the symposium, Arlington, VA, July 18-20,
1983 (A84-24626 09-12). New York: American
Institute of Aeronautics and Astronautics, pp.
145-57.

Cooper, Mary H. 1985. Arms control negotiations.
Editorial Research Reports, February 22, 147-
168.

Cooperation instead of confrontation. 1984.
Soviet Life, April, 15-16.

Courter, Rep. Jim. 1985. Addressing Soviet
treaty violations a must. Defense Science
2003+ 4 (April/May):67-69.

Covault, Craig. 1984. Spaceplane called a weapons
platform. Aviation Week and Space Technology,
July 23, 70-71.

———. 1985. Space Command, NORAD merging missile,
air and space warning roles. Aviation Week and
Space Technology, February 11, 60-62.

———. 1985. Strategic Defense Initiative will use
two shuttle flights a year. Aviation Week and
Space Technology, February 18, 20.

———. 1985. Laser firing and tracking test set
for 1987 Spacelab mission. Aviation Week and
Space Technology, August 19, 16-17.

Coxe, Donald. 1985. Oh, what a lovely star war:
if Uncle Sam wants us to make the world safe
for democracy, we should cash in on it.
Canadian Business, July, 130.

Crawford, Mark. 1985. In defense of Star Wars.
Science, May 3, 563.

Cross, M. 1985. Batteries that pack a Star Wars
punch. New Scientist 108 (no. 1476):34.

Crozier, Brian. 1985. The approaching summit.
National Review, October 18, 26.

———. 1985. The Star Wars debate. National Review, February 8, 24.

Cugston, Michael. 1985. A polite "no" to Star Wars. Macleans, September 16, 10-11.

Cullen, Robert B. 1985. A start to the Star Wars talks. Newsweek, July 9, 19.

Cunningham, Ann Marie, and Mariana Fitzpatrick. 1983. Future fire-weapons for the apocalypse. New York: Warner Books.

Currently-funded SDIO contractors named. 1985. Aviation Week and Space Technology, September 2, 20.

Dahlitz, Julie. 1985. The option of Star Wars: meaning and consequences. Bulletin of Peace Proposals 16 (no. 2):99-104.

Dallmeyer, Dorinda G., ed. 1986. The Strategic Defense Initiative: new perspectives on deterrence. Boulder, CO: Westview Press.

Daniels, Robert V. 1985. America's doubting allies. New Leader, June 3, 5-7.

———. 1985. Hidden agendas; the Star Wars summit. New Leader, September 23, 3-6.

Danielsson, S. Spring 1984. Examination of proposals relating to the prevention of an arms race in outer space. Journal of Space Law 12:1-11.

Daniloff, Nicholas. 1983. Space race: Russia takes shocks in stride. US News and World Report, October 31, 39.

David, Leonard. 1983. Reagan aims for the high ground. Space World, August-September, 15-18.

———. 1984. Star Wars - skeptics abound one year on. Nature 308 (no. 5959):485.

———. 1984. Star Wars: pre-election Congress turning sour. Nature 309 (no. 5963):3.

----. 1984. Star Wars - skeptical report from OTA. Nature 309 (no. 5968):485.

Davidson, J. 1984. BMD - Star wars in perspective. Aerospace America, January, 78-83.

The debate continues: reporting on the reports. 1984. Environment, June, 36-37.

Debate over Star Wars puts academic scientists in the middle. 1985. Research & Development 27 (December):33.

Delta SDI payload. 1985. Aviation Week and Space Technology, August 5, 19.

de Medici, Marino. 1985. Europe sees SDI as two-edged sword: strategic preoccupations counter-weigh technological rewards. Europe (European Communities) (July/August):10-11.

Deudney, Daniel. Spring 1985. Forging missiles into spaceships. World Policy Journal 2:271-303.

DeWitt, Hugh E. 1984. Labs drive the arms race. Bulletin of the Atomic Scientists 40 (November):40-42.

Dickson, David. 1985. France seeks joint European research. Science, May 10, 694.

----. 1985. A European defense initiative; the idea that European nations band together for a strictly European version of SDI is gaining support. Science, September 20, 1243.

----. 1985. British cabinet split on SDI. Science, December 13, 1251-52.

Didisheim, Peter. Winter/Spring 1986. The ASAT/SDI link, papers on strategic defense. Cambridge, MA: Union of Concerned Scientists.

Dietrich, Schroeer. 1984. Science, technology, and the nuclear arms race. New York: John Wiley and Sons.

Din, Allan W. 1985. Space defense to need anti-aircraft network. Army Times, January, 22.

----. 1985. Strategic defense technology; fact or fiction? International Defense Review 18:29-34.

Directed-energy weapons - where are they headed? 1983. Physics Today, August, 17-20.

Disarmament Conference agrees on space arms committee. 1985. UN Chronicle 12 (March):29.

Doener, William R. 1985. Shooting for the stars: space-based defense technology is still well over the horizon. Time, January 14, 20.

----. 1985. "Let's get started." Time, February 18, 18-19.

----. 1985. Putting it on the table; Star Wars is the big obstacle as the U.S. and Soviets return to Geneva. Time, March 11, 12-13.

Dornheim, Michael A. 1985. Missile destroyed in first SDI test at high-energy laser facility. Aviation Week and Space Technology, September 23, 17-22.

Douglass, Joseph, Jr., and Samuel T. Cohen. 1985. SDI: the hidden opportunity. Defense Science 2003+ 4 (August/September):5-8.

Downing Street muddle. 1985. National Review, May 3, 18.

Draft of the Treaty on the Prohibition of the Use of Force in Outer Space and From Outer Space with Regard to Earth. 1984. Soviet Life, April, 14.

Draper, Theodore. 1985. Pie in the sky. New York Review of Books, February 14, 20-27.

Drell, S.D. 1985. Star Wars. Nature 313 (no. 6004):619.

Drell, Sidney D., Philip J. Farley, and David Holloway. Fall 1984. Preserving the ABM Treaty: a critique of the Reagan Strategic Defense Initiative. International Security 9:51-91.

----. 1985. The Reagan Strategic Defense Initiative a technical, political, and arms control assessment. Cambridge, MA: Ballinger.

Drell, Sidney D., and Wolfgang K.H. Panofsky. 1984. The case against strategic defense: technical and strategic realities. Issues in Science and Technology 1 (no. 1):45-65.

Drinan, Robert F. 1983. Star Wars leap could escalate arms race. National Catholic Reporter, May 6, 21.

Dudney, Robert S. 1984. What Star Wars "czar" is up against. US News and World Report, April 9, 34.

----. 1985. Star Wars; the Soviet thrust. US News and World Report, February 18, 34-35.

Durr, Hans-Peter. 1985. Could Star Wars work? World Press Review, September, 23-29.

Dyer, J. L., and A. F. Jones. 1984. Centralized versus distributed architectures for the SDI BMD systems. Proceedings of the 17th Annual Electronics and Aerospace Conference, September 10-12, 1984, Washington, D.C. New York: Institute of Electrical and Electronics Engineer

Dyson, Freeman J. 1984. Role of strategic space forces in a non-nuclear world. Physics Today, June, 9-10.

----. 1984. Weapons and Hope. Cambridge, MA: Harper and Row.

Eason, Henry. 1984. Build a missile shield in space? Nation's Business, March, 54-55.

Easton, Tom. 1985. Assured survival: putting the Star Wars defense in perspective. Analog, September, 186.

Eberhart, Jonathan. 1985. ASAT target was working research satellite. Science News, September 28, 197.

----. 1985. Shuttle: four-for-four and SDI too. Science News, June 29, 405.

Edelson, Edward. 1984. Space weapons - the science behind the debate. Popular Science, July, 53-61.

Electromagnetic launcher facility scheduled to begin operation. 1985. Aviation Week and Space Technology, November 18, 117.

Elmer-DeWitt, Philip. 1985. Star Wars and software; the defense system's crucial link may be the program that runs it. Time, July 22, 73.

End illusions and Star Wars. 1984. National Catholic Reporter, April 27, 15.

Energy Department seeks research funds for Strategic Defense Initiative. 1985. Aviation Week and Space Technology, February 18, 61-62.

Esogbue, A.O. 1983. Dynamic programming, fuzzy sets, and the modeling of R&D management control systems. IEEE Transactions on Systems, Man and Cybernetics SMC-13 (January-February): 18-30.

"Eureka's" problems. 1986. World Press Review, January, 55.

Europeans link SDI participation to technology transfer issue. 1985. Aviation Week and Space Technology, February 18, 21.

Evans, David. 1985. The 99% fallacy: a Marine nuclear targeting officer says Star Wars can't do the job. Washington Monthly 17 (October): 45-46.

Face-off on nuclear defense. 1984. Technology Review, April, 38-40.

Fairhall, David. 1985. A new competition?
Controlling satellite weapons. World Press
Review, March, 35.

The fallacy of Star Wars: why space weapons can't
protect us. 1984. Publishers Weekly, October
19, 44.

A farewell to nuclear arms? 1985. Business Week,
March 25, 104.

Feazel, Michael. 1985. Shultz affirms European
role in SDI test, production aspects. Aviation
Week, October 21, 20-21.

Feld, B. T. 1985. Star Wars not viable. Bulletin
of the Atomic Scientists 41 (April):60-61.

Feurherd, Joseph. 1985. Star Wars expert calls
program a "massive fraud," supports coalition
to oppose plan. National Catholic Reporter,
May 31, 8.

Field, George, and David Spergel. 1986. Cost of
space-based laser ballistic missile defense.
Science, March 21, 1387-92.

Finch, E. R, Jr. Spring-Fall 1983. Law and
security in outer space - implications for priva
enterprise. Journal of Space Law 11:107-10.

Finn, William W., Jr. 1985. Ballistic missile
defense. Current History, November, 385.

Firms hone SDI-applicable R&D through Eureka.
1985. Aviation Week and Space Technology,
December 16, 15.

Flax, Alexander. Spring 1985. Ballistic missile
defense: concepts and history. Daedalus
114:33-51.

Fletcher, James C. 1984. The technologies for
ballistic missile defense. Issues in Science
and Technology 1 (no. 1):15-29.

---. 1985. Ballistic missile defense. Issues
in Science and Technology 1 (no. 3):15-16.

The flight that failed. 1986. Nation, February 8, 129.

Fontaine, Andre. 1985. Choices and conflicts; jeopardizing the Atlantic Alliance? World Press Review, March, 40.

Forbes, M. S., Jr. 1985. Defending Star Wars. Forbes, February 11, 31.

Ford, Daniel. 1985. The button: the Pentagon's strategic command and control system. New York: Simon and Schuster.

Foreign issues: interview with Brian Widlake of the British Broadcasting Corporation, October 29, 1985. Weekly Compilation of Presidential Documents 21 (November 4):1318-1323.

Foreign issues: responses to questions submitted by La Vanguardia of Spain, April 25, 1985. 1985. Weekly Compilation of Presidential Documents 21 (May 6):537-539.

Fossedal, Gregory A. 1985. The Reagan doctrine: you might have missed it, but it was boomed in January. American Spectator, March, 12-15.

---. Spring 1985. Beware of the union label: the metaphysics and politics of the UCS. Policy Review 32:47-49.

Fox, Eugene. 1985. The ballistic missile defense; a commitment to strategic defense. (transcript) Vital Speeches 52 (December 1):101-104.

France, Boyd. 1985. Why talks with the Soviets avoid the heart of the matter. Business Week, January 21, 31.

Freedman, Lawrence. 1984. The Reagan strategic defense initiative: a technical, political and arms control assessment. Bulletin of the Atomic Scientists 40 (December):27-28.

Freiwald, D. A., and T. E. Botts. 1985. Wanted - ground simulator for SDI. Aerospace America, July, 80-81.

Friel, Patrick J. 1984. U.S. ballistic missile defense technology: a technical overview. Comparative Strategy 4 (no. 4):319-347.

---. 1985. America's Strategic Defense Initiative. Chemtech 15 (no. 4):211-213.

From VE Day to Star Wars. 1985. New Statesman, May 3, 2-3.

Fromm, Joseph. 1983. Behind Reagan's Star Wars strategy: the President is out to stop more than Soviet nuclear missiles. US News and World Report, April 4, 28.

---. 1985. Star Wars: a nightmare for Gorbachev's land. US News and World Report, October 21, 44-45.

---. 1985. Now for the hard part. US News and World Report, January 21, 31-32.

Frum, David. 1986. In defense of strategic defense. Saturday Night, January, 13-20.

Fund Star Wars, at least for now. 1984. Business Week, May 14, 206.

Fusion Energy Foundation Scientific Staff 1984. Beam weapons--an alternative to nuclear destruction. Fallbrook, CA: Aero-Publishers.

Gal, G. 1983. Activities on orbit and on celestial bodies - two motions of peaceful uses? In Colloquium on the Law of Outer Space, 25th, Paris, France, September 27-October 2, 1982, Proceedings (A84-17026 05-84). New York: American Institute of Aeronautics and Astronautics. Report no. IAF PAPER 82-IISL-21, pp. 83-87.

Gallagher, Robert T. 1985. A French proposal could invigorate Europe's high-tech research. Electronics, July 22, 30-31.

Galloway, E. 1983. Expanding Article IV of the 1967 Space Treaty - a proposal. In Colloquium on the Law of Outer Space, 25th, Paris, France, September 27-October 2, 1982, Proceedings (A84-17026 05-84). New York: American Institute of Aeronautics and Astronautics. Report no. IAF PAPER 82-IISL-22, pp. 89-92.

Garwin, Richard. 1985. Technologies of ballistic missile defense. Paper presented at the 1985 American Association for the Advancement of Science Annual Meeting 8520021, Los Angeles, CA, May 26-31, 1985.

Garwin, Richard L., Kurt Gottfried, and Donald L. Hafner. 1984. Antisatellite weapons. Scientific American, June, 45-56.

Garwin, Richard L., and John Pike. 1984. Space weapons. Bulletin of the Atomic Scientists 40 (May):48-49.

Garwin, Richard L., John Pike, and Yevgeny P. Velikov. 1984. Space weapons. Bulletin of the Atomic Scientists 40 (May):supplement.

Garwin, Richard L., and Carl Sagan. 1983. Ban space weapons. Bulletin of the Atomic Scientists 39 (November):2-3.

Gavrilov, N. 1985. Military journal on U.S. intelligence satellites. Space, May, 101-9. Translated into English from Zarubezhnoye Voyennoye Obozreniye (Moscow), November 1984, 54-59. Arlington, VA: Joint Publications Research Service.

Gayler, Noel. 1985. Reagan's ASAT boomerang. Space World, December, 2.

Gee, Marcus. 1985. An impasse at the arms talks. Macleans, June 10, 38.

Gelb, Leslie H. 1985. Weapons in space - the controversy over Star Wars. Vision of space defense posing new challenges. New York Times, March 3.

---. 1985. Weapons in space. Star Wars advances: the plan vs. the reality. New York Times, December 5.

Geneste, Marc. Spring 1985. Strategic defense and the shield of Europe. Strategic Review 13:37-43.

Georgia Institute wins SDI parallel processing contract. 1985. Aviation Week and Space Technology, August 26, 73.

Gergen, David R. 1985. Why Reagan is turning his eyes to foreign policy. US News and World Report, December 9, 36.

Germans insist on technology gains as part of SDI cooperation. 1985. Aviation Week and Space Technology, April 8, 21.

Glaser, Charles L. Fall 1984. Why even good defense may be bad. International Security 9:92-123.

---. 1985. Star Wars bad even if it works. Bulletin of the Atomic Scientists 41 (March):13.

Glen, Maxwell. 1985. Star Wars future remains uncertain despite its early successes in Congres National Journal August 10:1832-1836.

Glynn, Lenny. 1984. An orbiting arms race. Macleans, June 25, 34.

Goddy, David. 1985. Space arms talks focus on Star Wars; negotiators on space weapons grapple with a U.S. plan for a shield against attack. Scholastic Update, November 15, 7.

Goldblat, Jozef. 1984. New means of ballistic missile defense: the question of legality and arms control implications. Arms Control and Disarmament 5 (September):176-80.

Golden, Frederic. 1985. Star Wars: the research heats up. Discover, September, 28-40.

Gollon, Peter J. 1986. SDI funds costly for scientists. Bulletin of the Atomic Scientists 42 (January):24-27.

Good intentions, dangerous results. 1985. Commonweal, December 20, 691-92.

Goodwin, Irwin. 1985. Star Wars and the debate among physicists. Physics Today, July, 58.

----. 1985. Senators and scientists object to SDI costs and uncertainties. Physics Today, July, 55-59.

Goorden, W. 1984. Directed-energy weapons. Ingenieur (Netherlands) 96 (February):18-21.

Gorbachev's post-summit press conference. 1985. Current Digest of Soviet Press, December 18, 10-17.

Gorbiel, A. 1985. Towards the entire demilitarization of outer space. Postepy Astronautyki (Poland) 18:25-56.

Gordon, Charles. 1985. Star Wars and dollar doldrums. Macleans, March 4, 9.

----. 1985. Laughing on the way to Geneva. Macleans, November 11, 13.

Gordon, Michael R. 1983. Proposed U.S. antisatellite system threatens arms control in space. National Journal, December 31, 2660-2665.

----. 1984. Reagan's Star Wars proposals prompt debate over future nuclear strategy. National Journal, January 7, 12-17.

----. 1984. Reagan's Star Wars talk spurs renewed interest in North American air defense. National Journal, September 8, 1663-1665.

----. 1985. U.S.-Soviet arms control negotiations: nuclear and space weapons. AEI (American Enterprise Institute) Foreign Policy and Defense Review 5 (no. 2): 21-44.

Gorove, S. 1983. Limiting the use of arms in
outer space - legal and policy issues. In
Colloquium on the Law of Outer Space, 25th,
Paris, France, September 27-October 2, 1982,
Proceedings (A84-17026 05-84). New York:
American Institute of Aeronautics and
Astronautics. Report no. IAF PAPER 82-IISL-23,
pp. 93-97.

Gottfried, Kurt, and Richard Lebow. Spring 1985.
Anti-satellite weapons: weighing the risks.
Daedalus 114:147-169.

Govoni, Stephen J. 1986. SDI's momentum.
Financial World, February 19, 28.

Graham, Daniel O. 1983. We must defend America--
and put an end to MADness. Chicago: Regnery
Gateway.

---. Summer 1984. It's time for high frontier.
Journal of Social, Political and Economic
Studies 9:180-83.

---. Winter 1984. High frontier: the next four
years. Journal of Social, Political and Economic
Studies 9:405-411.

Gray, Colin S. 1983. American military space
policy: information systems, weapons systems
and arms control. Cambridge, MA: Abt Books.

---. 1985. SDI necessary for national security.
Defense Science 2003+ 4 (February/March):14-19.

---. 1985 Emerging policy triad defense, offense
and arms control. Defense Science 2003+
4 (April/May): 26-40.

---. 1985. The Strategic Defense Initiative:
thirteen issues. Defense Science 2003+ 4
(June/July):36-46.

---. 1986. Denting the shield, blunting the
sword. Defense Science 2003+ 4
(December/January):11-19.

Great guns. 1985. Scientific American, October,
80-81.

Greb, G.A., and G.W. Johnson. 1983. Strategic arms limitation. Proceedings of a short course on physics, technology and the nuclear arms race. April 17, 1983, Baltimore, MD: AIP Conference Proceedings, No. 104, 246-261.

Greeley, Brendan M., Jr. 1986. Navy expanding its space command to bolster readiness. Aviation Week and Space Technology, February 3, 54-56.

Green, Brian. 1984. Strategic defense: the technology that makes it possible. Washington, D.C.: Heritage Foundation.

Greenberg, Daniel S. 1985. An end run for labs and a goal line stand against SDI. Discover, October, 118-119.

----. 1985. The hidden cost of Star Wars. New Scientist 105 (no. 1449):41.

----. 1986. Fundamental research vs. basic economics. Discover, January, 86-87.

Gregory, William H. 1983. Watershed on nuclear defense. Aviation Week and Space Technology, April 25, 13.

----. 1984. Reagan's space challenge. Aviation Week and Space Technology, January 30, 11.

----. 1984. Overreacting to Star Wars. Aviation Week and Space Technology, November 5, 9.

----. 1985. Dilemma for Europe. Aviation Week and Space Technology, June 24, 11.

----. 1985. Arms control once more. Aviation Week and Space Technology, January 21, 9.

Grey, J. 1984. A Soviet view of Star Wars. Aerospace America, September, 26.

Grier, Peter, and Scott Armstrong. 1985. Star Wars will it work? Christian Science Monitor, November 4, 5, 6, 7, 8, and 12.

Griffiths, Dave. 1985. Reagan and Gorbachev must learn to live with Star Wars. Business Week, November 25, 37.

Griffiths, Dave, Evert Clark, and Alan Hall. 1985. Why Star Wars is a shot in the arm for corporate R&D. Business Week, April 8, 77-78.

Griffiths, Dave, Ronald Taggiasco, Thane Peterson, and Frederic A. Miller. 1985. The selling of Star Wars to businesses abroad; behind the raging political debate, companies jockey for a piece of the action. Business Week, July 15, 68-69.

Gross, Richard C. 1985. Weinberger and the Soviet quest for the death star. Defense Science 2003+ 4 (June/July):7-9.

Growing doubts; a Star Wars invitation. 1985. Time, April 8, 50.

Gubarev, V. 1984. Space, (JPRS-USP-84-003) June, 28-29. Translated into English from Pravda (USSR), January 1, 3. Arlington, VA: Joint Publications Research Service.

Guertner, Gary L. Summer 1985. What is "proof"? Foreign Policy 59:73-84.

---. Autumn 1985. Strategic defense: new technologies, old tactics. Parameters 15:16-22.

Gwynne, P. 1985. America's scientists sign the pledge against Star Wars. New Scientist 107 (no. 1474):14.

Hafner, Donald L. Spring 1985. Assessing the President's vision: the Fletcher, Miller, and Hoffman panels. Daedalus 114:91-106.

---. 1985. Space weapons, national security, and arms control. Paper presented at the 1985 American Association for the Advancement of Science Annual Meeting 8520021, Los Angeles, CA, May 26-31, 1985.

Haley, P. Edward, and Jack Merritt, eds. 1986.
Strategic defense: folly or future? Boulder,
CO: Westview Press.

Hamilton, Meredith, Michael Kilian, Joe Lertola,
and Robert McCall. 1985. Battleground in the
heavens. Discover, September, 43-62.

Hammer, Armand. 1985. To share or not to share.
National Review, October 18, 20-21.

Hanrahan, M.R., and M. Nields. 1984. Defense
electronics and industry synergism. Digital
Design 14 (no. 6):100-107.

Harnly, Caroline D., ed. 1985. Space Weapons.
Oryx Science Bibliographies Series, Volume 2.
Phoenix, AZ: Oryx Press.

Harrowell, R.V. 1985. Price of Star Wars.
Nature 317 (no. 6037):470.

---. 1986. Debris that shatters the Star Wars
myth. New Scientist 109 (no. 1491):55.

Hartung, William. 1986. Star Wars pork barrel.
Bulletin of the Atomic Scientists 42
(January):20-24.

Hartung, William, and Rosy Nimroody. 1985. Cutting
up the Star Wars pie. Nation, September
14, 200-201.

---. 1985. Star Wars: what price strategic
defense? New York: Council on Economic
Priorities.

Hasselmann, C. G. 1983. Weapons of mass
destruction, Article IV Outer Space Treaty and
the relationship to general disarmament. In
Colloquium of the Law of Outer Space, 25th, Paris,
France, September 27-October 2, 1982, Proceedings (A84-17026 05-84). New York: American
Institute of Aeronautics and Astronautics, pp.
99-111. Report no. IAF PAPER 82-IISL-24.

Healy, Melissa. 1986. How the allies are lining up. US News and World Report, January 20, 28.

Hebblethwaite, Peter. 1985. Papal science agenda: Star Wars. National Catholic Reporter, February 1, 2.

Hecht, J. 1985. Star Wars - an astronomical bribe for scientists. New Scientist 106 (no. 1461):14-18.

High-power accelerator evaluates electron-beam weapon feasibility. 1985. Aviation Week and Space Technology, September 9, 72-73.

Himes, Kenneth R. 1985. Star Wars: safety or danger ahead? America, November 23, 341-345.

Hirsch, E. 1985. Evolutionary acquisition of command and control systems. Signal 40 (September):39-45.

Hirsch, R. 1986. Star Wars. New Scientist 109 (no. 1489):53.

Hobbs, David. 1986. An illustrated guide to space warfare: "Star Wars" technology diagrammed and explained. New York: Prentice-Hall.

Hogan, Brian J. 1985. Distributed-energy railgun can fire repeatedly. Design News, September 9, 84-87.

Hoffman, Fred S. 1983. 1983 summary report, ballistic missile defenses and U.S. national security. Washington, D.C.: Institute for Defense Analysis, October.

----. 1984. Active defense and Western security. Paper presented at the 26th Annual International Institute for Strategic Studies Conference at Avignon, France, September 13-16.

Hoffmann, Stanley. 1986. Fog over the summit. New York Review of Books, January 16, 22-25.

Hofstadter, Douglas R. 1986. Dreams of a magical shield. Newsweek, March 3, 8.

Holloway, David. 1985. Space weapons and U.S.-
U.S.S.R. relations. Paper presented at the
1985 American Association for the Advancement
of Science (AAAS) 1985 Annual meeting 8520021,
Los Angeles, CA, May 26-31, 1985.

----. Summer 1985. The Strategic Defense Initiative
and the Soviet Union. Daedalus 114:257-278.

Holm, Hans-Henrik. Spring 1985. SDI and European
security: does dependence assure security?
Alternatives (World Policy Institute) 10:517-
532.

Holzman, David. 1984. A cheap ballistic-missile
defense? Technology Review, August-September,
73-74.

Homsley, T.L. 1976. Application of angle-only
track to ballistic missile defense. Paper
presented at the 1976 Institute of Electrical
and Electronics Engineers (IEEE) Conference on
Decision and Control/15th Symposium on Adaptive
Processes A764155, Clearwater, FL, December 1-
3, 1976. In Conference Record No. 76CH1150-
2CS. New York: Institute of Electrical and
Electronics Engineers.

Horelick, Arnold. 1985. Interview. What worries
Soviets, U.S. about an arms pact. US News and
World Report, November 11, 33-34.

Hough, Jerry F., Stanley R. Sloan, Paul C.
Warnke, and David Linebaugh. 1985. Arms control
and the Strategic Defense Initiative: three
perspectives. Occasional Paper 36. Muscatine,
IA: Stanley Foundation, October.

House amendments would set commissions to monitor
SDI. 1985. Aviation Week and Space Technology,
July 8, 23.

House panel cuts $317 million from ballistic
missile defense. 1985. Aviation Week, May 7,
22-23.

Howe, Geoffrey. 1985. Interviewed by Hilary
Mackenzie. "Room for agreement." Macleans,
October 7, 32.

How to talk about Star Wars. 1985. *Nature* 313 (no. 5997):1-2.

Hoyt, H.C. 1985. A simple ballistic missile defense model to help decision-makers. *Interfaces* 15 (no. 5):54-62.

Hussain, F. 1985. Will space weapons sink Britain's Trident fleet? *New Scientist* 105 (no. 1437):8-9.

Ignizio, J.P. 1974. Resource allocation and scheduling in ballistic missile defense adaptive control systems. In *Proceedings, 7th International Congress on Cybernetics,* Namur, Belgium: Association Internationale de Cybernetique.

Ikle, Fred. Summer 1984. Arms control amnesia. *Journal of Social, Political and Economic Studies* 9:136-40.

----. Spring 1985. Nuclear strategy: can there be a happy ending? *Foreign Affairs* 63:810-26.

Incentive structures and the evil empire. 1985. *National Review,* March 8, 18.

Industry, scientists seek approaches to tap SDI's commercial potential. 1985. *Aviation Week and Space Technology,* November 25, 75-77.

An interview with Gorbachev; candid views about U.S.-Soviet relations and his goals for his people. 1985. *Time,* September 9, 22-28.

Is there a way out? 1985. *Harpers,* June, 35-45.

Israel explores participation in U.S. Strategic Defense Initiative. 1985. *Aviation Week and Space Technology,* June 17, 97.

Italian SDI bids. 1985. *Aviation Week and Space Technology,* July 22, 20.

Jacky, Jonathan. 1985. The Star Wars defense won't compute. *Atlantic,* June, 18-25.

Jacobsen, Carl G. 1985. Soviet-American arms
    control: hope or hoax? Current History,
    October, 317-23.

Janssen Van Rady, J. L. Summer 1984. Europe and
    ballistic missile defense. Journal of Social,
    Political and Economic Studies 9:196-198.

Jasani, Bhupendra. 1984. Space weapons: the
    arms control dilemma. London: Taylor and
    Francis.

Jastrow, Robert. 1983. How to make nuclear
    weapons obsolete. Boston: Little, Brown.

---. 1984. Reagan vs. the scientists: why the
    president is right about missile defense.
    Commentary, January, 23-32.

---. 1984. The war against Star Wars.
    Commentary, December, 19-25.

---. 1985. Space defense: the war against Star
    Wars. Current, March-April, 27-33.

---. 1985. First strike! American Legion,
    August, 12-16.

---. 1985. Interviewed by Anthony Liversidge.
    Omni, September, 60-63.

---. 1986. Why we need Star Wars. Reader's
    Digest, February, 78-82.

Johnson, Kermit D. 1986. Bishops deterred by
    deterrence. National Catholic Reporter,
    January 31, 11-12.

Johnson, N. L. 1984. The Soviet year in space -
    1983. Space World, November, 24-30.

Johnstone, B. 1985. SDI - Star Wars research not
    up to scratch. Nature 318 (no. 6046):497.

Jones, Arthur. 1985. Architect of SALT I
    agreement shoots down Star Wars "hoax." National
    Catholic Reporter, November 15, 1-2.

Jones, J. G. 1978. Ballistic-missile defense overview. Paper presented at the American Institute of Aeronautics and Astronautics (AIAA) Strategic Offensive/Defensive Missile Meeting 781 1032, Monterey, CA, February 1-3, 1978. Classified papers. New York: American Institute of Aeronautics and Astronautics.

Jones, Robert R. 1983. Is world peace hiding in a technological fix? Industrial Research 25 (May):11.

---. 1983. There is reason to doubt a technological fix. Industrial Research 25 (June):11.

Jones, Rodney W., and Steven A. Hildreth. Fall 1984. Star Wars: the problems of strategic defense. Washington Quarterly 7:104-111.

Joyce, C. 1985. Industry takes a shine to Star Wars. New Scientist 108 (no. 1486):18-19.

Joyce, James Avery. 1983. The "verification" escape hatch. Christian Century, November 9, 1004-1005.

Kaplan, Fred. 1983. The wizards of Armageddon. New York: Simon and Schuster.

Karas, Thomas. 1983. The Star Wars scenario. Nation, April 9, 444-446.

---. 1983. The new high ground: systems and weapons of space age war. New York: Simon & Schuster.

Karenin, Alexei. 1984. Perverted logic: the U.S. ABM plans lead to a new arms spiral. New Times (Moscow), June, 6-8.

Kass, Ilana, and Ethan S. Burger. 1985. Soviet responses to the U.S. Strategic Defense Initiative: the ABM gambit revisited? Air University Review 36 (March/April):55-64.

---, ed. 1985. People in space: policy perspectives for a Star Wars century. New Brunswick, NJ: Transaction Books.

Kegley, Charles W., Jr., and Eugene R. Wittkopf. 1985. The nuclear reader. New York: St. Martin's Press.

Kelley, James B. 1983. The new high ground. America, November 5, 275.

Kennet, W. 1985. Star Wars - Europe's polite waffle. Bulletin of the Atomic Scientists (September) 41:7-11.

Kessel, Jeffrey. 1984. What you should know about ASAT's: Star Wars' opening gun. Nation, November 3, 445-47.

Keyworth, George A. 1984. Space-based defense. Signal 38 (January):39-41.

----. 1984. A sense of obligation - the Strategic Defense Initiative. Aerospace America, April, 56.

----. 1985. Security and stability: the role for strategic defense. Institute on Global Conflict and Cooperation, Policy Papers, No. 1, University of California, San Diego.

Khozin, G. S. 1985. U.S., Soviet space program aims contrasted. Space, (JPRS-USP-85-001), 104-110. Translated into English from Zelmya i Vselennaya (USSR), March-April 1984, 14-18. Arlington, VA: Joint Publications Research Service.

Kidd, Jack. 1985. "Star light" can be an alternative to Star Wars. Humanist 45 (September-October): 27-29.

King, M. 1984. Ballistic-missile defense. Aviation Week and Space Technology, April 16, 212.

Kiser, John W. Fall 1985. How the arms race really helps Moscow. Foreign Policy (no. 60):40-51.

Kistiakowsky, Vera. 1986. Should university researchers acept SDI funding? Technology Review, January, 10-12.

Kittle, Robert A. 1985. Even with Star Wars, U.S. open to attack. US News and World Report, March 18, 27-28.

---. 1985. Will Star Wars zap U.S.-Soviet arms talks? US News and World Report, October 28, 34.

---. 1985. It's "big birds" vs. laser rays at Geneva. US News and World Report, November 11, 30-31.

Klass, Philip J. 1984. SDI plans comprehensive option study. Aviation Week and Space Technology, October 8, 20-21.

---. 1985. Defense Department halts Lockheed's Talon Gold program. Aviation Week and Space Technology, January 14, 26-27.

---. 1985. Defense, Energy departments negotiate new space power development. Aviation Week and Space Technology, February 4, 89-90.

---. SDI office pushes innovative science, technology research. Aviation Week and Space Technology, April 29, 225-26.

---. 1985. OTA weighs ballistic missile defense options. Aviation Week and Space Technology, September 30, 22-23.

Kluger, Jeff. 1983. The never-never gun: space lasers: will they work? Science Digest, August, 46.

Kogut, John, and Michael Weissman. 1986. Taking the pledge against Star Wars. Bulletin of the Atomic Scientists 42 (January):27-30.

Kolcum, Edward H. 1985. Discovery crew tests laser tracker, surpasses mission goals. Aviation Week and Space Technology, July 1, 19-20.

Kondracke, Morton. 1985. The President's view; Reagan discusses Star Wars, MX and the arms talks. Newsweek, March 18, 21-22.

---. 1985. In search of the deal; don't count on Star Wars as a bargaining chip. Newsweek, November 25, 43.

Kopal, V. 1983. Article IV of the 1967 Space Treaty - its present meaning and possibilities of further development. In Colloquium on the Law of Outer Space, 25th, Paris, France, September 27-October 2, 1982, Proceedings (A84-17026 05-84). New York: American Institute of Aeronautics and Astronautics. Report no. IAF PAPER 82-IISL-27, pp. 119-125.

---. Spring 1984. Evolution of the main principles of space law in the institutional framework of the United Nations. Journal of Space Law 12:12-25.

Koppes, C. R. 1984. Star Wars. Sciences 24 (no. 4):2.

Kosovac, S.M. 1976. Ballistic missile defense simulation validation. Paper presented at the 1976 Summer Computer Simulation Conference A763050, Washington, D.C., July 12-14, 1976. Montvale, NJ:AFIPS Press.

Kozicharow, E. 1985. Research aims at development of laser-guided electron beam. Aviation Week and Space Technology, February 18, 18-19.

---. 1985. SDI revives Navy laser effort. Aviation Week and Space Technology, February 25, 26.

---. 1985. U.S. launches program to bring NATO into SDI research role. Aviation Week and Space Technology, March 11, 55-56.

---. 1985. Strategic Defense Initiative tries to maintain structured funding pace. Aviation Week and Space Technology, March 18, 35.

---. 1985. SDI organization moves to promote non-U.S. share of research work. Aviation Week and Space Technology, April 29, 215-21.

Kramer, Ken. 1983. Space and new strategic ethics. Space World, May, 2-3.

Kramer, Michael. 1985. Scoping the summit. New York, November 11, 34-40.

Krauthammer, Charles. 1984. The illusion of Star Wars: the worst offense is a bad defense. New Republic, May 14, 13-17.

----. 1985. Will Star Wars kill arms control: a deal for Geneva. New Republic, January 21, 12-15.

Krebs, Thomas H. 1985. Ballistic missile defense: Soviet countermeasures. Defense Science 2003+ 4 (August/September):65-75.

Krepon, Michael. 1986. Dormant threat to the ABM Treaty. Bulletin of the Atomic Scientists 42 (January):31-34.

Kupperman, Robert H. Summer 1983. Mutual arms reduction: an impossible dream? Washington Quarterly 6:50-54.

Kuznetsov, Vladlen. 1985. The White House and SALT: the U.S. is out to scrap the Strategic Arms Limitation Treaty. New Times (Moscow), June, 7-8.

Lach, Joseph. 1985. The fallacy of Star Wars. Bulletin of the Atomic Scientists (June-July) 41:50-51.

Lamb, J. 1985. Star Wars software will not work. New Scientist 107 (no. 1472):19.

----. 1985. The bugs in the Star Wars program. New Scientist 108 (no. 1483):27-29.

Lampman, S. 1985. On Star Wars. Bulletin of the Atomic Scientists 41 (August):62.

Landis, G. A. 1984. Ballistic missile defense. Physics Today, October, 126.

Laser-tracking tests. 1985. Aviation Week and Space Technology, July 15, 19.

Lasers and rail guns arrive. 1984. Popular Mechanics, July, 87.

Lasers link university, industry and Star Wars. New Scientist 108 (no. 1477):29.

Laurin, T. C. 1985. Stampede to Star Wars. Photonics Spectra 19 (no. 7):14.

Laver, Ross. 1985. A secret plan for defending the north. Macleans, November 11, 20-21.

Lawyer, John E. 1984. Beyond deterrence: the strategic defense option. Air University Review 36 (November-December):32-41.

Leber, W. P. 1974. Deterrent value of ballistic missile defense. Paper presented at the 10th Annual Meeting of the American Institute of Aeronautics and Astronautics A741059, Washington, D.C., January 28-30, 1974. New York: American Institute of Aeronautics and Astronautics.

Lefevere, Patricia Scharber. 1985. Peace pastoral influenced Star Wars, contends Reagan adviser. National Catholic Reporter, May 10, 2.

Lehrman, Lewis E. Winter 1985. The case for strategic defense: new shield of the republic. Policy Review (no. 31):42-46.

Lehrman, Lewis, and Gregory A. Fossedal. 1986. How to decide about strategic defense. National Review, January 31, 32-37.

Lellouche, Pierre. Summer/Fall 1985. SDI and the Atlantic Alliance. SAIS (School of Advanced International Studies) Review 5:67-80.

Lenorovitz, Jeffrey M. 1985. European ministers meet in Paris to discuss Eureka prospects. Aviation Week and Space Technology, July 15, 21-22.

Leon, Steven J. 1985. Scott Carpenter speaks out; America's second man in orbit talks about project Mercury, militarization, and the moon. Space World, July, 49-50.

Lerner, E. J. 1985. Star Wars - feasibility key to policy debate. Aerospace America, August, 38-42.

----. 1985. Star Wars - survivability and stability. Aerospace America, September, 80-84.

----. 1985. Star Wars - who wins the cost exchange? Aerospace America, October, 62.

----. 1985. Star Wars - countermeasures and the uses of SDI. Aerospace America, November, 60-63.

Levin, Bob. 1985. The Star Wars summit. Macleans, November 25, 22-23.

Lienert, Paul. 1985. A Star Wars thrust from abroad. Nation's Business, April, 24.

Lin, Herbert. 1984. The BMD debate: deja vu. Technology Review, April, 50.

----. 1985. The software for Star Wars: an Achilles heel? Technology Review, July, 16-18.

----. 1985. The development of software for ballistic-missile defense. Scientific American, December, 46-53.

Lining up for ABM contracts. 1983. Fortune, April 18, 7.

Long, Franklin A., Donald Hafner, and Jeffrey Boutwell, eds. 1986. Weapons in Space New York: W. W. Norton & Company.

Longstreth, Thomas K. 1985. U.S., Soviet programs threaten ABM Treaty. Bulletin of the Atomic Scientists 41 (April):11-15.

Longstreth, Thomas K., John Pike, and John B. Rhinelander. 1985. The impact of U.S. and Soviet ballistic missile defense programs on the ABM Treaty. Washington, D.C.: National Campaign to Save the ABM Treaty, March.

Lupton, Lt. Col. David. Fall 1983. Space doctrine. Strategic Review:36-47.

Lytle, D. 1984. Star Wars - the anti's strike back. Photonics Spectra 18 (no. 8):26-27.

---. 1985. Star Wars - where do we go from here? Photonics Spectra 19 (no. 8):30-31.

McCartney, Laton. 1985. Laying odds on Star Wars; the heart of the Initiative promises to be an investor's dream. Science Digest, November, 38.

McClelland, L. A. 1985. The bright outlook for lasers. Defense Electronics 17 (July):71.

McDonald, Marci. 1985. In defense of Star Wars. Macleans, October 28, 34.

---. 1985. Leaping into space. Macleans, November 25, 24-28.

McFarlane, Robert C. 1985. Strategic Defense Initiative. Department of State Bulletin 85 (June):57-59.

---. 1985. Interview. Meet the Press, October 6, 1-10.

McFarlane describes Soviet SDI-type program. 1985. Aviation Week and Space Technology, November 4, 16.

Mackenzie, Hilary. 1985. Divisions on free trade and Star Wars. Macleans, September 2, 13.

---. 1985. Scientists puzzled as Thatcher backs Star Wars. New Scientist 105 (no. 1445):3-4.

McLaughlin, John. 1985. The summit according to Henry. National Review, November 15, 24.

---. 1985. Star Wars and politics. National Review, December 31, 22.

McLucas, J. L. 1984. Star Wars. Sciences 24 (no. 4):2.

McManus, Jim. 1986. U.S. rejects test ban pleas; space defense tests begin - arms control, bishops' conditions put on hold. National Catholic Reporter, January 10, 1-2.

McNamara, Robert S., and Hans A. Bethe. 1985. Reducing the risk of nuclear war. Atlantic, July, 43-51.

Maddox, J. 1985. Piecemeal ballistic-missile defense. Nature 315 (no. 6018):365.

Magno, P. 1983. Military space programmes. In Colloquium on the Law of Outer Space, 25th, Paris, France, September 27-October 2, 1982, Proceedings (A84-17026 05-84). New York: American Institute of Aeronautics and Astronautics, pp. 127-30. Report no. IAF PAPER 82-IISL-28.

Magnuson, Ed. 1984. Volleys over outer space; Washington deftly returns a suggestion for Star Wars talks. Time, July 16, 30-31.

Maier, M. H., and T. J. Venanzi. 1985. Return of the death ray - the Star Wars defense plan is a costly remake of an old fantasy. Sciences 25 (no. 2):30-33.

Main directions and principles of international cooperation in the peaceful exploration of outer space in the conditions of its nonmilitarization. 1985. Soviet Life, November, 44-45.

Mann, Paul. 1985. Missile defense worries NATO. Aviation Week and Space Technology, March 11, 57-58.

---. 1985. Reagan rules out ending SDI effort in exchange for Soviet missile cuts. Aviation Week and Space Technology, September 30, 93-95.

---. 1985. SDI, offensive arms disputes weigh
equally in Geneva talks. Aviation Week and
Space Technology, November 18, 14-15.

---. 1986. SDI, current defense contracts spared
in first fiscal 1986 budget cuts. Aviation
Week and Space Technology, January 20, 23-24.

Marbach, William D. 1985. Realistic defense or
leap of faith? Newsweek, June 17, 41-43.

Markoff, John. 1985. Defense spending cushions
Silicon Valley's slump. National Catholic
Reporter, October 11, 5.

Marsh, Gerald E. 1985. SDI: the stability
question. Bulletin of the Atomic Scientists 41
(October):23-24.

---. 1985. The anatomy of Star Wars. New
Scientist 108 (no. 1482):32-37.

Marshall, Eliot. 1985. Space junk grows with
weapons tests. Science, October 25, 425-426.

---. 1985. Keyworth quits White House post.
Science, December 13, 1249-1251.

Marshall, H. R., Jr. Fall 1984. Commercialization
of space - incentives, impediments and
alternatives. Journal of Space Law
12:163-73.

Martin, H. V. 1984. Seeking the high ground -
US/USSR philosophies, assets vary dramatically.
Defense Systems Review and Military
Communications 2 (February):12.

Martin, Jim. 1985. SDI: analyzing the opinion
war. Defense Science 2003+ 4
(February/March):23-31.

---. 1985. SDI: the technical alternatives.
Defense Science 2003+ 4 (April/May):49-59.

Mason, R. 1984. Star Wars - an alternate view.
Aerospace America, July, 24.

Massive space defense effort sought. 1984. Space
World, January, 35-36.

Mates, Leo. 1985. Star Wars and arms talks.
Review of International Affairs 36
(February):9-11.

May, Michael M. 1986. Safeguarding our military
space systems. Science, April 18, 336-340.

Meacham, James, Achin Vanaik, Denise Harrington,
and Ian Davidson. 1984. The arms race:
slowing? World Press Review, November, 35-40.

Means, M. L., and J. F. Voss. 1985. Star Wars - a
developmental study of expert and novice
knowledge structures. Journal of Memory and
Language 24 (no. 6):746-757.

Meinel, Carolyn. 1984. Fighting mad. Technology
Review, April, 31-39.

Menaul, Stewart. Summer 1984. Europe's stake in
ballistic missile defense. Journal of Social,
Political and Economic Studies 9:184-95.

Mendelsohn, Jack. 1985. Put the Genie back in
the bottle. New Statesman, July 5, 17-18.

Menshikov, S. 1985. What is behind the Star Wars
debate. International Affairs (Moscow), June,
67-77.

Meyers, N. 1985. Star Wars - Israel attracted by
spin-off. Nature 314 (no. 6013):660.

Mikhaylov, O. 1985. Militarization of space
activity in United States. Space (JPRS-USP-
85-003), March, 137-144. Translated into
English from Politicheskoye Samoobrazovaniye
(USSR), June 1984, 115-20. Arlington, VA: Joint
Publications Research Service.

Miller, Robert. 1985. A Star Wars scenario.
Macleans, November 25, 30-31.

Mische, Patricia M. 1985. Star Wars and the state of our souls: deciding the future of planet earth. Minneapolis, MN: Winston Press.

Missile defense effort includes directed-energy, other means. 1983. Aviation Week and Space Technology, May 30, 332-33.

Mock, Gregory. 1985. Star Wars comes to the supermarket. Science'85, September, 76.

Mohr, Charles. 1985. Weapons in space - the controversy over Star Wars. What Moscow might do in replying to Star Wars. New York Times, March 6.

----. 1985. Weapons in space - Star Wars in strategy: the Russian response. New York Times, December 17.

Mordoff, Keith F. 1985. Test ASAT launched autonomously from USAF F-15 carrier aircraft. Aviation Week and Space Technology, October 7, 18-19.

Morganthau, Tom. 1986. An answer for Gorbachev; Reagan's new arms response. Newsweek, March 3, 28.

Morrison, David C. 1985. The miracle workers: they aim for the stars - and miss. Progressive, July, 28-29.

Moscow's bold blueprint; Gorbachev outlines a nuclear-free world. 1986. US News and World Report, January 27, 6-7.

Movement against Star Wars gathers pace. 1985. New Scientist 108 (no. 1479):15.

Much ado about statement D (Anti-Ballistic Missile Treaty of 1972). 1985. National Review, November 15, 18.

Mulroney says no? 1985. Nation, October 5, 301.

Murtagh, Pat. 1984. The Canadian connection. Canadian Forum, April, 13-14.

258 / Bibliography

Myers, Ware. 1986. The Star Wars software debate. Bulletin of the Atomic Scientists 42 (February):31-36.

NASA's link to strategic defense effort grows with new spacecraft. 1985. Aviation Week and Space Technology, August 26, 18-20.

Nelson, V. P. 1985. Hardware acquisition for the enhancement of a fault-tolerance/distributed computing laboratory. Auburn University, AL. Engineering Experiment Station. August. Report no. AD-A158439; AU-EE-85-0006-1; ARO-18964.1-EL-EQ.

New Army command. 1985. Aviation Week and Space Technology, July 8, 23.

New Star Wars row. 1985. Nature 314 (no. 6009):302.

Newell, David. 1985. ABM: the shift that never was; a McFarlane gaffe sparks an uproar. Newsweek, October 21, 55.

The newest Star Wars battle. 1984. Time, July 23, 82.

Newhouse, John. 1985. The diplomatic round: test. New Yorker, July 22, 37-54.

Nichols, J. P. 1985. Strategic Defense Initiative. Martin Marietta Energy Systems, Inc., Oak Ridge, TN. Report no. DE85-012778; DOE/OR-21400/T124.

Nitze, Paul H. 1985. The objectives of arms control. Department of State Bulletin 85 (May):57-63.

---. 1985. SDI and the ABM Treaty. Department of State Bulletin 85 (August):37-39.

---. 1985. SDI: the Soviet program. Department of State Bulletin 85 (September):40-42.

---. 1985. The ABM Treaty and the SDI program.

Current Policy Paper no. 755. Washington, D.C.: U.S. Department of State, Bureau of Public Affairs, October.

Norman, Colin. 1985. Scientists at the White House. Science, March 1, 1015.

---. 1985. Memo sets policy for Star Wars publications. Science, August 30, 843.

Norton, Robert E. 1985. High-tech stardust; as fallout from Star Wars, the Pentagon has $100 million for funding frontier R&D. Fortune, September 30, 122.

Nuclear bargains. 1985. Nation, October 12, 332-333.

A nuclear-free world? 1986. National Catholic Reporter, January 24, 14.

Nuclear war by accident - is it impossible? 1983. US News and World Report, December 19, 27-28.

Oberg, James E. 1984. Pearl Harbor in space. Omni, July, 42-46.

---. 1984. Space weapons. Bulletin of the Atomic Scientists 40 (July):47-48.

---. 1986. Congress covers up Soviet space weapons. National Review, February 14, 25.

Off balance - but on cue. 1985. Newsweek, March 11, 47.

Offensive talk. 1985. Progressive, November, 11-12.

Offutt, J., and J. B. Danese. 1985. Communications for SDI. Signal (July) 39:37-43.

O'Lessker, Karl. 1984. High frontiers of strategic defense: the fate of the earth could be survival. American Spectator, April, 12-15.

O'Lone, Richard G. 1985. North Atlantic Assembly declares support for SDI after lobbying effort. Aviation Week and Space Technology, October 21, 18-19.

One shrewd comrade. 1985. America, December 14, 414-415.

Onosko, Tim. 1983. Showdown on the high frontier. Omni, November, 72-76.

Outer space should serve peace. 1985. Soviet Life, October, 2.

Outer space sub-committee discusses spacecraft and satellite issues. 1985. UN Chronicle 12 (February):14.

Outer space legal questions discussed by subcommittee. 1985. UN Chronicle 22 (May):64-65.

Ovinnikov, R. 1985. Star Wars programme: a new phase in Washington's militaristic policy. International Affairs (Moscow), August, 13-22.

Paine, Christopher. 1983. The ABM Treaty: looking for the loopholes. Bulletin of Atomic Scientists 39 (August/September):13-17.

Panel affirms feasibility of producing SDI software. 1985. Aviation Week and Space Technology, December 9, 19.

Panofsky, Wolfgang K. H. 1985. The Strategic Defense Initiative: perception vs reality. Physics Today, June, 34.

Papp, D. S. 1983. Ballistic missile defense, space-based weapons, and the defense of the west. U.S. Army War College, Carlisle Barracks, PA. Strategic Studies Institute. Report no. AD-A140280.

Parnas, David Lorge. 1985. Software aspects of Strategic Defense Systems. SIGSOFT Software Engineering Notes 10 (October):15-23.

----. 1985. Why Star Wars software won't work. Harper's, March, 17-18.

----. 1985. Software aspects of strategic defense systems. American Scientist, September/October, 432-440.

Payne, Keith B., ed. 1983. Laser weapons in space: policy and doctrine. Boulder, CO: Westview Press.

----. 1986. Strategic defense: "Star Wars" in perspective. Lanham, MD: Hamilton Press.

Payne, Keith B., and Colin S. Gray. Spring 1984. Nuclear policy and the defensive transition. Foreign Affairs 62:820-845.

----. 1985. Toward ballistic missile defense. In The nuclear reader. Charles W. Kegley, Jr., and Eugene R. Wittkopf, eds. New York: St. Martin's Press.

Payne, Keith B., Colin S. Gray, and Adam M. Garfinkle. Summer 1984. Forum: the Strategic Defense Initiative. Orbis 28:215-255.

Peace through strength and dialogue; ballistic missile defense. 1984. Vital Speeches 51 (December 1):101-103.

Peaceful uses of outer space: progress and problems. 1984. UN Chronicle 11 (April):32-39.

Pearson, Natalie, and Raoul Schonemann. 1986. Star Wars: questions and answers on the space weapons debate. Progressive, January, 41.

Pen pals. (Yuri Andropov's appeal to ban space weapons) 1983. Time, May 9, 57.

Perle, Richard. 1985. Interview. "We can't trust the Russians - nor should we." US News and World Report, September 30, 26.

Persh, J. 1985. Materials and structures, science and technology requirements for the DOD

Strategic Defense Initiative. *American Ceramic Society Bulletin* 64 (no. 4):555-559.

Perspectives on Star Wars. Summer 1985. *International Security* 10:3-57.

Peterson, Ivars. 1985. Secrecy, security and SDI. *Science News*, October 19, 248.

Pirani, Felix. 1985. SDI is pie in the sky. *New Statesman*, July 5, 18-20.

----. 1985. Total defense against missiles just isn't on. *New Statesman*, November 1, 21-22.

----. 1986. Stifling Star Wars. *New Statesman*, January 3, 18.

Platonov, A. 1985. Militarization of outer space: a threat to mankind. *International Affairs*, (Moscow) February, 28-36.

Pluenneke, John E. 1985. After the West German spy scandal: are Star Wars' secrets safe? *Business Week*, October 7, 53.

----. 1985. Helmut Kohl: the man in the middle of the superpower summit. *Business Week*, October 28, 48-50.

Pluenneke, John, Friedrich Thelen, and Frank J. Comes. 1985. Star Wars is zapping Nato unity on nuclear defense. *Business Week*, March 4, 51.

"Pork barrel in the sky." 1985. *Time*, May 6, 23.

Posner, Michael, Peter Lewis, Marci McDonald, and David North. 1985. Raising toasts to a new era. *Macleans*, December 2, 32-35.

Potemkin wars. 1986. *Scientific American*, February, 54-55.

Powell, Bill. 1985. Star Wars on Wall Street. *Newsweek*, August 19, 48-49.

President Reagan's policy statement. 1985.
Congressional Digest 64 (March):65-71.

The President's Strategic Defense Initiative.
1985. Department of State Bulletin 85
(March):65-71.

Pressler, Larry. 1986. Star Wars: debating the
Strategic Defense Initiative. New York: Praeger.

Prime minister says Japan considering role in
SDI. 1985. Aviation Week and Space Technology,
April 8, 21.

Principles of directed-energy weapons. 1984.
Environment, June, 10-11.

Project chief asks full funds for Strategic
Defense Initiative. 1984. Aviation Week and
Space Technology May 21, 23.

Projected cost growth cited in SDI optics program cut. 1985. Aviation Week and Space
Technology, September 2, 21.

Quammen, David. 1985. The conscience of the
young scientist. Esquire, December, 223-
225.

Quinn, Hal. 1985. Star Wars at the summit.
Macleans, May 6, 32-33.

Railgun experiments strive for high velocity,
repetition. 1986. Aviation Week and Space
Technology, January 27, 21.

Raloff, Janet. 1985. Star Wars defense: is it
legal? Science News, January 19, 39.

---. 1985. Star Wars: lasers can guide electrons.
Science News, April 13, 230.

Ralston, A. 1985. Star Wars program. Science,
May 31, 1040.

---. 1985. Star Wars - what is the professional
responsibility of computer scientists? Abacus
(New York) 3 (no. 1):2-3.

264 / Bibliography

Rankine, R. R., Jr. 1984. Research and technology
for strategic defense. Aerospace America,
April, 64.

Rathjens, George. 1984. The Strategic Defense
Initiative: the imperfections of "perfect
defense." Environment, June, 6-16.

Rathjens, George, and Jack Ruina. Summer 1985.
BMD and strategic instability. Daedalus
114:239-255.

Reagan, Ronald. 1985. The case for Star Wars -
in Reagan's own words. US News and World
Report, January 14, 24.

----. 1985. A message from the president.
Defense Science 2003+4 (April/May):13-14.

----. 1985. Strategic Defense Initiative: radio
address to the nation, July 13, 1985. Weekly
Compilation of Presidential Documents, July 22,
901-2.

Reagan, Gorbachev fail to agree on space-based
weapons limits. 1985. Aviation Week and Space
Technology, November 25, 14-15.

Reagan orders test of antisatellite vehicle
against space target. 1985. Aviation Week and
Space Technology, August 26, 23-24.

Reagan's Star Wars. 1984. New York Review of
Books, April 26, 47-52.

Research produces results for missile defense
program. 1985. Aviation Week and Space
Technology, December 23, 58-59.

Resolving a Star Wars skirmish. 1985. Time,
October 28, 45.

Rettig, James. 1985. Space weapons. Wilson
Library Bulletin 60 (November):65.

RFP readied for strategic defense concepts. 1984.
Aviation Week and Space Technology, July 2, 48.

Richardson, Robert C., III. Fall 1983. Technology, bureaucracy, and defense: the prospects for the US "High Frontier" program. Journal of Social, Political and Economic Studies 8:291-99.

----. Summer 1984. Security in the nuclear age: a new strategy in space. Journal of Social, Political and Economic Studies 9:199-210.

----. Summer 1985. Star Wars: some less-frequently discussed considerations. Journal of Social, Political and Economic Studies 10:131-53.

Rivkin, David B., Jr. Summer 1985. What does Moscow think? Foreign Policy 59:85-105.

Rivkin, David B., Jr., and Manfred R. Hamm. 1985. In strategic defense, Moscow is ahead. Washington,D.C.: Heritage Foundation.

Roberts, A. 1985. Star Wars. New Society 74 (no.1195):339-40.

Roberts, Leslie. 1983. Reactors in orbit. Science'83, December, 46-50.

Robertson, R. P. 1985. Star Wars in medicine - good and bad fallout. Western Journal of Medicine 143 (no. 6):744.

Robinson, Clarence A., Jr. 1983. Beam weapon advances emerge. Aviation Week and Space Technology, July 18, 18-21.

----. 1983. Shuttle may aid in space weapons test. Aviation Week and Space Technology, October 31, 74-78.

----. 1984. Strategic defense group speeds effort. Aviation Week and Space Technology, June 11, 16-18.

----. 1984. BMD research draws strategic focus. Aviation Week and Space Technology, June 18, 83-87.

----. 1984. Army testing hit-to-kill, radar-guided interceptor. Aviation Week and Space Technology, July 9, 38-42.

----. 1984. Defense Department developing orbital guns. Aviation Week and Space Technology, July 23, 61-65.

Robinson, M. 1986. Star Wars - can technology solve all our problems? Electronic Design 34 (no. 1):11.

Rockwood, S. D. 1985. Strategic defense initiatives at Los Alamos National Laboratory. Paper presented at the Southwest Conference on Optics, Albuquerque, NM, March 4, 1985. Los Alamos National Laboratory, NM. Report no.: DE85-014093; LA-UR-85-2177; CONF-850345-25.

Ropelewski, Robert R. 1985. Battle management, C3I network challenge resources of SDI office. Aviation Week and Space Technology, July 15, 19-21.

----. 1985. Gains in directed energy projects may cut SDI operational lead time. Aviation Week and Space Technology, October 14, 21-22.

----. 1986. Experts claim battle management paramount to missile defense. Aviation Week and Space Technology, January 13, 22-23.

Rogers, General Bernard. 1986. Interview. US News and World Report, January 20, 29.

Rose, Craig D. 1985. SDI won't fly, say computer experts. Electronics, October 28, 18-19.

Rosenberg, Tina. 1986. The authorized version. Atlantic, February, 26-28.

Rosin, J. 1985. Opposition to Star Wars. Chemical and Engineering News 63 (no. 40):2.

Rothschild, Matthew, and Keenen Peck. 1985. Star Wars: the final solution. Progressive, July, 20-26.

Rowny, Edward L., and Robert S. McNamara. 1985.
Star Wars debate: one for, one against.
Scholastic Update, November 15, 8-9.

Ruhe, Volker, Bernhard Gonsior, Roald Sagdeyev,
Michel Tatu, Radovan Vukadinovic, Hideki
Tomizawa, Taranjit Singh Sandhu, Moshe Zaq, and
John Honderich. 1986. The Star Wars debate;
sampling opinion in a global controversy.
World Press Review, February, 25-28.

Ruina, Jack P. 1985. Ballistic missile defense.
Issues in Science and Technology 1 (no. 3):14-
15.

---. 1986. Perspectives on hard-site defense.
Issues in Science and Technology 2 (no. 2):
128-133.

Rykunov, Vladimir. 1984. Strategy of space terrorism. New Times (Moscow), January, 21-23.

Safire, William. 1985. New name for Star Wars.
New York Times Magazine, March 24, 14-15.

Sagan, Carl. 1984. Interviewed by Julie
Kosterlitz and Deborah Baldwin. Common Cause
Magazine, May/June, 20-25.

Sagan, Carl. 1985. Why Star Wars concept is a
crock. National Catholic Reporter, May 10, 14.

Sartori, Leo. 1985. From H-bombs to Star Wars:
the politics of strategic decision-making.
Bulletin of the Atomic Scientists 41
(March):57-58.

Schecter, Jerrold L. 1984. Defending the final
frontier. Esquire, November, 103-4.

Scheibla, Shirley Hobbs. 1985. The other Star
Wars; a battle looms over the space station.
Barrons, April 15, 36.

---. Non-nuclear umbrella; the strategic defense
initiative is vital to the free world.
Barrons, July 15, 9.

Schlageter, Mark D., David C. Phillips, B.B.
Stoller, B. Bruce-Briggs, R.H. Cunningham,
Sinclair Kossoff, Alan J. Saly, Joseph Forbes,
Alexis A. Gilliland, Nicholas T. Sakell, and
Bruce McKinney. 1984. Star Wars. Commentary,
June, 2-12.

Scholl, Jaye. 1984. The force is with them; Star
Wars defense will benefit a slew of companies.
Barrons, April 30, 8-10.

Schurzmann, Franz. 1986. Star Wars as Marshall
Plan. National Catholic Reporter, January 31,
18.

Schwartz, David N. 1983. Ballistic missile
defense: reflections on current issues. Annals
of the American Academy of Political and Social
Science 469 (September):58-67.

Schwartzbart, Elias M. 1985. Negotiating with
the Russians: Geneva prospects. Freedom at
Issue, May/June, 3-9.

Scientists' opposition to Star Wars growing.
1985. Chemical & Engineering News 63
(no. 29):7-8.

SDI and the "Challenge of Peace." 1985. America,
November 23, 337-338.

SDI awards optical coating contract. 1985.
Aviation Week and Space Technology,
March 11, 55.

SDI budget seeks to capitalize on advances gained
from research. Aviation Week and Space
Technology, February 10, 27.

SDI chief highlights European contracts,
technical gains. 1985. Aviation Week and Space
Technology, December 2, 23-24.

SDI civil benefits. 1985. Aviation Week and
Space Technology, October 14, 22.

The SDI debate: to deal or not to deal. 1985.
Newsweek, December 2, 46-47.

SDI: its nature and rationale. (transcript) 1985. Department of State Bulletin 85 (December):69-71.

SDI Organization studies surveillance-tracking configuration. 1985. Aviation Week and Space Technology, July 29, 15.

SDI policy linked to protection of people. 1985. Aviation Week and Space Technology, April 29, 225.

SDI pursues hypercube technology effort. 1985. Aviation Week and Space Technology, March 4, 81.

SDI pushes space surveillance effort. 1984. Aviation Week and Space Technology, December 10, 57.

SDI: setting the record straight. 1985. Department of State Bulletin 85 (October):42-45.

SDI south of the border; Buenos Aires. 1986. National Review, February 28, 46.

SDIO achieving program goals while resolving technical issues. 1985. Aviation Week and Space Technology, December 9, 18.

SDIO discusses research disclosure policy. 1985. Aviation Week and Space Technology, August 26, 59.

SDIO plans to issue RFP for test facility. 1985. Aviation Week and Space Technology, November 25, 18.

Second beam distortion compensation test demonstrates tracking concept. 1985. Aviation Week, November 25, 71.

The selling of Star Wars. 1985. Harpers, June, 22.

The selling of Star Wars. 1985. New Scientist 106 (no. 1458):3.

Senator calls for halt to U.S. ASAT testing.
1985. Aviation Week and Space Technology,
October 21, 19-20.

Senators propose SDI funding cut. 1985. Aviation
Week and Space Technology, April 29, 216.

Services coordinate SDI architecture work. 1985.
Aviation Week and Space Technology, December 9,
51.

Sewall, Sarah. 1983. Militarizing the last frontier: the space weapons race. Defense Monitor
12 (no. 5):whole issue.

Shadwick, Martin. 1985. Canadian air defense.
International Perspectives (Canada),
March/April, 11-15.

Shafran, J. S. 1973. Adaptive real time control
for ballistic missile defense systems: hierar-
chical controls of multiple radar/data processing units. In Proceedings of 6th Hawaii
International Conference on System Sciences.
Conference held in Honolulu, HI, January 9-11,
1973. New York: Institute of Electrical and
Electronics Engineers.

Shapiro, Walter. 1985. An ambitious arms agenda.
Newsweek, March 18, 18-22.

Shenfield, Stephen. 1985. Soviets and Star Wars.
Bulletin of the Atomic Scientists 41
(September):53-54.

----. 1985. Soviets may not imitate Star Wars.
Bulletin of the Atomic Scientists 41 (June-
July):38-39.

Sherr, Alan B. 1984. Legal issues of the "Star
Wars" defense program. Boston: Lawyers'
Alliance for Nuclear Arms Control, June.

Shevardnadze, Eduard. 1985. For the peaceful
exploration of outer space. (letter to Javier
Perez de Cuellar). Soviet Life, November, 44.

Shultz, George P. 1985. Interview. Meet the
Press, January 13, 1-8.

---. 1986. Interview. "No thought to departing."
US News and World Report, February 3, 36.

Shultz-bashing. 1985. National Review, August
23, 14-15.

Sidey, Hugh. 1985. "The alternative is so
terrible." Time, January 28, 29.

Sietz, Konrad. SDI: the technological challenge
for Europe. 1985. World Today (London),
August/September, 154-57.

Signing off. 1986. Scientific American, January,
60.

Skantze, Lawrence A. 1986. Military space; a new
era for force structure decisions. Vital
Speeches 52 (January 15):205-7.

Skees, H. 1985. Star Wars uneconomical.
Chemical & Engineering News 63 (no.32):2.

Sloan, J. H. 1984. Space development - the
strategic implications. In New opportunities
in space; Proceedings of the Twenty-first Space
Congress, Cocoa Beach, FL, April 24-26, 1984
(A85-37151 17-12). Cape Canaveral, FL:
Canaveral Council of Technical Societies, pp.
9-1.

Sloss, Leon. Summer 1984. The return of strategic defense. Strategic Review 12:37-44.

Slouching toward superiority. 1985. Commonweal,
September 6, 451-452.

Smith, Dan. 1985. Captain Marvel's final fix.
New Statesman, July 12, 24-25.

Smith, Gerard C. 1985. Star Wars is shooting
down arms-control talks. Business Week, August
19, 14.

---. 1985. Ballistic missile defense. Issues in
Science and Technology 1 (no. 2):4.

Smith, M. S. 1983. Protecting the earth and outer space environment - problems of on-orbit space debris. In Colloquium on the Law of Outer Space, 25th, Paris, France, September 27-October 2, 1982, Proceedings (A84-17026 05-84). New York: American Institute of Aeronautics and Astronautics. Report no. IAF PAPER 82-IISL-12, pp. 45-51.

Smith, R. Jeffrey. 1983. Star Wars plan gets green light. Science, November 25, 901-902.

----. 1984. Star Wars panels highlight uncertainties. Science, April 6, 33.

----. 1984. Weapons bureaucracy spurns Star Wars goal. Science, April 6, 32-34.

----. 1984. Pentagon names Star Wars czar. Science, April 13, 131.

----. 1984. Aerospace experts challenge ASAT decision. Science, May 18, 693-697.

----. 1984. A dim future for weapons talks. Science, August 10, 601.

----. 1984. Star Wars chief takes aim at critics. Science, August 10, 600-601.

----. 1984. Schlesinger attacks Star Wars plan. Science, November 9, 673.

----. 1985. A fresh start for arms negotiations. Science, January 25, 389-390.

----. 1985. Star Wars grants attract universities. Science, April 19, 304.

----. 1985. Academic consortia receive first Star Wars grants. Science, May 10, 696-697.

----. 1985. Negotiators report no progress at arms talks. Science, May 24, 971-972.

----. 1985. An unhealthy trend. Science, June 14, 1293.

----. 1985. Caltech, MIT deny role in Star Wars research. Science, June 21, 1411.

----. 1985. Star Wars tests and the ABM Treaty. Science, July 5, 29-31.

----. 1985. New doubts about Star Wars' feasibility. Science, July 26, 367-368.

----. 1985. Reagan announces a new ASAT test. Science, September 6, 946-947.

----. 1985. OTA study highlights Star Wars difficulties. Science, October 4, 50.

----. 1985. Star Wars boycott gains strength. Science, October 11, 152.

----. 1985. Soviets propose new arms agreement. Science, October 18, 301-302.

----. 1985. Experts cast doubts on X-ray laser. Science, November 8, 646-648.

----. 1985. Reagan reinterprets the ABM Treaty. Science, November 8, 644.

----. 1985. Lab officials squabble over X-ray laser. Science, November 22, 923.

----. 1985. Livermore acknowledges X-ray laser problem. Science, November 29, 1023.

Smith, T. 1974. Utilization of discrimination data for real-time ballistic missile defense (BMD) control decisions. Papers in classified proceedings, January 1974. New York: American Institute of Aeronautics and Astronautics.

Snow, Donald. 1983. Ballistic missile defense and the strategic future. Parameters: Journal of the Army War College (June):11-12.

----. 1984. Space weapons policy. Congressional Digest (March):entire issue.

274 / Bibliography

----. 1985. BMD, SDI, and future policy: issues
and prospects. Air University Review 36
(July/August):4-13.

Some lame duck. 1986. National Review, February
14, 18.

Sommer, Theo, Achin Vanaik, Richard Gwyn, Andre
Fontaine, and David Watt. 1984. Reagan and
Moscow: world press report. World Press
Review, September, 35-40.

Somov, M. 1986. Star peace, not star wars.
International Affairs. (Moscow), March,
54-62

Sorenson, David S. 1985. Ballistic missile
defense for Europe. Comparative Strategy
5 (no. 2):159-78.

Southern, J. R., C. G. Davis, and M. P. Edwards.
1985. Army Battle Management/C/ sup 3/ in the
SDI program. Signal 39 (July):37-43.

Soviet military power: the Pentagon's 1984 view.
1984. Space World, July, 22-25.

Soviet threat in space said to be on rise. 1983.
Aviation Week and Space Technology, May 16, 46-
47.

Space defense and its attackers. 1985. National
Review, February 22, 16.

Space defense and Strategic Defense Initiative
(SDI) Market. 1984. New York: Frost & Sullivan.

Space power project moves to SDI office. 1984.
Aviation Week and Space Technology, October 29,
19.

Space wars' new weaponry. 1983. Macleans, April
4, 32-34.

Space weapons policy: pro & con. 1984.
Congressional Digest 63 (March):67-96.

Space weapons: the whole world is watching.
1983. Technology Review, January, 80.

Spector, Daniel. 1985. Reagan's Star Wars:
first strike against disarmament. Political
Affairs 64 (July):25-30.

Speser, P., and K. Mancuso. 1984. R&D
opportunities in the Strategic Defense Initiative.
Laser Focus 20 (no. 8):14.

Stanglin, Douglas. 1985. Behind new U.S.-Soviet
struggle for Europe. US News and World Report,
December 23, 23-24.

Star Wars. 1983. National Review, April 15,
415-416.

Star Wars bargain. 1985. Nature 313
(no. 6003):516.

The Star Wars controversy: pro and con. 1985.
Congressional Digest 64 (March):69-96.

Star Wars: counting the cost. 1985. Commonweal,
March 22, 163-65.

The Star Wars debate: world press report. 1985.
World Press Review, March, 35-40.

Star Wars defense: fact or science fiction?
1985. American Legion, August, 14-15.

Star Wars defense; the technology is still in
its infancy, but the allure is clear: weapons
kill weapons instead of people. 1983.
Newsweek, April 4, 18-20.

Star Wars dissenters shout out. 1985. New
Scientist 107 (no. 1467):15.

The Star Wars gambit riles the experts. 1983.
Business Week, April 11, 30-31.

The Star Wars general gets a taste of hostile
fire. 1984. Business Week, May 14, 180-181.

Star Wars, MX and Geneva. 1985. New Statesman, March 29, 2-3.

Star Wars or star peace? 1985. Labor Today, November, 1.

Star Wars - Pentagon's defensive criticism turned. 1984. Nature 310 (no. 5976):353.

Star Wars poll; overwhelming response evokes passion and politics. Science Digest, January, 60.

Star Wars should be negotiable. 1985. Business Week, November 25, 152.

Star Wars test successful. 1984. Space World, October, 15-18.

Star Wars threat to ABM treaty. 1985. Nature 315 (no. 6014):1-2.

Star Wars unworkable. 1984. Nature 309 (no. 5965):196.

Star Wars whiz kids. 1984. Nation, February 11, 145.

Star Wars "will ruin all arms-control negotiations." 1985. US News and World Report, September 30, 27.

Stares, Paul B. 1983. Space and U.S. National Security. Journal of Strategic Studies 6 (December):31-48.

---. 1985. Space weapons and US strategy: origins and development. London: Croom Helm Ltd.

---. Spring 1985. U.S. and Soviet military space programs: a comparative assessment. Daedalus 114:127-72.

Stein, Jonathan B. 1984. From h-bomb to Star Wars: the politics of strategic decision making. San Diego, CA: Lexington Books.

----. 1985. Political push, technological pull. Bulletin of the Atomic Scientists 41 (June-July):40-41.

Stein, Kenneth J. 1984. Current technologies could aid in implementing Reagan's SDI policy. Aviation Week and Space Technology, December 10, 75-76.

Steinberg, Gerald M. 1985. Comparing technological risks in large scale national projects. Policy Sciences (Amsterdam) 18 (March):79-93.

Steinbreder, H. John. 1985. Pitching Star Wars. Fortune, November 25, 7-8.

Stengel, Richard. 1985. The great Star Wars p.r. war: kindergarten imagery obscures a vital and complex debate. Time, December 9, 31-32.

Stevens, Sayre. 1985. Ballistic missile defense in the Soviet Union. Current History, October, 313-320.

Stine, G. H. 1984. Star Wars. Sciences 24 (no. 4):2.

Stone, Marvin. 1985. Star Wars: pie in the sky? US News and World Report, February 25, 82.

----. 1985. When Soviets run scared. US News and World Report, March 18, 82.

Strategic Defense Initiative. 1984. Department of State Bulletin 84 (May):71-72.

The Strategic Defense Initiative. Summer 1984. Orbis 28:215-55.

The Strategic Defense Initiative; special issue. 1984. Arms Control Today 14 (July-August):whole issue.

Strategic Defense Initiative. 1985. Department of State Bulletin 85 (February):24.

The Strategic Defense Initiative. 1985.
Department of State Bulletin 85 (September):42-
47.

Strategic Defense Initiative: interview of Preside
Reagan, March 4, 1985. 1985. Weekly Compilation
of Presidential Documents 21 (March 18):276-82.

Strategic Defense Initiative to use Delta
launchers. 1985. Aviation Week and Space
Technology, July 29, 22.

Strategic Defense Office awards phase 2 contract.
1985. Aviation Week and Space Technology,
August 5, 25.

Strategists ponder Star Wars implications. 1986.
Laser Focus 22 (no. 1):52.

Strategy for peace: twenty-fifth annual US
foreign policy conference report, October 11-
13, 1984. Strategy for Peace Conference.
Muscatine, IA: Stanley Foundation.

Stubbing, Richard. 1985. Buildup or binge? The
defense program. Current, October, 29-40.

Stuttaford, Genevieve. 1984. Assured survival:
putting the Star Wars defense in prespective.
Publishers Weekly, September 21, 80-81.

Subrahmanyam, K. 1983. The Star Wars delusion:
some deeper implications of the new strategy.
World Press Review, June, 21-24.

Summers, H. G., Jr. 1986. Europe's Star Wars
worries; analysis: if Reagan's plan works, will
NATO's armies be at risk? US News and World
Report, January 20, 27-28.

Sweet, William. 1985. Riesenhuber favors cuts
for CERN, is cautious on SDI. Physics Today,
July, 69-70.

----. 1985. Star Wars petitions attract strong
support at some schools. Physics Today,
November, 95-96.

Swinbanks, D. 1985. Star Wars - United States pressure on Japan. Nature 314 (no. 6013):661.

Takase, Shoji. 1985. What Star Wars means to Japan. Japan Quarterly 32 (July-September):240-247.

Talbott, Strobe. 1984. The case against Star Wars weapons. Time, May 7, 81-82.

----. 1985. Wild card on the table; Star Wars complicates prospects for an arms-control agreement. Time, January 21, 30-31.

----. 1985. Upsetting the delicate balance; will defensive weapons undermine deterrence and spark a new arms race? Time, March 11, 14-17.

----. 1985. Holier-than-thou on Star Wars; the Soviets conveniently overlook their own efforts. Time, July 1, 26-27.

----. 1985. Maneuvering around square one; the only arms-control progress was a desire to look ahead. Time, December 2, 39.

----. 1986. Breakthrough or breakout? Time, January 20, 19.

Technology in space. Summer 1985. Journal of International Affairs 39:1-174.

Teitelbaum, Sheldon. 1985. Israel and Star Wars: the shape of things to come. New Outlook 28 (May/June):59-62.

Teller, Edward. 1984. Bringing Star Wars down to earth. Popular Mechanics, July, 84-89.

----. 1985. Science and technology in the Strategic Defense Initiative. Defense Science 2003+ 4 (April/May):17-24.

----. 1985. Interview. Meet the Press, July 8, 1-8.

----. 1985. Interview. "Go tell it on the mountain." Progressive, November, 10-12.

Teller, Edward, and Carl Sagan. 1985. Pro and con. Discover, September, 66-74.

Ten companies, teams win strategic defense studies. 1985. Aviation Week and Space Technology, January 7, 26.

Texas Center developing electromagnetic rail gun. 1985. Aviation Week and Space Technology, April 15, 70.

They get the money... but they don't pay taxes. 1985. Labor Today, November, 4-5.

Thomas, Evan. 1985. Once more to Geneva: the big question: will Star Wars be put on the bargaining table? Time, January 7, 64-65.

----. 1985. Bigger bucks for smarter bombs; weapons research gets carte blanche, and stirs controversy. Time, March 4, 21-22.

----. 1985. Setting the summit table; as the Soviet foreign minister arrives, Reagan holds the line on Star Wars. Time, September 30, 22-24.

----. 1985. A mix of hope and hokum; Gorbachev's arms-control plan could yield fruit, but beware the fine print. Time, October 14, 26-29.

Thomsen, Dietrich E. 1985. Strategic defense of X-ray initiative. Science News, December 14, 375.

Thompson, E. P. 1985. The real meaning of Star Wars. Nation, March 9, 257-260.

----. 1986. Star Wars: science fiction, fantasy, or serious probability? New York: Pantheon.

Tierney, John. 1984. Star Wars: the scientists strike back. Science'84, June, 14-15.

----. 1985. Why Star Wars is not like the Manhattan Project. Washington Monthly 17 (March):32-36.

Time interviews Gorbachev. 1985. Current Digest of Soviet Press, September 25, 15-22.

Tircuit, E. C. 1985. An anthology: rationale for a US ballistic missile defense (1969-1984). Student Report. Air Command and Staff College, Maxwell Air Force Base, AL. Report no. AD-A156781; ACSC-85-2715.

Tirman, John. 1983. Star Wars - from scenario to fact: destabilizing space. Nation, December 24, 661-64.

----. 1984. Walking out of Star Wars; Richard Garwin. Esquire, October, 110-116.

----, ed. 1984. The fallacy of Star Wars. New York: Random House.

Tolkunov, A. 1983. Pravda scores US plans for space-based defensive system. Space 24 (JPRS-84161), 75-77. Translated into English from Pravda (Moscow), May 10, 1983, 5. Arlington, VA: Joint Publications Research Service.

Toomay, J.C. 1984. VHSIC in midcourse. Aerospace America, June, 41-46.

----. Summer 1985. The case for ballistic missile defense. Daedalus 114:219-237.

Topping, John. Summer 1985. The legality of President Reagan's proposed space-based ballistic missile defense system. Georgia Journal of International and Comparative Law 14:329-356.

Towell, Pat. 1984. Reagan, critics square off on space weaponry: Pentagon cites Soviet moves. Congressional Quarterly Weekly Report 42 (April 14):837-840.

----. 1985. A summit outlook: arms control, Star Wars. Congressional Quarterly Weekly Report 43 (November 9):2278-2283.

Trevethan, L. 1985. On Star Wars. Bulletin of the Atomic Scientists 41 (August):61-62.

Trewhitt, Henry. 1985. Moscow's weak points - as
seen by Washington. US News and World Report,
November 4, 32.

----. 1985. Eyeing the stakes. US News and World
Report, November 18, 28-29.

----. 1985. Back to earth, summit foes face the
same old problems. US News and World Report,
December 9, 35.

Trimming nuclear arsenals - the Kremlin view. 1985.
US News and World Report, November 11, 33.

Tsipis, Kosta. 1984. Why Reagan's Star Wars plan
won't work. Playboy, June, 59-61.

----. 1985. Third generation nuclear weapons. In
World Armaments and Disarmament - SIPRI
Yearbook. Stockholm, Sweden: Stockholm
International Peace Research Institute.

Tucker, Jonathan B. 1984. The fallacy of laser
defense. Technology Review, April, 30.

Turner, Admiral Stanfield (U.S.N., ret.), former
director, Central Intelligence Agency. 1984.
Interview. Meet the Press, May 27, 1-9.

Two-billion-dollar limit proposed for SDI. 1985.
Aviation Week and Space Technology, January 28,
27.

Ulam, Adam, Jeane Kirkpatrick, Lucian Pye,
Sanford J. Ungar, and Walter Laquer. 1985.
Promises and pitfalls for U.S.; from Star Wars
to terrorism: five experts assess foreign policy.
US News and World Report, December 30,
48-51.

United States allies urged to participate in
antiballistic missile system. 1984. Aviation
Week and Space Technology, August 13, 169.

"Unk-unks" and "golden arches": the new lingo of
Star Wars. 1985. US News and World Report,
December 9, 50.

The urgency of the Geneva talks. 1985. Business Week, January 21, 130.

U.S. allies urged to participate in antiballistic missile system. 1984. Aviation Week and Space Technology, August 13, 169.

U.S.-British memorandum addresses missile defense technology transfer. 1986. Aviation Week and Space Technology, January 27, 20.

U.S. Congress. 1985. Fiscal year 1986 arms control impact statements: statements submitted to the Congress by the president. 99th Congress, 1st session.

U.S. Congress. House. Committee on Appropriations. Hearings on Department of Defense Appropriations for 1984, Part 8. 98th Congress, 1st session. March 23, April 19, May 3, 11, June 22, 1983.

———. Hearing on Department of Defense Appropriations for 1985. Part 1: Secretary of Defense and Chairman, Joint Chiefs of Staff. 98th Congress, 2nd session, March 1, 1984.

———. Hearings on Department of Defense Appropriations for 1985. Part 5. 98th Congress, 2nd session, March 29, April 5, 11, May 1, 9, 17, 1984.

———. Hearings on Department of Defense Appropriations for 1986, Part 1. 99th Congress, 1st session. February 27, April 17, 1985.

———. Hearings on Department of Defense Appropriations for 1986, Part 7. 99th Congress, 1st session. March 28, April 2, 18, 25, May 7, 23, 1985.

———. Committee on Armed Services. Hearings on Defense Department Authorization and Oversight. Part 5: Research, Development Test, and Evaluation. 98th Congress, 1st sesssion. March 1, 2, 9, 15, 17, 23, 24, April 12, 18-20, 22, 27, 28, 1983.

---. Hearing on H.R. 3073, People Protection
Act. 98th Congress, 1st session, November 10,
1983.

---. Hearings on Defense Department
Authorization and Oversight. Part 4: Research,
Development, Test, and Evaluation. 99th
Congress, 1st session. March 6-8, 19-20, 26-29,
April 2-4, 16, 1985.

---. Hearings on MX Missile and the Strategic
Defense Initiative--Their Implications on Arms
Control Negotiations. 99th Congress, 1st
session. February 27, 28, March 12-14, 20,
1985.

---. Committee on Foreign Affairs. Staff study
prepared by Robert T. Huber (et al) on U.S.-
Soviet Relations: New Promise or Peril. 99th
Congress, 1st session. June 1985.

---. Hearings on Arms Control in Outer Space.
98th Congress. 2nd session. November 10, 1983,
April 10, May 2, July 26, 1984.

---. Hearing on Arms Control and Disarmament
Agency Authorization for FY86-FY87. 99th Congress, 1st session. March 20, May 8, 14, 1985.

---. Hearings on Implications of the President's
Strategic Defense Initiative and Antisatellite
Weapons Policy. 99th Congress, 1st session.
April 24, May 1, 1985.

---. Hearings on Arms Control and the Atomic Bomb
40 Years Later. 99th Congress, 1st session.
May 13, 1985.

---. Report prepared by Mark M. Lowenthal on
Fundamentals of Nuclear Arms Control, Part IV:
Treaty Compliance and Nuclear Arms Control.
99th Congress, 1st session. June 19, 1985.

---. Report on the Fundamentals of Nuclear Arms
Control. Part III: Structuring Nuclear Arms
Control Proposals and Agreements. 99th Con-
gress, 1st session. September 12, 1985.

---. Committee on Science and Technology.
Report prepared by Marcia S. Smith. Space
Activities of the U.S., Soviet Union, and Other
Launching Countries/Organizations: 1957-1982.
97th Congress, 1st session, April 1983.

---. House Document 98-257, prepared by B. F.
Mangan and Marcia S. Smith. Should the U.S.
Federal Government Significantly Increase the
Exploration and/or Development of Space Beyond
the Earth's Mesosphere? 98th Congress, 2nd
session. 1984.

---. Senate. Committee on Appropriations.
Hearings on Department of Defense
Appropriations, FY86, Part 1: Budget Overview.
99th Congress, 1st session. February 21, March
5, 7, 26, June 25, 1985.

---. Committee on Armed Services. Hearings
on Department of Defense Authorization
for Appropriations for FY84. Part 5: Strategic
and Theater Nuclear Forces. 98th Congress, 1st
session. March 15, 18, 21, 23, April 7, 15,
May 2, 1983.

---. Hearing on Department of Energy FY84
National Defense Programs Authorization. 98th
Congress, 1st session. April 12, 1983.

---. Hearings on Department of Defense
Authorization for Appropriations for FY85.
Part 6: Strategic Defense Initiative.
98th Congress, 2nd session. March 8, 22, April
24, 1984.

---. Hearings on Department of Defense
Authorization for Appropriations for FY85.
Part 7: Strategic and Theater Nuclear Forces.
98th Congress, 2nd session. March 6, 9, 13, 15, 29,
April 12, 26, May 1, 4, 1984.

---. Hearing on Department of Energy FY85
National Security Programs Authorization. 98th
Congress, 2nd session. March 27, 1984.

---. Hearing on Department of Defense
Authorization for Appropriations for FY86.
Part 1: U.S. Military Posture. 99th Congress,
1st session. February 4, 1985.

---. Committee on Foreign Relations. Hearings
on Senate Resolution 43 and Senate Joint Resolution 28: Controlling Space Weapons. 98th
Congress, 1st session. April 14 and May 18,
1983.

---. Hearings on Strategic Defense and Anti-
satellite Weapons. 98th Congress, 2nd session.
April 25, 1984.

---. Unpublished staff paper prepared by Lawrence
J. Cavaiola and Bonita J. Pombey. Analysis of
the costs of the Administration's Strategic
Defense Initiative, 1985-89. 98th Congress,
2nd session. May 23, 1984.

U.S. Congressional Budget Office. 1984.
Analysis of the costs of the administration's
Strategic Defense Initiative, 1985-1989.
Washington, D.C.: U.S. Congressional Budget
Office.

U.S. Department of Defense. 1984, 1985, 1986.
Soviet military power. Washington, D.C.:
U.S. Government Printing Office.

---. 1984. The Strategic Defense Initiative
defensive technologies study. Washington,
D.C.: U.S. Government Printing Office, April.

---. 1985. Report to Congress on the Strategic
Defense Initiative. Washington, D.C.: U.S
Governement Printing Office.

U.S. Department of Defense and Department of
State. 1985. Soviet strategic defense
programs. Washington, D.C.: U.S. Government
Printing Office, October.

U.S. Department of State. 1985. Bureau of Public
Affairs. The ABM Treaty and the SDI Program.
Current Policy Paper no. 755. Washington,
D.C.: U.S. Government Printing Office, October.

---. 1985. The Strategic Defense Initiative.
Special Report no. 129. Washington, D.C.: U.S.
Government Printing Office, June.

U.S. Office of Technology Assessment. 1985.
Anti-satellite weapons, countermeasures, and
arms control. Washington, D.C.: U.S.
Government Printing Office, September.

---. 1985. Ballistic Missile Defense Technologies.
Washington, D.C.: U.S. Government Printing
Office, September.

U.S. pursues multilayered ballistic missile
defense. 1984. Aviation Week and Space
Technology, March 12, 31-36.

U.S.S.R. Ministry of Defense Staff. 1985. Star
Wars: delusions and dangers. USSR: Progress
Publications. Distributed by Four Continent
Book Corporation, New York.

U.S. to test ASAT device. 1985. Department of
State Bulletin 85 (October):46.

U.S. urged to negotiate treaty based upon
freedom of space. 1984. Aviation Week and
Space Technology, May 28, 118.

U.S.-U.S.S.R. negotiations on nuclear and space
arms. 1986. Department of State Bulletin 86
(January):40.

U.S. White House. 1985. The President's
Strategic Defense Initiative. Washington,
D.C.: U.S. Government Printing Office, January.

Valley, Bruce L. 1985. The ultimate defense.
United States Naval Institute Proceedings 111
(February):30-37.

Van Cleave, William. 1986. Fortress USSR.
Stanford, CA: Hoover Institution Press.

Van Tilborg, A. 1982. Towards real-time
decentralized operating systems for ballistic
missile defense (HICSS-15) 8215005. In
Proceedings Fifteenth Annual Hawaii
International Conference on System Science,

Honolulu, HA, January 6-8, 1982.   North Hollywood
CA: Western Periodicals Company.

Van Tilborg, A. M., and T. J. Jasinski. 1981.
Circumvention against logic upset in ballistic
missile defense multi-computer systems.   In
IEEE Transactions on Nuclear Science NS-28,
December 1981.   New York: Institute of Electrical
and Electronics Engineers, pp. 4384-4388.

Vereshchetin, V.S. 1983.   Against arbitrary
interpretation of some important provisions of
international space law.   In Colloquium on the
Law of Outer Space, 25th, Paris, France,
September 27-October 2, 1982, Proceedings (A84-
17026 05-84).   New York: American Institute of
Aeronautics and Astronautics, pp. 153-158.
Report no. IAF PAPER 82-IISL-34.

Vibration damping studied for weapons in space.
1984.   Aviation Week and Space Technology, July
2, 54-56.

Vigilante, Richard. 1985.   A down-to-earth guide
to Star Wars.   Reason 17 (September):35-41.

Vogt, D. A., and T. N. Mervosh. 1983.   Space arms
control - a difficult process.   In Colloquium
on the Law of Outer Space, 25th, Paris, France,
September 27-October 2, 1982, Proceedings (A84-
17026 05-84).   New York: American Institute of
Aeronautics and Astronautics, pp. 167-169.

von Hippel, Frank. 1985.   Attacks on Star Wars
critics a diversion.   Bulletin of the Atomic
Scientists 41 (April):8-10.

Vukadinovic, Radovan. 1985.   The Soviet Union and
space defense.   Report on International Affairs
36 (August 5-20):20-22.

The vulnerable frontier. 1985.   National Review,
September 20, 16-17.

Walczak, Lee. 1984.   Congress will aim at weapons
in space.   Business Week, January 9, 125.

Waldrop, M. Mitchell. 1983. A PAC for star wars.
Science, October 21, 304-5.

Walgate, R. 1985. Star Wars - France rallies
European forces. Nature 314 (no. 6013):660-61.

----. 1985. Star Wars - Franco-German accord.
Nature 314 (no. 6016):171.

Waller, Larry. 1985. Are hard times ahead for
defense industry? Electronics, October 21, 23.

----. 1985. The big bucks in SDI are getting
smaller; some high-risk, high-payoff projects
are in jeopardy. Electronics, October 21, 45-
46.

Wallop, Malcolm, and George E. Brown, Jr. 1985.
Should Congress approve the president's
Strategic Defense Initiative? American Legion,
May, 11.

Walmsley, Ann. 1983. Developing space weaponry.
World Press Review, July, 55.

Watson, Russell. 1985. Tough talks on Star Wars.
Newsweek, September 30, 38-30.

----. 1985. Showdown in Geneva; Reagan and
Gorbachev meet. Newsweek, November 25, 32-35.

----. 1985. Behind closed doors; in five hours of
one-on-one conversation, Reagan and Gorbachev
take each other's measure. Newsweek, December
2, 28-32.

----. 1986. Getting to zero; Gorbachev springs a
new plan on arms. Newsweek, January 27, 30-31.

Wautelet, M. 1984. Science versus fiction: laser
weapons. European Journal of Physics (Great
Britain) 5: 184-189.

Weeks, Albert. 1986. Trying to "look innocent"
while seeking highest ground. Defense Science
2003+ 4 (December/January):22-27.

Weerakon, Gamini. 1985. The final trump? The stakes: arms-control concessions. World Press Review, March, 39-40.

Weigel, Jack W. 1984. The fallacy of Star Wars: based on studies conducted by the Union of Concerned Scientists. Library Journal, November 15, 2141.

Weinberg, Alvin M., and Jack N. Barkenbus. Spring 1984. Stabilizing Star Wars. Foreign Policy (no. 54):164-170.

Weinberger, Caspar. 1985. Interview. "There isn't any way" Reagan will trade Star Wars. US News and World Report, November 25, 34-35.

---. 1985. U.S. Defense Strategy. Foreign Affairs 64: 675-697.

Wellborn, Stanley N. 1985. Sons of Star Wars: fallout of a huge project. US News and World Report, December 9, 48-50.

Welling, Kathryn M. 1983. Playing Star Wars: Fred Kittler picks his favorite high-tech defense stocks. Barrons, August 1, 6-8.

Westway and Star Wars. 1985. National Review, March 22, 17.

What Americans expect from summit. 1985. US News and World Report, November 18, 28-29.

What worries Soviets; U.S. about an arms pact. 1985. US News and World Report, November 11, 33-34.

Whence the threat to peace. 1984. USSR: Military Publishing House. Distributed by the Soviet Embassy, Washington, D.C.

Whelan, C.R. 1985. Developing the technology for the SDI Battle Management/C/sup 3/ system. Signal 39 (July):44-46.

Whitaker, Mark. 1985. What's next for Star Wars; diplomacy is now in a race against technology. Newsweek, December 2, 45-47.

Who is serious about arms control? 1985. New
Republic, October 21, 10-12.

Wieseltier, Leon. 1985. Nuclear idealism,
nuclear realism: what's really wrong with Star
Wars. New Republic, March 11, 20-23.

Wilkinson, John. Summer 1985. Foreign
perspectives on the SDI. Daedalus 114:297-
313.

Wilson, Robert R. 1985. What should APS (American
Physical Society) be doing about SDI? Physics
Today, August, 9-10.

Wirick, Gregory. 1984. Reagan's space wars. The
Canadian Forum, April, 10-12.

Wolfe, Alexander. 1985. Star Wars is the force
driving weapons research. ElectronicsWeek,
May 13, 28-30.

---. 1985. Optical computing is beginning to
take on the glow of reality. ElectronicsWeek,
June 10, 24-26.

Wood, Chris, Hilary Mackenzie, Ken MacQueen,
Michael Rose, David Todd, and Jane O'Hara.
1985. The debate over Star Wars. Macleans,
August 12, 10-11.

Working Group of the Committee of Soviet
Scientists for Peace Against Nuclear Threat.
1986. Consequences of creating a space-based
anti-missile system using directed-energy weapons.
Defense Science 2003+ 4 (December/January):47.

Workshop on Arms Control in Space. 1984. Office
of Technology Assessment, Washington, D.C.
Workshop held in Washington, D.C., January 30-
31, 1984. Report no. LC-84-601064.

World armaments and disarmament: SIPRI yearbook,
1985. Stockholm International Peace Research
Institute (SIPRI), Almqvist, Stockholm. London:
Taylor and Francis.

Wright, J. 1986. Uncertainty and the Strategic Defense Initiative. Nature 319 (no. 6051):275-279.

Wulf, N. Spring-Fall 1983. Arms control--outer space. Journal of Space Law 11:67-72.

X-ray laser and secrecy. 1986. Bulletin of the Atomic Scientists 42 (January):2.

Xu, Z., and F. Lusheng. 1981. Defense against space weapons. Air Force Systems Command, Wright-Patterson Air Force Base, OH. Foreign Technology Division. Translated into English from Hangkong Zhishi (China), December 1981, 8-9. Report no. AD-A126159; FTD-ID(RS)T-1384-82.

Yonas, Gerold. 1984. Physics and technology requirements of the Strategic Defense Initiative. In Conference Record of the 1984 IEEE International Conference on Plasma Science 53. May 14-16, 1984. St. Louis, Mo. New York: Institute of Electrical and Electronics Engineers.

---. Spring 1985. The Strategic Defense Initiative. Daedalus 114:73-90.

---. 1985. Strategic Defense Initiative. Paper presented at the 1985 American Association for the Advancement of Science Annual Meeting 8520021, Los Angeles, CA, May 26-31, 1985.

---. 1985. Strategic Defense Initiative: the politics and science of weapons in space. Physics Today, June, 24-32.

Yonas, Gerold, and Hans Bethe. 1985. Can Star Wars make us safe? Science Digest, September, 30-38.

York, Herbert F. Spring 1985. Nuclear deterrence and the military uses of space. Daedalus 114:17-31.

Yost, David S. Fall 1984. European anxieties about ballistic missile defense. Washington Quarterly 7:112-129.

---. Summer 1985. Soviet ballistic missile defense and NATO. Orbis 29:281-292.

Young, Alwyn. Winter 1984. Ballistic missile defense: capabilities and constraints. Fletcher Forum 8:147-175.

Zapping back: a panel shoots down Star Wars. 1984. Time, April 2, 18.

Zhuang, Q. 1984. PRC journal discusses Star Wars space program. Science and Technology (JPRS-CST-84-039), December, 1-8. Translated into English from Shijie Zhishi (China), October 1, 1984, 7-9. Arlington, VA: Joint Publications Research Service.

---. 1985. Behind the drive: military, political, and economic implications. World Press Review, March, 38-39.

Ziska, R.F. 1984. High energy lasers: a primer on directed-energy weapons for space use. M.S. thesis. Naval Postgraduate School, Monterey, CA. Report no. AD-A151279.

Zraket, Charles A. Spring 1985. Strategic defense: a systems perspective. Daedalus 114:109-123.

Zuckerman, Mortimer B. 1985. The central issue. US News and World Report, November 18, 92-93.

Appendix A:
Documents and Treaties
Related to the SDI
and Arms Control

THE CONCLUSION OF PRESIDENT REAGAN'S SPEECH
ON DEFENSE SPENDING AND DEFENSE TECHNOLOGY

Now, thus far tonight I've shared with
you my thoughts on the problems of national
security we must face together. My predecessors
in the Oval Office have appeared before you on
other occasions to describe the threat posed by
Soviet power and have proposed steps to address
that threat. But since the advent of nuclear
weapons, those steps have been increasingly the
promise of retaliation.

This approach to stability through
offensive threat has worked. We and our allies
have succeeded in preventing nuclear war for more
than three decades. In recent months, however,
my advisors, including in particular the Joint
Chiefs of Staff, have underscored the necessity
to break out of a future that relies solely on
offensive retaliation for our security.

Over the course of these discussions,
I've become more and more deeply convinced that
the human spirit must be capable of rising above
dealing with other nations and human beings by
threatening their existence. Feeling this way, I
believe we must thoroughly examine every
opportunity for reducing tensions and for
introducing greater stability into the strategic
calculus on both sides.

One of the most important contributions
we can make is, of course, to lower the level of
all arms, and particularly nuclear arms. We're

engaged right now in several negotiations with the Soviet Union to bring about a mutual reduction of weapons. I will report to you a week from tomorrow my thoughts on that score. But let me just say, I'm totally committed to this course.

If the Soviet Union will join with us in our effort to achieve major arms reduction, we will have succeeded in stabilizing the nuclear balance. Nevertheless, it will still be necessary to rely on the specter of retaliation, on mutual threat. And that's sad commentary on the human condition. Wouldn't it be better to save lives than to avenge them? Are we not capable of demonstrating our peaceful intentions by applying all our abilities and our ingenuity to achieving a truly lasting stability? I think we are. Indeed, we must.

After careful consultation with my advisers, including the Joint Chiefs of Staff, I believe there is a way. Let me share with you a vision of the future which offers hope. It is that we embark on a program to counter the awesome Soviet missile threat with measures that are defensive. Let us turn to the very strengths in technology that spawned our great industrial base and that have given us the quality of life we enjoy today.

What if free people could live secure in the knowledge that their security did not rest upon the threat of instant U.S. retaliation to deter a Soviet attack, that we could intercept and destroy strategic ballistic missiles before they reached our own soil or that of our allies?

I know this is a formidable, technical task, one that may not be accomplished before the end of this century. Yet, current technology has attained a level of sophistication where it's reasonable for us to begin this effort. It will take years, probably decades of effort on many fronts. There will be failures and setbacks, just as there will be successes and breakthroughs. And as we proceed, we must remain constant in preserving the nuclear deterrent and maintaining a solid capability for flexible response. But isn't it worth every investment necessary to free the world from the threat of nuclear war? We know it is.

In the meantime, we will continue to pursue real reductions in nuclear arms, negotiating from a position of strength that can be ensured only by modernizing our strategic forces. At the same time, we must take steps to reduce the risk of conventional conflict escalating to nuclear war by improving our non-nuclear capabilities.

America does possess--now--technologies to attain very significant improvements in the effectiveness of our conventional, non-nuclear forces. Proceeding boldly with these new technologies, we can significantly reduce any incentive that the Soviet Union may have to threaten attack against the United States or its allies.

As we pursue our goal of defensive technologies, we recognize that our allies rely upon our strategic offensive power to deter attacks against them. Their vital interests and ours are inextricably linked. Their safety and ours are one. And no change in technology can or will alter that reality. We must and shall continue to honor our commitments.

I clearly recognize that defensive systems have limitations and raise certain problems and ambiguities. If paired with offensive systems, they can be viewed as fostering an aggressive policy, and no one wants that. But with these considerations firmly in mind, I call upon the scientific community in our country, those who gave us nuclear weapons, to turn their great talents now to the cause of mankind and world peace, to give us the means of rendering these nuclear weapons impotent and obsolete.

Tonight, consistent with our obligations of the ABM treaty and recognizing the need for closer consultation with our allies, I'm taking an important first step. I am directing a comprehensive and intensive effort to define a long-term research and development program to begin to achieve our ultimate goal of eliminating the threat posed by strategic nuclear missiles. This could pave the way for arms control measures to eliminate the weapons themselves. We seek neither military superiority nor political advantage. Our only purpose--one all people share--is to search for ways to reduce the danger of nuclear war.

My fellow Americans, tonight we're launching an effort which holds the promise of changing the course of human history. There will be risks, and results take time. But I believe we can do it. As we cross this threshold, I ask for your prayers and your support. Thank you, good night, and God bless you.

TREATY BANNING NUCLEAR WEAPON TESTS IN THE ATMOSPHERE, IN OUTER SPACE AND UNDER WATER

Signed at Moscow August 5, 1963. Ratification advised by U.S. Senate September 24, 1963. Ratified by U.S. President October 7, 1963. U.S. ratification deposited at Washington, London, and Moscow October 10, 1963. Proclaimed by U.S. President October 10, 1963. Entered into force October 10, 1963.

The Governments of the United States of America, the United Kingdom of Great Britain and Northern Ireland, and the Union of Soviet Socialist Republics, hereinafter referred to as the "Original Parties,"

Proclaiming as their principal aim the speediest possible achievement of an agreement on general and complete disarmament under strict international control in accordance with the objectives of the United Nations which would put an end to the armaments race and eliminate the incentive to the production and testing of all kinds of weapons, including nuclear weapons,

Seeking to achieve the discontinuance of all test explosions of nuclear weapons for all time, determined to continue negotiations to this end, and desiring to put an end to the contamination of man's environment by radio-active substances,

Have agreed as follows:

Article I

1. Each of the Parties to this Treaty undertakes to prohibit, to prevent, and not to carry out any nuclear weapon test explosion, or any other nuclear explosion, at any place under its jurisdiction or control:

(a) in the atmosphere; beyond its limits, including outer space; or under water, including territorial waters or high seas; or

(b) in any other environment if such explosion causes radioactive debris to be present outside the territorial limits of the State under whose jurisdiction or control such explosion is conducted. It is understood in this connection that the provisions of this subparagraph are without prejudice to the conclusion of a treaty resulting in the permanent banning of all nuclear test explosions, including all such explosions underground, the conclusion of which, as the Parties have stated in the Preamble to this Treaty, they seek to achieve.

2. Each of the Parties to this Treaty undertakes furthermore to refrain from causing, encouraging, or in any way participating in, the carrying out of any nuclear weapon test explosion, or any other nuclear explosion, anywhere which would take place in any of the environments described, or have the effect referred to, in paragraph 1 of this Article.

Article II

1. Any party may propose amendments to this Treaty. The text of any proposed amendment shall be submitted to the Depositary Governments which shall circulate it to all Parties to this Treaty. Thereafter, if requested to do so by one-third or more of the Parties, the Depositary Governments shall convene a conference, to which they shall invite all the Parties, to consider such amendment.

2. Any amendment to this Treaty must be approved by a majority of the votes of all the Parties to this Treaty, including the votes of all of the Original Parties. The amendment shall

enter into force for all Parties upon the deposit of instruments of ratification by a majority of all the Parties, including the instruments of ratification of all of the Original Parties.

Article III

1. This Treaty shall be open to all States for signature. Any State which does not sign this Treaty before its entry into force in accordance with paragraph 3 of this Article may accede to it at any time.
2. This Treaty shall be subject to ratification by signatory States. Instruments of ratification and instruments of accession shall be deposited with the Governments of the Original Parties--the United States of America, the United Kingdom of Great Britain and Northern Ireland, and the Union of Soviet Socialist Republics-- which are hereby designated the Depositary Governments.
3. This Treaty shall enter into force after its ratification by all the Original Parties and the deposit of their instruments of ratification.
4. For States whose instruments of ratification or accession are deposited subsequent to the entry into force of this Treaty, it shall enter into force on the date of the deposit of their instruments of ratification or accession.
5. The Depositary Governments shall promptly inform all signatory and acceding States of the date of each signature, the date of deposit of each instrument of ratification of and accession to this Treaty, the date of its entry into force, and the date of receipt of any requests for conferences or other notices.
6. This Treaty shall be registered by the Depositary Governments pursuant to Article 102 of the Charter of the United Nations.

Article IV

This Treaty shall be of unlimited duration. Each Party shall in exercising its national sovereignty have the right to withdraw from the Treaty if it decides that extraordinary events, related to the subject matter of this Treaty, have jeopardized the supreme interests of its country. It shall give notice of such withdrawal to all other Parties to the Treaty three months in advance.

Article V

This Treaty, of which the English and Russian texts are equally authentic, shall be deposited in the archives of the Depositary Governments. Duly certified copies of this Treaty shall be transmitted by the Depositary Governments to the Governments of the signatory and acceding States.

IN WITNESS WHEREOF the undersigned, duly authorized, have signed this Treaty.

DONE in triplicate at the city of Moscow the fifth day of August, one thousand nine hundred and sixty-three.

For the Government of the United States of America;

For the Government of the United Kingdom of Great Britain and Northern Ireland;

For the Government of the Union of Soviet Socialist Republics

DEAN RUSK   HOME   A. GROMYKO

TREATY ON PRINCIPLES GOVERNING THE ACTIVITIES OF STATES IN THE EXPLORATION AND USE OF OUTER SPACE, INCLUDING THE MOON AND OTHER CELESTIAL BODIES

Signed at Washington, London, Moscow, January 27, 1967. Ratification advised by U.S. Senate April

25, 1967. Ratified by U.S. President May 24, 1967. U.S. ratification deposited at Washington, London, and Moscow, October 10, 1967. Proclaimed by U.S. President October 10, 1967. Entered into force October 10, 1967.

The State Parties to the Treaty,
    Inspired by the great prospects opening up before mankind as a result of man's entry into outer space,
    Recognizing the common interest of all mankind in the progress of the exploration and use of outer space for peaceful purposes,
    Believing that the exploration and use of outer space should be carried on for the benefit of all peoples irrespective of the degree of their economic or scientific development,
    Desiring to contribute to broad international co-operation in the scientific as well as the legal aspects of the exploration and use of outer space for peaceful purposes,
    Believing that such co-operation will contribute to the development of mutual understanding and to the strengthening of friendly relations between States and peoples,
    Recalling resolution 1962 (XVIII), entitled "Declaration of Legal Principles Governing the Activities of States in the Exploration and Use of Outer Space," which was Adopted unanimously by the United Nations General Assembly on 13 December 1963,
    Recalling resolution 1884 (XVIII), calling upon States to refrain from placing in orbit around the Earth any objects carrying nuclear weapons or any other kinds of weapons of mass destruction or from installing such weapons on celestial bodies, which was adopted unanimously by the United Nations General Assembly on 17 October 1963,
    Taking account of United Nations General Assembly resolution 110 (II) of 3 November 1947, which condemned propaganda designed or likely to provoke or encourage any threat to the peace, breach of the peace or act of aggression, and considering that the aforementioned resolution is applicable to outer space,

Convinced that a Treaty on Principles Governing the Activities of States in the Exploration and Use of Outer Space, including the Moon and Other Celestial Bodies, will further the Purposes and Principles of the Charter of the United Nations,
Have agreed on the following:

Article I

The exploration and use of outer space, including the moon and other celestial bodies, shall be carried out for the benefit and in the interests of all countries, irrespective of their degree of economic or scientific development, and shall be the province of all mankind.

Outer space, including the moon and other celestial bodies, shall be free for exploration and use by all States without discrimination of any kind, on a basis of equality and in accordance with international law, and there shall be free access to all areas of celestial bodies.

There shall be freedom of scientific investigation in outer space, including the moon and other celestial bodies, and States shall facilitate and encourage international cooperation in such investigation.

Article II

Outer space, including the moon and other celestial bodies, is not subject to national appropriation by claim of sovereignty, by means of use or occupation, or by any other means.

Article III

States Parties to the Treaty shall carry on activities in the exploration and use of outer space, including the moon and other celestial bodies, in accordance with international law, including the Charter of the United Nations, in the interest of maintaining international peace and security and promoting international co-operation and understanding.

Article IV

States Parties to the Treaty undertake not to place in orbit around the Earth any objects carrying nuclear weapons or any other kinds of weapons of mass destruction, install such weapons on celestial bodies, or station such weapons in outer space in any other manner.

The moon and other celestial bodies shall be used by all States Parties to the Treaty exclusively for peaceful purposes. The establishment of military bases, installations and fortifications, the testing of any type of weapons and the conduct of military maneuvers on celestial bodies shall be forbidden. The use of military personnel for scientific research or for any other peaceful purposes shall not be prohibited. The use of any equipment or facility necessary for peaceful exploration of the moon and other celestial bodies shall also not be prohibited.

Article V

States Parties to the Treaty shall regard astronauts as envoys of mankind in outer space and shall render to them all possible assistance in the event of accident, distress, or emergency landing on the territory of another State Party or on the high seas. When astronauts make such a landing, they shall be safely and promptly returned to the State of registry of their space vehicle.

In carrying on activities in outer space and on celestial bodies, the astronauts of one State Party shall render all possible assistance to the astronauts of other States Parties.

States Parties to the Treaty shall immediately inform the other States Parties to the Treaty or the Secretary-General of the United Nations of any phenomena they discover in outer space, including the moon and other celestial bodies, which could constitute a danger to the life or health of astronauts.

Article VI

States Parties to the Treaty shall bear international responsibility for national activities in outer space, including the moon and other celestial bodies, whether such activities are carried on by governmental agencies or by non-governmental entities, and for assuring that national activities are carried out in conformity with the provisions set forth in the present Treaty. The activities of non-governmental entities in outer space, including the moon and other celestial bodies, shall require authorization and continuing supervision by the appropriate State Party to the Treaty. When activities are carried on in outer space, including the moon and other celestial bodies, by an international organization, responsibility for compliance with this Treaty shall be borne both by the international organization and by the States Parties to the Treaty participating in such organization.

Article VII

Each State Party to the Treaty that launches or procures the launching of an object into outer space, including the moon and other celestial bodies, and each State Party from whose territory or facility an object is launched, is internationally liable for damage to another State Party to the Treaty or to its natural or juridical persons by such object or its component parts on the Earth, in air space or in outer space, including the moon and other celestial bodies.

Article VIII

A State Party to the Treaty on whose registry an object launched into outer space is carried shall retain jurisdiction and control over such object, and over any personnel thereof, while in outer space or on a celestial body. Ownership of objects launched into outer space,

including objects landed or constructed on a
celestial body, and of their component parts, is
not affected by their presence in outer space or
on a celestial body or by their return to the
Earth. Such objects or component parts found
beyond the limits of the State Party to the
Treaty on whose registry they are carried shall
be returned to that State Party, which shall,
upon request, furnish identifying data prior to
their return.

Article IX

In the exploration and use of outer
space, including the moon and other celestial
bodies, States Parties to the Treaty shall be
guided by the principle of co-operation and
mutual assistance and shall conduct all their
activities in outer space, including the moon and
other celestial bodies, with due regard to the
corresponding interests of all other States
Parties to the Treaty. States Parties to the
Treaty shall pursue studies of outer space,
including the moon and other celestial bodies,
and conduct exploration of them so as to avoid
their harmful contamination and also adverse
changes in the environment of the Earth resulting
from the introduction of extra-terrestrial matter
and, where necessary, shall adopt appropriate
measures for this purpose. If a State Party to
the Treaty has reason to believe that an activity
or experiment planned by it or its nationals in
outer space, including the moon and other
celestial bodies, would cause potentially harmful
interference with activities of State Parties in
the peaceful exploration and use of outer space,
including the moon and other celestial bodies, it
shall undertake appropriate international
consultations before proceeding with any such
activity or experiment. A State Party to the
Treaty which has reason to believe that an
activity or experiment planned by another State
Party in outer space, including the moon and
other celestial bodies, would cause potentially
harmful interference with activities in the
peaceful exploration and use of outer space,

including the moon and other celestial bodies, may request consultation concerning the activity or experiment.

Article X

In order to promote international cooperation in the exploration and use of outer space, including the moon and other celestial bodies, in conformity with the purposes of this Treaty, the States Parties to the Treaty shall consider on a basis of equality any requests by other States Parties to the Treaty to be afforded an opportunity to observe the flight of space objects launched by those States.

The nature of such an opportunity for observation and the conditions under which it could be afforded shall be determined by agreement between the States concerned.

Article XI

In order to promote international cooperation in the peaceful exploration and use of outer space, States Parties to the Treaty conducting activities in outer space, including the moon and other celestial bodies, agree to inform the Secretary General of the United Nations as well as the public and the international scientific community, to the greatest extent feasible and practicable, of the nature, conduct, locations and results of such activities. On receiving the said information, the Secretary General of the United Nations should be prepared to disseminate it immediately and effectively.

Article XII

All stations, installations, equipment and space vehicles on the moon and other celestial bodies shall be open to representatives of other States Parties to the Treaty on a basis of reciprocity. Such representatives shall give reasonable advance notice of a projected visit, in order that appropriate consultations may be held and that maximum precautions may be taken to assure safety and to avoid interference with normal operations in the facility to be visited.

Article XIII

The provisions of this Treaty shall apply to the activities of States Parties to the Treaty in the exploration and use of outer space, including the moon and other celestial bodies, whether such activities are carried on by a single State Party to the Treaty or jointly with other States, including cases where they are carried on within the framework of international inter-governmental organizations.

Any practical questions arising in connection with activities carried on by international inter-governmental organizations in the exploration and use of outer space, including the moon and other celestial bodies, shall be resolved by the States Parties to the Treaty either with the appropriate international organization or with one or more States members of that international organization, which are Parties to this Treaty.

Article XIV

1. This Treaty shall be open to all States for signature. Any State which does not sign this Treaty before its entry into force in accordance with paragraph 3 of this article may accede to it at any time.
2. This Treaty shall be subject to ratification by signatory States. Instruments of ratification and instruments of accession shall be deposited with the Governments of the United States of America, the United Kingdom of Great Britain and Northern Ireland and the Union of Soviet Socialist Republics, which are hereby designated the Depositary Governments.
3. This Treaty shall enter into force upon the deposit of instruments of ratification

by five Governments including the Governments designated as Depositary Governments under this Treaty.

4. For States whose instruments of ratification or accession are deposited subsequent to the entry into force of this Treaty, it shall enter into force on the date of deposit of their instruments of ratification or accession.

5. The Depositary Governments shall promptly inform all signatory and acceding States of the date of each signature, the date of deposit of each instrument of ratification of an accession to this Treaty, the date of its entry into force and other notices.

6. This Treaty shall be registered by the Depositary Governments pursuant to Article 102 of the Charter of the United Nations.

Article XV

Any State Party to the Treaty may propose amendments to this Treaty. Amendments shall enter into force for each State Party to the Treaty accepting the amendments upon their acceptance by a majority of the State Parties to the Treaty and thereafter for each remaining State Party to the Treaty on the date of acceptance by it.

Article XVI

Any State Party to the Treaty may give notice of its withdrawal from the Treaty one year after its entry into force by written notification to the Depositary Governments. Such withdrawal shall take effect one year from the date of receipt of this notification.

Article XVII

This Treaty, of which the English, Russian, French, Spanish and Chinese texts are equally authentic, shall be deposited in the

archives of the Depositary Governments. Duly
certified copies of this Treaty shall be
transmitted by the Depositary Governments to the
Governments of the signatory and acceding States.

IN WITNESS WHEREOF the undersigned, duly
authorized, have signed this Treaty.

DONE in triplicate, at the cities of Washington,
London and Moscow, this twenty-seventh day of
January one thousand nine hundred sixty seven

TREATY ON THE NON-PROLIFERATION
OF NUCLEAR WEAPONS

Signed at Washington, London, and Moscow
July 1, 1968. Ratification advised by U.S. Senate
March 13, 1969. Ratified by U.S. President
November 24, 1969. U.S. ratification deposited
at Washington, London, and Moscow March 5, 1970
Proclaimed by U.S. President March 5, 1970
Entered into force March 5, 1970.

The States concluding this Treaty,
hereinafter referred to as the "Parties to the
Treaty",
Considering the devastation that would be
visited upon all mankind by a nuclear war and the
consequent need to make every effort to avert the
danger of such a war and to take measures to
safeguard the security of peoples,
Believing that the proliferation of
nuclear weapons would seriously enhance the
danger of nuclear war,
In conformity with resolutions of the
United Nations General Assembly calling for the
conclusion of an agreement on the prevention of
wider dissemination of nuclear weapons,
Undertaking to cooperate in facilitating
the application of international Atomic Energy
Agency safeguards on peaceful nuclear activities,
Expressing their support for research,

development and other efforts to further the
application, within the framework of the
International Atomic Energy Agency safeguards
system, of the principle of safeguarding
effectively the flow of source and special
fissionable materials by use of instruments and
other techniques at certain strategic points,
Affirming the principle that the benefits
of peaceful applications of nuclear technology,
including any technological by-products which may
be derived by nuclear-weapon States from the
development of nuclear explosive devices, should
be available for peaceful purposes to all Parties
of the Treaty, whether nuclear-weapon or non-
nuclear weapon States,
Convinced that, in furtherance of this
principle, all Parties to the Treaty are entitled
to participate in the fullest possible exchange
of scientific information for, and to contribute
alone or in cooperation with other States to, the
further development of the applications of atomic
energy for peaceful purposes,
Declaring their intention to achieve at
the earliest possible date the cessation of the
nuclear arms race and to undertake effective
measures in the direction of nuclear disarmament,
Urging the cooperation of all States in
the attainment of this objective,
Recalling the determination expressed by
the Parties to the 1963 Treaty banning nuclear
weapon tests in the atmosphere, in outer space
and underwater in its Preamble to seek to achieve
the discontinuance of all test explosions of
nuclear weapons for all time and to continue
negotiations to this end,
Desiring to further the easing of
international tension and the strengthening of
trust between States in order to facilitate the
cessation of the manufacture of nuclear weapons,
the liquidation of all their existing stockpiles,
and the elimination from national arsenals of
nuclear weapons and the means of their delivery
pursuant to a treaty on general and complete
disarmament under strict and effective
international control,
Recalling that, in accordance with the
Charter of the United Nations, States must

refrain in their international relations from the
threat or use of force against the territorial
integrity or political independence of any State,
or in any other manner inconsistent with the
Purposes of the United Nations, and that the
establishment and maintenance of international
peace and security are to be promoted with the
least diversion for armaments of the world's
human and economic resources,

Have agreed as follows:

Article I

Each nuclear-weapon State Party to the
Treaty undertakes not to transfer to any
recipient whatsoever nuclear weapons or other
nuclear explosive devices or control over such
weapons or explosive devices directly, or
indirectly; and not in any way to assist,
encourage, or induce any non-nuclear weapon State
to manufacture or otherwise acquire nuclear
weapons or other nuclear explosive devices, or
control over such weapons or explosive devices.

Article II

Each non-nuclear-weapon State Party to
the Treaty undertakes not to receive the transfer
from any transferor whatsoever of nuclear weapons
or other nuclear explosive devices or of control
over such weapons or explosive devices directly,
or indirectly, not to manufacture or otherwise
acquire nuclear weapons or other nuclear
explosive devices; and not to seek or receive any
assistance in the manufacture of nuclear weapons
or other nuclear explosive devices.

Article III

1. Each non-nuclear weapon State
Party to the Treaty undertakes to accept
safeguards, as set forth in an agreement to be
negotiated and concluded with the International
Atomic Energy Agency in accordance with the
Statute of the International Atomic Energy Agency

and the Agency's safeguards system, for the exclusive purpose of verification of the fulfillment of its obligations assumed under this Treaty with a view to preventing diversion of nuclear energy from peaceful uses to nuclear weapons or other nuclear explosive devices. Procedures for the safeguards required by this article shall be followed with respect to source or special fissionable material whether it is being produced, processed or used in any principal nuclear facility or is outside any such facility. The safeguards required by this article shall be applied to all source or special fissionable material in all peaceful nuclear activities within the territory of such State, under its jurisdiction, or carried out under its control anywhere.

2.   Each State Party to the Treaty undertakes not to provide: (a) source or special fissionable material, or (b) equipment or material especially designed or prepared for the processing, use or production of special fissionable material, to any non-nuclear-weapon State for peaceful purposes, unless the source or special fissionable material shall be subject to the safeguards required by this article.

3.   The safeguards required by this article shall be implemented in a manner designed to comply with article IV of this Treaty, and to avoid hampering the economic or technological development of the Parties or international cooperation in the field of peaceful nuclear activities, including the international exchange of nuclear material and equipment for the processing, use or production of nuclear material for peaceful purposes in accordance with the provisions of this article and the principle of safeguarding set forth in the Preamble of the Treaty.

4.   Non-nuclear-weapon States Party to the Treaty shall conclude agreements with the International Atomic Energy Agency to meet the requirements of this article either individually or together with other States in accordance with the Statute of the International Atomic Energy Agency. Negotiation of such agreements shall commence within 180 days from the original entry

into force of this Treaty. For States depositing their instruments of ratification or accession after the 180-day period, negotiation of such agreements shall commence not later than the date of such deposit. Such agreements shall enter into force not later than eighteen months after the date of initiation of negotiations.

Article IV

1.   Nothing in this Treaty shall be interpreted as affecting the inalienable right of all the Parties to the Treaty to develop research, production and use of nuclear energy for peaceful purposes without discrimination and in conformity with articles I and II of this Treaty.

2.   All the Parties to the Treaty undertake to facilitate, and have the right to participate in, the fullest possible exchange of equipment, materials and scientific and technological information for the peaceful uses of nuclear energy. Parties to the Treaty in a position to do so shall also cooperate in contributing alone or together with other States or international organizations to the further development of the applications of nuclear energy for peaceful purposes, especially in the territories of non-nuclear-weapon States Party to the Treaty, with due consideration for the needs of the developing areas of the world.

Article V

Each party to the Treaty undertakes to take appropriate measures to ensure that, in accordance with this Treaty, under appropriate international observation and through appropriate international procedures, potential benefits from any peaceful applications of nuclear explosions will be made available to non-nuclear-weapon States Party to the Treaty on a nondiscriminatory basis and that the charge to such Parties for the explosive devices used will be as low as possible and exclude any charge for research and

development. Non-nuclear-weapon States Party to
the Treaty shall be able to obtain such benefits,
pursuant to a special international agreement or
agreements, through an appropriate international
body with adequate representation of non-nuclear
weapon States. Negotiations on this subject
shall commence as soon as possible after the
Treaty enters into force. Non-nuclear weapon
States party to the Treaty so desiring may also
obtain such benefits pursuant to bilateral
agreements.

Article VI

Each of the Parties to the Treaty
undertakes to pursue negotiations in good faith
on effective measures relating to cessation of
the nuclear arms race at an early date and to
nuclear disarmament, and on a treaty on general
and complete disarmament under strict and
effective international control.

Article VII

Nothing in this Treaty affects the right
of any group of States to conclude regional
treaties in order to assure the total absence of
nuclear weapons in their respective territories.

Article VIII

1.   Any Party to the Treaty may
propose amendments to this Treaty. The text of
any proposed amendment shall be submitted to the
Depositary Governments which shall circulate it
to all Parties to the Treaty. Thereupon, if
requested to do so by one-third or more of the
Parties to the Treaty, the Depositary Governments
shall convene a conference, to which they shall
invite all the Parties to the Treaty, to consider
such an amendment.
2.   Any amendment to this Treaty must
be approved by a majority of the votes of all the
Parties to the Treaty, including the votes of all

nuclear-weapon States Party to the Treaty and all
other Parties which, on the date the amendment is
circulated, are members of the Board of Governors
of the International Atomic Energy Agency. The
amendment shall enter into force for ratification
of the amendment upon the deposit of such
instruments of ratification by a majority of all
the Parties, including the instruments of
ratification of all nuclear-weapon States Party
to the Treaty and all other Parties which, on the
date the amendment is circulated, are members of
the Board of Governors of the International
Atomic Energy Agency. Thereafter, it shall enter
into force for any other Party upon the deposit
of its instrument of ratification of the
amendment.

3.   Five years after the entry into
force of this Treaty, a conference of Parties to
the Treaty shall be held in Geneva, Switzerland,
in order to review the operation of this Treaty
with a view to assuring that the purposes of the
Preamble and the provisions of the Treaty are
being realized. At intervals of five years
thereafter, a majority of the Parties to the
Treaty may obtain, by submitting a proposal to
this effect to the Depositary Governments, the
convening of further conferences with the same
objective of reviewing the operation of the
Treaty.

Article IX

1.   This Treaty shall be open to all
States for signature. Any State which does not
sign the Treaty before its entry into force in
accordance with paragraph 3 of this article may
accede to it any time.

2.   This Treaty shall be subject to
ratification by signatory States. Instruments of
ratification and instruments of accession shall
be deposited with the Governments of the United
States of America, the United Kingdom of Great
Britain and Northern Ireland and the Union of
Soviet Socialist Republics, which are hereby
designated the Depositary Governments.

3.   This Treaty shall enter into

force after its ratification by the States, the Governments of which are designated Depositaries of the Treaty, and forty other States signatory to this Treaty and the deposit of their instruments of ratification. For the purposes of this treaty, a nuclear-weapon State is one which has manufactured and exploded a nuclear weapon or other nuclear explosive device prior to January 1, 1967.

4.   For States whose instruments of ratification or accession are deposited subsequent to the entry into force of this Treaty, it shall enter into force on the date of the deposit of their instruments of ratification or accession.

5.   The Depositary Governments shall promptly inform all signatory and acceding States of the date of each signature, the date of deposit of each instrument of ratification or of accession, the date of the entry into force of this Treaty, and the date of receipt of any requests for convening a conference or other notices.

6.   This Treaty shall be registered by the Depositary Governments pursuant to article 102 of the Charter of the United Nations.

Article X

1.   Each Party shall in exercising its national sovereignty have the right to withdraw from the Treaty if it decides that extraordinary events, related to the subject matter of this Treaty, have jeopardized the supreme interests of its country. It shall give notice of such withdrawal to all other Parties to the Treaty and to the United Nations Security Council three months in advance. Such notice shall include a statement of the extraordinary events it regards as having jeopardized its supreme interests.

2.   Twenty-five years after the entry into force of the Treaty, a conference shall be convened to decide whether the Treaty shall continue in force indefinitely, or shall be extended for an additional fixed period or

periods. This decision shall be taken by a majority of the Parties to the Treaty.

Article XI

This Treaty, the English, Russian, French, Spanish and Chinese texts of which are equally authentic, shall be deposited in the archives of the Depositary Governments. Duly certified copies of this Treaty shall be transmitted by the Depositary Governments to the Governments of the signatory and acceding States.

IN WITNESS WHEREOF the undersigned, duly authorized, have signed this Treaty.

DONE in triplicate, at the cities of Washington, London and Moscow, this first day of July one thousand nine hundred sixty-eight.

TEXTS OF THE 1972 ABM TREATY AND ITS AGREED INTERPRETATIONS, AND ITS 1976 PROTOCOL TREATY BETWEEN THE UNITED STATES OF AMERICA AND THE UNION OF SOVIET SOCIALIST REPUBLICS ON THE LIMITATION OF ANTI-BALLISTIC MISSILE SYSTEMS

Signed at Moscow May 26, 1972. Ratification advised by U.S. Senate August 3, 1972. Ratified by U.S. President September 30, 1972. Proclaimed by U.S. President October 3, 1972 Instruments of ratification exchanged October 3, 1972. Entered into force October 3, 1972.

The United States of America and the Union of Soviet Socialist Republics, hereinafter referred to as the Parties,

Proceeding from the premise that nuclear war could have devastating consequences for all mankind,

Considering that effective measures to limit anti-ballistic missile systems would be a substantial factor in curbing the race in strategic offensive arms and would lead to a decrease in the risk of outbreak of war involving nuclear weapons,

Proceeding from the premise that the limitation of anti-ballistic missile systems, as well as certain agreed measures with respect to the limitation of strategic offensive arms, would contribute to the creation of more favorable conditions for further negotiations on limiting strategic arms,

Mindful of their obligations under Article VI of the Treaty on the Non-Proliferation of Nuclear Weapons,

Declaring their intention to achieve at the earliest possible date the cessation of the nuclear arms race and to take effective measures toward reductions in strategic arms, nuclear disarmament, and general and complete disarmament,

Desiring to contribute to the relaxation of international tension and the strengthening of trubst between States

Have agreed as follows:

Article I

1.   Each party undertakes to limit anti-ballistic missile (ABM) systems and to adopt other measures in accordance with the provisions of this Treaty.

2.   Each Party undertakes not to deploy ABM systems for a defense of the territory of its country and not to provide a base for such a defense, and not to deploy ABM systems for defense of an individual region except as provided for in Article III of this Treaty.

Article II

1.   For the purpose of this Treaty an ABM system is a system to counter strategic ballistic missiles or their elements in flight trajectory, currently consisting of:

(a)   ABM interceptor missiles, which are interceptor missiles constructed and deployed for an ABM role, or of a type tested in an ABM mode;

        (b)   ABM launchers, which are launchers constructed and deployed for launching ABM interceptor missiles, and;

        (c)   ABM radars, which are radars constructed and deployed for an ABM role, or of a type tested in an ABM mode.

        2.   The ABM system components listed in paragraph 1 of this Article include those which are:

        (a)   operational;
        (b)   under construction;
        (c)   undergoing testing;
        (d)   undergoing overhaul, repair or conversion; or
        (e)   mothballed

Article III

Each Party undertakes not to deploy ABM systems or their components except that:

        (a)   within one ABM system deployment area having a radius of one hundred and fifty kilometers and centered on the Party's national capital, a Party may deploy: (1) no more than one hundred ABM launchers and no more than one hundred ABM interceptor missiles at launch sites, and (2) ABM radars within no more than six ABM radar complexes, the area of each complex being circular and having a diameter of no more than three kilometers; and

        (b)   within one ABM system deployment area having a radius of one hundred and fifty kilometers and containing ICBM silo launchers, a Party may deploy: (1) no more than one hundred launchers and no more than one hundred ABM interceptor missiles at launch sites, (2) two large phased-array ABM radars comparable in potential to corresponding ABM radars operational or under construction on the date of signature of the Treaty in an ABM system deployment area containing ICBM silo launchers and (3) no more than eighteen ABM radars each having a potential less than the potential of the smaller of the above-mentioned two large phased-array ABM radars.

Article IV

The limitations provided for in Article III shall not apply to ABM systems or their components used for development or testing, and located within current or additionally agreed test ranges. Each Party may have no more than a total of fifteen ABM launchers at test ranges.

Article V

1.   Each Party undertakes not to develop, test, or deploy ABM systems or components which are sea-based, air-based, space-based, or mobile land-based.
2.   Each Party undertakes not to develop, test, or deploy ABM launchers for launching more than one ABM interceptor missile at a time from each launcher, not to modify deployed launchers to provide them with such a capability, not to develop, test, or deploy automatic or semi-automatic or other similar systems for rapid reload of ABM launchers.

Article VI

To enhance assurance of the effectiveness of the limitations on ABM systems and their components provided by the Treaty, each Party undertakes:
(a)   not to give missiles, launchers, or radars, other than ABM interceptor missiles, ABM launchers, or ABM radars, capabilities to counter strategic ballistic missiles or their elements in flight trajectory, and not to test them in an ABM mode; and
(b)   not to deploy in the future radars for early warning of strategic ballistic missile attack except at locations along the periphery of its national territory and oriented outward.

Article VII

Subject to the provisions of this Treaty, modernization and replacement of ABM systems or their components may be carried out.

Article VIII

ABM systems or their components in excess of the numbers or outside the areas specified in this Treaty, as well as ABM systems or their components prohibited by this Treaty, shall be destroyed or dismantled under agreed procedures within the shortest possible agreed period of time.

Article IX

To assure the viability and effectiveness of this Treaty, each Party undertakes not to transfer to other States, and not to deploy outside its national territory, ABM systems or their components limited by this Treaty.

Article X

Each Party undertakes not to assume any international obligations which would conflict with this Treaty.

Article XI

The Parties undertake to continue active negotiations for limitations on strategic offensive arms.

Article XII

1.   For the purpose of providing assurance of compliance with the provisions of this Treaty, each Party shall use national technical means of verification at its disposal

in a manner consistent with generally recognized principles of international law.

2. Each Party undertakes not to interfere with the national technical means of verification of the other Party operating in accordance with paragraph 1 of this Article.

3. Each Party undertakes not to use deliberate concealment measures which impede verification by national technical means of compliance with the provisions of this Treaty. This obligation shall not require changes in current construction, assembly, conversion, or overhaul practices.

Article XIII

1. To promote the objectives and implementation of the provisions of this Treaty, the Parties shall establish promptly a Standing Consultative Commission, within the framework of which they will:

(a) consider questions concerning compliance with the obligations assumed and related situations which may be considered ambiguous;

(b) provide on a voluntary basis such information as either Party considers necessary to assure confidence in compliance with the obligations assumed;

(c) consider questions involving unintended interference with national technical means of verification;

(d) consider possible changes in the strategic situation which have a bearing on the provisions of this Treaty;

(e) agree upon procedures and dates for destruction or dismantling of ABM systems or their components in cases provided for by the provisions of this Treaty;

(f) consider, as appropriate, possible proposals for further increasing the viability of this Treaty; including proposals for amendments in accordance with the provisions of this Treaty;

(g) consider, as appropriate, proposals for further measures aimed at limiting strategic arms.

2.   The Parties through consultation shall establish, and may amend as appropriate, Regulations for the Standing Consultative Commission governing procedures, composition and other relevant matters.

Article XIV

1.   Each Party may propose amendments to this Treaty. Agreed amendments shall enter into force in accordance with the procedures governing the entry into force of this Treaty.
2.   Five years after entry into force of this Treaty, and at five-year intervals thereafter, the Parties shall together conduct a review of this Treaty.

Article XV

1.   This Treaty shall be of unlimited duration.
2.   Each Party shall, in exercising its national sovereignty, have the right to withdraw from this Treaty if it decides that extraordinary events related to the subject matter of this Treaty have jeopardized its supreme interests. It shall give notice of its decision to the other Party six months prior to withdrawal from the Treaty. Such notice shall include a statement of the extraordinary events the notifying Party regards as having jeopardized its supreme interests.

Article XVI

1.   This Treaty shall be subject to ratification in accordance with the constitutional procedures of each Party. The Treaty shall enter into force on the day of the exchange of instruments of ratification.
2.   This Treaty shall be registered pursuant to Article 102 of the Charter of the United Nations.

DONE at Moscow on May 26, 1972, in two copies, each in the English and Russian languages, both texts being equally authentic.

FOR THE UNION OF SOVIET SOCIALIST REPUBLICS
General Secretary of the Central Committee
of the CPSU

FOR THE UNITED STATES OF AMERICA
President of the United States

AGREED STATEMENTS, COMMON UNDERSTANDINGS, AND UNILATERAL STATEMENTS REGARDING THE TREATY BETWEEN THE UNITED STATES OF AMERICA AND THE UNION OF SOVIET SOCIALIST REPUBLICS ON THE LIMITATION OF ANTI-BALLISTIC MISSILES

1. Agreed Statements

The document set forth below was agreed upon and initialed by the Heads of the Delegations on May 26, 1972 (letter designations added);
Agreed Statements Regarding the Treaty Between the United States of America and the Union of Soviet Socialist Republics on the Limitation of Anti-Ballistic Missile Systems.

[A] The Parties understand that, in addition to the ABM radars which may be deployed in accordance with subparagraph (a) of Article III of the Treaty, those non-phased-array ABM radars operational on the date of signature of the Treaty within the ABM system deployment area for defense of the national capital may be retained.

[B] The Parties understand that the potential (the product of mean emitted power in watts and antenna area in square meters) of the smaller of the two large phased-array ABM radars referred to in subparagraph (b) of Article III of the Treaty is considered for purposes of the Treaty to be three million.

[C] The Parties understand that the center of the ABM system deployment area centered on the national capital and the center of the ABM system deployment area containing ICBM silo launchers for each Party shall be separated by no less than thirteen hundred kilometers.

[D] In order to insure fulfillment of the obligation not to deploy ABM systems and their components except as provided in Article III of the Treaty, the Parties agree that in the event ABM systems based on other physical principles and including components capable of substituting for ABM interceptor missiles, ABM launchers, or ABM radars are created in the future, specific limitations on such systems and their components would be subject to discussion in accordance with Article XIII and agreement in accordance with Article XIV of the Treaty.

[E] The Parties understand that Article V of the Treaty includes obligations not to develop, test or deploy ABM interceptor missiles for the delivery by each ABM interceptor missile of more than one independently guided warhead.

[F] The Parties agree not to deploy phased-array radars having a potential (the product of mean emitted power in watts and antenna area in square meters) exceeding three million, except as provided for in Articles III, IV and VI of the Treaty, or except for the purposes of tracking objects in outer space or for use as national technical means of verification.

[G] The Parties understand that Article IX of the Treaty includes the obligation of the US and the USSR not to provide to other states technical descriptions or blue prints specially worked out for the construction of ABM systems and their components limited by the Treaty.

2. Common Understandings

Common understanding of the parties on the following matters was reached during the negotiations:

A. Location of ICBM Defenses

The U.S. Delegation made the following statement on May 26, 1972:

Article III of the ABM Treaty provides for each side one ABM system deployment area centered on its national capital and one ABM system deployment area containing ICBM silo launchers. The two sides have registered agreement on the following statement: "The Parties understand that the center of the ABM system deployment area centered on the national capital and the center of the ABM system deployment area containing ICBM silo launchers for each Party shall be separated by no less than thirteen hundred kilometers." In this connection, the U.S. side notes that its ABM system deployment area for defense of ICBM silo launchers, located west of the Mississippi River, will be centered in the Grand Forks ICBM silo launcher deployment area. (See Agreed Statement [C]).

B. ABM Test Ranges

The U.S. Delegation made the following statement on April 26, 1972:

Article IV of the ABM Treaty provides that "the limitations provided for in Article III shall not apply to ABM systems or their components used for development or testing, and located within current or additionally agreed test ranges." We believe it would be useful to assure that there is no misunderstanding as to current ABM test ranges. It is our understanding that ABM test ranges encompass the area within which ABM components are located for test purposes. The current U.S. ABM test ranges are at White Sands, New Mexico, and at Kwajalein Atoll, and the current Soviet ABM test range is near Sary Shagan in Kazakhstan. We consider that the non-phased array radars of types used for range safety or instrumentation purposes may be located outside of ABM test ranges. We interpret the reference in Article IV to "additionally agreed test ranges" to mean that ABM components will not be located at any other test ranges without prior agreement between our Governments that there will be such additional ABM test ranges.

On May 5, 1972, the Soviet Delegation stated that there was a common understanding on what ABM test ranges were, that the use of the types of non-ABM radars for range safety or instrumentation was not limited under the Treaty, that the reference in Article IV to "additionally agreed" test ranges was sufficiently clear, and that national means permitted identifying current test ranges.

C. Mobile ICBM Systems

On January 29, 1972, the U.S. Delegation made the following statement:

Article V(1) of the Joint Draft Text of the ABM Treaty includes an undertaking not to develop, test, or deploy mobile land-based ABM systems and their components. On May 5, 1971, the U.S. side indicated that, in its view, a prohibition of deployment of mobile ABM systems and components would rule out the deployment of ABM launchers and radars which were not permanent fixed types. At that time, we asked for the Soviet view of this interpretation. Does the Soviet side agree with the U.S. side's interpretation put forward on May 5, 1971?

On April 13, 1972, the Soviet Delegation said there is a general common understanding on this matter.

D. Standing Consultative Commission

Ambassador Smith made the following statement on May 22, 1972:

The United States proposes that the sides agree that, with regard to initial implementation of the ABM Treaty's Article XIII of the Standing Consultative Commission (SCC) and of the consultation Articles to the Interim Agreement on offensive arms and the Accidents Agreement, (1) agreement establishing the SCC will be worked out early in the follow-on SALT negotiations; until that is completed, the following arrangements will prevail: when SALT is in session, any consultation desired by either side under these Articles can be carried out by the two SALT Delegations; when SALT is not in session, ad hoc arrangements for any desired consultations under these Articles may be made through diplomatic channels.

Minister Semenov replied that, on an ad referendum basis, he could agree that the U.S. statement corresponded to the Soviet understanding.

E. Standstill

On May 6, 1972, Minister Semenov made the following statement:

In an effort to accommodate the wishes of the U.S. side, the Soviet Delegation is prepared to proceed on the basis that the two sides will in fact observe the obligations of both the Interim Agreement and the ABM Treaty beginning from the date of signature of these two documents.

----

1. See Article 7 of the Agreement to Reduce the Risk of Outbreak of Nuclear War Between the United States of America and the Union of Soviet Socialist Republics, signed September 30, 1971.

In reply, the U.S. Delegation made the following statement on May 20, 1972:

The U.S. agrees in principle with the Soviet statement made on May 6 concerning observance of obligations beginning from date of signature but we would like to make clear our understanding that this means that, pending ratification and acceptance, neither side would take any action prohibited by the agreements after they had entered into force. This understanding would continue to apply in the absence of notification by either signatory of its intention not to proceed with ratification or approval.

The Soviet Delegation indicated agreement with the U.S. statement.

3. Unilateral Statements

The following noteworthy unilateral statements were made during the negotiations by the United States Delegation.

A. Withdrawal from ABM the Treaty

On May 9, 1972, Ambassador Smith made the following statement:

The U.S. Delegation has stressed the importance the U.S. Government attaches to achieving agreement on more complete limitations on strategic offensive arms, following agreement on an ABM Treaty and on an Interim Agreement on certain measures with respect to the limitation of strategic offensive arms. The U.S. Delegation believes that an objective of the follow-on negotiations should be to constrain and reduce on a long-term basis threats to the survivability of our respective strategic retaliatory forces. The USSR Delegation has also indicated that the objectives of SALT would remain unfulfilled without the achievement of an agreement providing for more complete limitations on strategic offensive arms. Both sides recognize that the initial agreements would be steps toward the achievement of more complete limitations on strategic arms. If an agreement providing for more complete strategic offensive arms limitations were not achieved within five years, U.S. supreme interests could be jeopardized. Should that occur, it would constitute a basis for withdrawal from the ABM Treaty. The U.S. does not wish to see such a situation occur, nor do we believe that the USSR does. It is because we wish to prevent such a situation that we emphasize the importance the U.S. Government attaches to achievement of more complete limitations on strategic offensive arms. The U.S. Executive will inform the Congress, in connection with Congressional consideration of the ABM Treaty and the Interim Agreement, of this statement of the U.S. position.

B. Tested in ABM Mode

On April 7, 1972, the U.S. Delegation made the following statement:

Article II of the Joint Text Draft uses the term "tested in an ABM mode," in defining ABM components, and Article VI includes certain obligations concerning such testing. We believe that the sides should have a common understanding of this phrase. First, we would note that the testing provisions of the ABM Treaty are intended to apply to testing which occurs after the date of signature of the Treaty, and not to any testing which may have occurred in the past. Next, we would amplify the remarks we have made on this subject during the previous Helsinki phase by setting forth the objectives which govern the U.S. view on the subject, namely, while prohibiting testing of non-ABM components for ABM purposes: not to prevent testing of ABM components, and not to prevent testing of non-ABM components for non-ABM purposes. To clarify our interpretation of "tested in an ABM mode," we note that we would consider a launcher, missile or radar to be "tested in an ABM mode" if, for example, any of the following events occur: (1) a launcher is used to launch an ABM interceptor missile, (2) an interceptor missile is flight tested against a target vehicle which has a flight trajectory with characteristics of a strategic ballistic missile flight trajectory, or is flight tested in conjunction with the test of an ABM interceptor missile or an ABM radar at the same test range, or is flight tested to an altitude inconsistent with interception of targets against which air defenses are deployed, (3) a radar makes measurements on a cooperative target vehicle of the kind referred to in item (2) above during the reentry portion of its trajectory or makes measurements in conjunction with the test of an ABM interceptor missile or an ABM radar at the same test range. Radars used for purposes such as range safety or instrumentation would be exempt from application of these criteria.

C. No-Transfer Article of ABM Treaty

On April 18, 1972, the U.S. Delegation made the following statement:

In regard to this Article [IX], I have a brief and I believe self-explanatory statement to make. The U.S. side wishes to make clear that the provisions of this Article do not set a precedent for whatever provision may be considered for a Treaty on Limiting Strategic Offensive Arms. The question of transfer of strategic offensive arms is a far more complex issue, which may require a different solution.

D. No Increase in Defense of Early Warning Radars

On July 28, 1970, the U.S. Delegation made the following statement:

Since Hen House radars [Soviet ballistic missile early warning radars] can detect and track ballistic missile warheads at great distances, they have a significant ABM potential. Accordingly, the U.S. would regard any increase in the defenses of such radars by surface-to-air missiles as inconsistent with an agreement.

PROTOCOL TO THE TREATY BETWEEN
THE UNITED STATES OF AMERICA AND THE
UNION OF SOVIET SOCIALIST REPUBLICS ON THE
LIMITATION OF ANTI-BALLISTIC MISSILE SYSTEMS

Signed at Moscow July 3, 1974. Ratification advised by U.S. Senate November 10, 1975. Ratified by U.S. President March 19, 1976. Instruments of ratification exchanged May 24, 1976. Proclaimed by U.S. President July 6, 1976 Entered into force May 24, 1976.

The United States of America and the Union of Soviet Socialist Republics, hereinafter referred to as the Parties,
Proceeding from the Basic Principles of Relations between the United States of America and the Union of Soviet Socialist Republics signed on May 29, 1972,
Desiring to further the objectives of the Treaty between the United States of America and the Union of Soviet Socialist Republics on the Limitation of Anti-Ballistic Missile Systems signed on May 26, 1972, hereinafter referred to as the Treaty,
Reaffirming their conviction that the adoption of further measures for the limitation of strategic arms would contribute to strengthening international peace and security,
Proceeding from the premise that further limitation of anti-ballistic missile systems will create more favorable conditions for the completion of work on a permanent agreement on more complete measures for the limitation of strategic offensive arms,
Have agreed as follows:

Article I

1. Each Party shall be limited at any one time to a single area out of the two provided in Article III of the Treaty for deployment of anti-ballistic missile (ABM) systems or their components and accordingly shall not exercise its right to deploy an ABM system or its components in the second of the two ABM system deployment areas permitted by Article III of the Treaty, except as an exchange of one permitted area for the other in accordance with Article II of this Protocol.

2. Accordingly, except as permitted by Article II of this Protocol: the United States of America shall not deploy an ABM system or its components in the area centered on its capital, as permitted by Article III(a) of the Treaty, and the Soviet Union shall not deploy an ABM system or its components in the deployment area of intercontinental ballistic missile (ICBM) silo launchers as permitted by Article III(b) of the Treaty.

Article II

1. Each Party shall have the right to dismantle or destroy its ABM system and the components thereof in the area where they are presently deployed and to deploy an ABM system or its components in the alternative area permitted by Article III of the Treaty, provided that prior to initiation of construction, notification is given in accord with the procedure agreed to in the Standing Consultative Commission, during the year beginning October 3, 1977 and ending October 2, 1978, or during any year which commences at five year intervals thereafter, those being the years for periodic review of the Treaty, as provided in Article XIV of the Treaty. This right may be exercised only once.

2. Accordingly, in the event of such notice, the United States would have the right to dismantle or destroy the ABM system and its components in the deployment area of ICBM silo launchers and to deploy an ABM system or its

components in an area centered on its capital, as permitted by Article III(a) of the Treaty, and the Soviet Union would have the right to dismantle or destroy the ABM system and its components in the area centered on its capital and to deploy an ABM system or its components in an area containing ICBM silo launchers, as permitted by Article III(b) of the Treaty.

3.   Dismantling or destruction and deployment of ABM systems or their components and the notification thereof shall be carried out in accordance with Article VIII of the ABM Treaty and procedures agreed to in the Standing Consultative Commission.

Article III

The rights and obligations established by the Treaty remain in force and shall be compiled with by the Parties except to the extent modified by this Protocol. In particular, the deployment of an ABM system or its components within the area selected shall remain limited by the levels and other requirements established by the Treaty.

Article IV

This Protocol shall be subject to ratification in accordance with the constitutional procedures of each Party. It shall enter into force on the day of the exchange of instruments of ratification and shall thereafter be considered an integral part of the Treaty.

DONE at Moscow on July 3, 1974, in duplicate, in the English and Russian languages, both texts being equally authentic.

For the United States of America:
     Richard Nixon
President of the United States of America
For the Union of Soviet Socialist Republics:
     L.I. Brezhnev
General Secretary of the Central Committee of the CPSU

TREATY BETWEEN THE UNITED STATES OF AMERICA AND
THE UNION OF SOVIET SOCIALIST REPUBLICS ON THE
LIMITATION OF UNDERGROUND NUCLEAR WEAPON TESTS

Signed at Moscow July 3, 1974

The United States of America and the
Union of Soviet Socialist Republics, hereinafter
referred to as the Parties,
Declaring their intention to achieve at
the earliest possible date the cessation of the
nuclear arms race and to take effective measures
toward reductions in strategic arms, nuclear
disarmament, and general and complete disarmament
under strict and effective international control,
Recalling the determination expressed by
the Parties to the 1963 Treaty Banning Nuclear
Weapon Tests in the Atmosphere, in Outer Space
and Under Water in its Preamble to seek to
achieve the discontinuance of all test explosions
of nuclear weapons for all time, and to continue
negotiations to this end,
Noting that the adoption of measures for
the further limitation of underground nuclear
weapon tests would contribute to the achievement
of these objectives and would meet the interests
of strengthening peace and the further relaxation
of international tension,
Reaffirming their adherence to the
objectives and principles of the Treaty Banning
Nuclear Weapon Tests in the Atmosphere, in Outer
Space and Under Water and of the Treaty on the
Non-Proliferation of Nuclear Weapons.
Have agreed as follows:

Article I

1.   Each Party undertakes to
prohibit, to prevent, and not to carry out any
underground nuclear weapon test having a yield
exceeding 150 kilotons at any place under its
jurisdiction or control, beginning March 31,
1976.

2.   Each Party shall limit the number of its underground nuclear weapon tests to a minimum.

3.   The Parties shall continue their negotiations with a view toward achieving a solution to the problem of the cessation of all underground nuclear weapon tests.

Article II

1.   For the purpose of providing assurance of compliance with the provisions of this Treaty, each Party shall use national technical means of verification at its disposal in a manner consistent with the generally recognized principles of international law.

2.   Each Party undertakes not to interfere with the national technical means of verification of the other Party operating in accordance with paragraph 1 of this Article.

3.   To promote the objectives and implementation of the provisions of this Treaty the Parties shall, as necessary, consult with each other, make inquiries and furnish information in response to such inquiries.

Article III

The provisions of this Treaty do not extend to underground nuclear explosions carried out by the Parties for peaceful purposes. Underground nuclear explosions for peaceful purposes shall be governed by an agreement which is to be negotiated and concluded by the Parties at the earliest possible time.

Article IV

This Treaty shall be subject to ratification in accordance with the constitutional procedures of each Party. This Treaty shall enter into force on the day of the exchange of instruments of ratification.

Article V

1.   This Treaty shall remain in force for a period of five years. Unless replaced earlier by an agreement in implementation of the objectives specified in paragraph 3 of Article 1 of this Treaty, it shall be extended for successive five-year periods unless either Party notifies the other of its termination no later than six months prior to the expiration of the Treaty. Before the expiration of this period the Parties may, as necessary, hold consultations to consider the situation relevant to the substance of this Treaty and to introduce possible amendments to the text of the Treaty.

2.   Each party shall, in exercising its national sovereignty, have the right to withdraw from this Treaty if it decides that extraordinary events related to the subject matter of this Treaty have jeopardized its supreme interests. It shall give notice of its decision to the other Party six months prior to withdrawal from this Treaty. Such notice shall include a statement of the extraordinary events the notifying Party regards as having jeopardized its supreme interests.

3.   This Treaty shall be registered pursuant to Article 102 of the Charter of the United Nations.

DONE at Moscow on July 3, 1974, in duplicate, in the English and Russian languages, both texts being equally authentic.

For the United States of America:

RICHARD NIXON,
      The President of the United
      States of America

For the Union of Soviet Socialist Republics:

L. BREZHNEV,
      General Secretary of the Central
      Committee of the CPSU.

Appendix B:
Acronyms and Terminology
Related to the SDI

ACRONYMS

The following explanation of acronyms
commonly used in the strategic defense literature
is adapted from the glossary of acronyms found in
the Office of Technology Assessment, _Ballistic
Missile Defense Technologies_, U.S. Government
Printing Office, September 1985.

ABM	anti-ballistic missile
ALCM	air-launched cruise missile
ASAT	anti-satellite
BMD	ballistic missile defense
C3I	command, control, communications, and intelligence
CONUS	continental United States
DOD	Department of Defense
DEW	directed-energy weapon
DSAT	defensive satellite
GLCM	ground-launched cruise missile
HOE	homing overlay experiment
ICBM	intercontinental ballistic missile
IR	infrared
IRBM	intermediate-range ballistic missile
KEW	kinetic-energy weapon
KKV	kinetic-kill vehicle
LWIR	long-wave infrared
MaRV	maneuverable reentry vehicle
MIRV	multiple independently targeted reentry vehicle
MILSAT	military satellite

MPS	multiple protective shelters, once intended for use in basing the MX
MWIR	medium-wave infrared
MX	experimental missile, newest addition to U.S. ICBM arsenal, also called "Peacekeeper"
OTA	Office of Technology Assessment
PBV	post-boost vehicle
RV	reentry vehicle
SDI	Strategic Defense Initiative
SDIO	Strategic Defense Initiative Organization
SLBM	submarine-launched ballistic missile
SLCM	sea-launched cruise missile
SWIR	short-wave infrared
UV	ultraviolet

TERMINOLOGY

The explanation of SDI terminology is adapted from Lieutenant General James A. Abrahamson, "The Strategic Defense Initiative," Defense 84, August, 1984; and from the glossary of terms found in Office of Technology Assessment, Ballistic Missile Defense Technologies, U.S. Government Printing Office, September 1985.

Ablative Shield: A shield that evaporates when heated, absorbing laser energy and protecting the object behind it from heat damage.

ABM Treaty: A treaty of 1972, signed and ratified by the Soviet Union and the United States, prohibiting development of many types of anti-ballistic missile systems and limiting deployments on each side to a specified number of land-based units, that use only rocket interceptors and ground-based radar.

Acquisition: Detection of a potential target by the sensors of a weapons system.

Active Sensor: One that illuminates a target, producing return secondary radiation, which is then detected in order to track and/or identify the target.

Adaptive Optics: Optical systems that can be modified (e.g., by controlling the shape of a mirror) to compensate for distortions. An example is the use of information from a beam of light passing through the atmosphere, to compensate for the distortion suffered by another beam of light on its passage through the atmosphere. Used to eliminate the "twinkling" of stars in observational astronomy and to reduce the dispersive effect of the atmosphere on laser beam weapons.

Airborne Sensor: Sensors carried as an airborne optical adjunct to a ground-based radar system designed to detect, track, and discriminate incoming warheads. The sensors are typically optical or infrared devices carried in an aircraft stationed above the clouds.

Air-breathing: Describes a flying weapon that travels through the atmosphere and uses air in its propulsion system. Examples are jet aircraft and cruise missiles. Specifically does not include ballistic missiles.

Analog Processing: Problem solving in a computer by means of direct manipulation of the magnitudes of a physical quantity. For example, the sizes of different voltage pulses may be compared, added, subtracted, etc., in the course of solving a problem.

Anti-satellite Weapons (ASAT): A weapon designed to destroy satellites in space.

Anti-simulation: The deception of adversary sensors by making a strategic target look like a decoy.

Architecture: The physical structure of a computer system, which can include both hardware and software.

Area Defense: An ABM defense covering a large area. Usually implies the capability to protect "soft" (i.e., not hardened missile silos or bunkers) targets.

Ballistic Missile Defense (BMD): A defense system that is designed to protect territory from attacking ballistic missiles. Usually conceived as having several independent layers.

Battle Management: The set of instructions and rules and the corresponding hardware controlling the operation of a BMD system. Sensors and interceptors are allocated by the system, and the updated battle results are presented to the (human) command for analysis and possible intervention.

Birth-to-death Tracking: The tracking of objects from the time that they are deployed from a booster or post-boost vehicle until they are killed or detonated.

Blackout: The disabling of radar by means of a nuclear explosion. The intense electromagnetic energy released generates a large background that obscures signals and renders many types of radar useless for minutes or longer.

Booster: The rocket that boosts the payload to accelerate it from the earth's surface into a ballistic trajectory, during which no additional force is applied to the payload.

Boost Phase: The phase of a missile trajectory from launch to burnout of the final stage. For ICBMs, this phase typically lasts from 3 to 5 minutes, but studies indicate that reductions on the order of 1 minute could be possible.

Brightness: The amount of power that can be delivered per unit solid angle by a directed-energy weapon.

Bus Deployment Phase: That portion of a missile flight during which multiple warheads are deployed on different paths to different targets (also referred to as the post-boost phase). The warheads on a single missile are carried on a platform or "bus" (also referred to as a post-boost vehicle), which has small rocket motors to move the bus slightly from its original path.

Chemical Laser: A laser in which chemical action is used to produce pulses of intense light.

Coherence: The matching, in space and time, of the wave structure of different parallel rays of a single frequency of electromagnetic radiation. This results in the mutual reinforcing of the energy of the

different components of a larger beam.
Lasers can produce coherent radiation.

Command Guidance: The steering and control of a
missile by transmitting commands to it.

Common Mode Failure: Refers to a type of system
failure in which diverse components are
disabled by the same single cause.

Constellation Size: The number of defensive
weapon satellites placed in orbit about the
Earth as part of a BMD system.

Counter-countermeasures: Measures taken by the
defense to defeat offensive countermeasures.

Countermeasures: Measures taken by the offense
to overcome aspects of a BMD system.

Cruise Missile: A missile traveling within the
atmosphere at aircraft speeds and, usually,
low altitude, whose trajectory is prepro-
grammed. It is capable of achieving high
accuracy in striking a distant target. It
is maneuverable during flight, is constantly
propelled, and therefore does not follow a
ballistic trajectory. Cruise missiles may
be nuclear armed, but do not have to be.

Dazzling: The temporary blinding of a sensor by
overloading it with an intense signal of
electromagnetic radiation (e.g., from a
laser or a nuclear explosion).

Decoy: An object that is designed to make an
observer believe that the object is more
valuable than is actually the case. Usually
a decoy refers to a light object, not
containing a warhead, designed to look like
a nuclear-armed reentry vehicle.

Defensive-satellite Weapon (DSAT): A device that
is intended to defend satellites in space by
destroying attacking ASAT weapons.

Defensive Technologies Study Team (DTST): A
committee, generally known as the "Fletcher
Panel," after its chair, appointed by
President Reagan to investigate the
technologies of potential BMD systems.

Diffraction: The spreading out of
electromagnetic radiation as it leaves an
aperture, such as a mirror. The angle of
spread, which cannot be eliminated by
focusing, is proportional to the ratio of
the wavelength of radiation to the diameter
of the aperture.

Digital Processing: The most familiar type of computing, in which problems are solved through the mathematical manipulation of streams of numbers.

Directed-energy Weapon: A weapon that kills its target by delivering energy to it at or near the speed of light. Includes lasers and particle-beam weapons.

Discrimination: The ability of a defensive system to differentiate decoys or other nonthreatening objects from targets (e.g., a threatening booster rocket, post-boost vehicle, or RV).

Early Warning: Early detection of an enemy ballistic missile launch, usually by means of surveillance satellites and long-range radar.

Electromagnetic Radiation: A form of propagated energy, arising from electric charges in motion, that produces a simultaneous wavelike variation of electric and magnetic fields in space. The highest frequencies (or shortest wavelength) of such radiation are possessed by gamma rays, which originate from processes within atomic nuclei. As one goes to lower frequencies, the electromagnetic spectrum includes X-rays, ultraviolet light, visible light, infrared light, microwaves, and radio waves.

Electron-volt: The energy gained by an electron in passing through a potential difference of one volt.

Endo-atmospheric: Literally, within the atmosphere. An endo-atmospheric interceptor reaches its target within the atmosphere.

Exo-atmospheric: Outside the atmosphere. An exo-atmospheric interceptor reaches its target in space.

Fast-burn Booster: A ballistic missile that can burn out much more quickly than current versions, possibly before exiting the atmosphere entirely. Such rapid burnout complicates a boost-phase defense.

Fission: The breaking apart of the nucleus of an atom, usually by means of a neutron. For very heavy elements, such as uranium, a significant amount of energy is produced by

this process. When controlled, this process
yields energy that may be extracted for
civilian uses, such as commercial electric
generation. When uncontrolled, energy is
liberated very rapidly. Such fission is the
energy source of uranium and plutonium-
based nuclear weapons; it also provides
the trigger for fusion weapons.

Fratricide: The destructive effect of the
earlier-detonating weapons in a barrage on
those weapons that arrive later.

Functional Kill: The destruction of a target by
disabling vital components in a way not
immediately detectable, but nevertheless
able to prevent the target from functioning
properly. An example is the destruction of
electronics in a guidance system by a
neutral particle beam.

Galosh: The Soviet ABM built near to Moscow.

Geosynchronous Orbit: An orbit about 22,300
miles above the equator. A satellite placed
in such an orbit revolves around the Earth
once per day, maintaining the same position
relative to the surface of the Earth. It
then appears to be stationary and is useful
as a communications relay or as a
surveillance post.

Hard Kill: Destruction of a target in such a way
as to produce unambiguous visible evidence
of its neutralization.

Hardness: A property of a target, measured by
the power needed per unit area to destroy
the target by means of a directed-energy
weapon. A hard target is more difficult to
kill than a soft target.

Homing Device: A device, mounted on a missile,
that uses sensors to detect the position or
to help predict the future position of a
target, and then directs the missile to
intercept the target. It usually updates
frequently during the flight of the missile.

Homing Overlay Experiment: A non-nuclear test
conducted by the United States in which a
rocket was fired to intercept a warhead by
spreading out a kind of wire net that caused
the destruction of the warhead by the force
of impact between the two objectives.

Hypervelocity Gun: A gun that can accelerate projectiles to several miles a second or more (e.g., electromagnetic gun or rail gun).

Imaging: The process of identifying an object by obtaining a high-quality image of it.

Impulse Kill: The destruction of a target, using directed energy, by ablative shock. The intensity of directed energy is such that the surface of the target violently and rapidly boils off, delivering a mechanical shock wave to the rest of the target and causing structural failure.

Infrared Sensor: A sensor designed to detect the infrared radiation from a cold body such as a missile reentry vehicle.

Ionization: The removal or addition of one or more electrons to a neutral atom, forming a charged ion.

Keep-out Zone: A volume around a space asset, off limits to parties not owners of the asset. A keep-out zone can be negotiated or unilaterally declared. The right to defend such a zone by force and the legality of unilaterally declared zones under the Outer Space Treaty remain to be determined.

Kill Assessment: The detection and assimilation of information indicating the destruction of an object under attack. Kill assessment is one of the many functions to be performed by a battle management system.

Kinetic-energy Weapon: A weapon that uses kinetic energy, or energy of motion, to kill an object. Among the weapons that use kinetic energy are a rock, a bullet, a nonexplosively armed rocket, and an electromagnetic railgun.

Ladar: A technique analogous to radar, but one that uses laser light rather than radio waves or microwaves. The light is bounced off a target and then detected, with the return beam providing information on the distance and velocity of the target.

Laddering Down: A hypothetical technique for overcoming a terminal-phase missile defense. Successive salvos of salvage-fused RVs attack. The detonations of one salvo disable local ABM abilities so that following salvos are able to approach the target more closely before being, in turn, intercepted. Eventually, by repeating the process, the target is reached and destroyed.

Lasant: A material that can be stimulated to produce laser light.

Laser: A device that produces a narrow beam of coherent radiation through a physical process known as stimulated emission. Lasers are able to focus large quantities of energy at great distances and are among the leading candidates for BMD weapons.

Laser Imaging: A new technology whereby a laser beam can be used in a way similar to the use of a radar beam to produce a high-quality image of an object.

Laser Tracker: The process of using a laser to illuminate a target so that specialized sensors can detect the reflected laser light and track the target.

Layered Defenses: The use of several layers of BMD at different phases of the missile trajectory. Each layer is designed to be as independent as possible of the others, and each would probably use its own distinctive set of missile defense technologies.

Leakage: The percentage of warheads that get through a defensive system intact and operational.

Leverage: Refers to the advantage gained by boost-phase intercept, when a single booster kill may eliminate many RVs and decoys before they are deployed. This could provide a favorable cost-exchange ratio for the defense; it may also reduce stress on later layers of the defense system.

Limited Test Ban Treaty: The multilateral treaty signed and ratified by the United States and the USSR in 1963 prohibiting nuclear tests in all locations except underground.

Megawatt: One million watts; a unit of power. A typical commercial electric plant generates about 500 to 1,000 megawatts.

Mev: One million electron-volts. A unit of energy usually used in reference to nuclear processes. Equivalent to the energy that an electron gains in crossing a potential of 1 million volts.

Midcourse Phase: The phase of a ballistic missile trajectory in which the RVs travel through space on a ballistic course toward their targets. This phase lasts up to 20 minutes.

Military Satellite (MILSAT): A satellite used for military purposes, such as navigation or intelligence gathering.

Multiple Independently-targetable Reentry Vehicle (MIRV): One of several RVs on the same post-boost vehicle that can be independently placed on a ballistic course toward a target after completion of the boost phase.

Multiple Phenomenology: A system using repeated observations of potential targets by means of different physical principles and different sensor systems. In the case of sensor systems, the use of multiple phenomenology makes it more difficult for an adversary to deceive such systems.

Optical processing: A type of analog processing in which the behavior of light beams passed through optical systems is used in problem solving.

Outer Space Treaty of 1967: A signed and ratified agreement between the Soviet Union, the United States, and other nations, forbidding the basing of nuclear or other weapons of mass destruction in space.

Parallel Processing: The use of different paths in a computer to work simultaneously on different calculations needed to solve a single problem, thus reducing the time needed for the overall calculation.

Particle Beam: A stream of atoms or subatomic particles (electrons, protons, or neutrons) accelerated to nearly the speed of light.

Passive Sensor: One that detects naturally occurring emissions from a target for tracking and/or identification purposes.

Penetration Aid: A device mounted on a post-boost vehicle with RVs that is used to confuse defenses. It may be a decoy or anything else that renders more difficult the defense's job of detecting and killing the RVs or the PBV.

Phased-array Radar (PAR): A radar with elements that are physically stationary, but with a beam that is electronically steerable and can switch rapidly from one target to another. Used for tracking many objects, often at great distances.

Pointing: The aiming of sensors or defense weapons at a target with sufficient accuracy either to track the target or to aim with sufficient accuracy to destroy it.

Post-boost Phase: The phase of a missile trajectory, after the booster's stages have finished firing, in which the various RVs are independently placed on ballistic trajectories toward their targets. In addition, penetration aids are dispensed from the post-boost vehicle. The length of this phase is typically 3 to 5 minutes, but could be drastically reduced.

Post-boost Vehicle: That portion of a rocket payload that carries the multiple warheads and has maneuvering capability to place each warhead on its final trajectory to a target (also referred to as a "bus").

Preferential Defense: The concentration of defensive assets on a subset of targets.

Preferential Offense: The concentration of offensive assets on a subset of targets.

Pumping: The raising of the molecules or atoms of a lasant to an energy state above the normal lowest state, in order to produce laser light. This results when they fall back to a lower state. Pumping may be done using electrical, chemical, or nuclear energy.

Redout: The blinding or dazzling of infrared detectors due to high levels of infrared radiation produced in the upper atmosphere by a nuclear explosion.

Reentry: The return of objects, originally launched from Earth, into the atmosphere.

Reentry Vehicle (RV): Reentry vehicles are small containers holding nuclear warheads. They are released from the last stage of a booster rocket or from a post-boost vehicle early in the ballistic trajectory. They are thermally insulated to survive rapid heating during the high velocities of reentry into the atmosphere, and are designed to protect their contents until detonation at their targets.

Responsive Threat: The threat after taking into account modernization and BMD counter-measures.

Robust: When describing a system, this term indicates its ability to endure and perform its mission against a reactive adversary. Also used to indicate ability to survive under direct attack.

Safeguard: A U.S. midcourse and terminal-phase defense for ICBMs, deployed in 1975 and deactivated in 1976 due to its limited cost-effectiveness.

Salvage-fused: Describes a warhead that is set to detonate when attacked. Usually refers to a nuclear warhead.

Selectivity: Refers to the choice of a subset of targets, either for attack or defense. See preferential defense and preferential offense.

Semi-active Sensor: One that does not generate radiation itself, but instead detects radiation reflected by targets when they are illuminated by other BMD components. Such devices are used for tracking and identification and can operate without revealing their own locations.

Sensors: Electronic instruments that can detect radiation from objects at great distances. The information can be used for tracking, aiming, discrimination, attacking, kill assessment, or all of the above. Sensors may detect any type of electromagnetic radiation or several types of nuclear particles.

Sentinel: ABM system designed for light area defense against low-level ballistic missile attack on the United States. Developed into the Safeguard system in late 1960s.

Shoot-back: The technique of defending a space asset by shooting an attacker.

Signature: Distinctive type of radiation emitted or reflected by a target, which can be used to identify that target.

Simulation: The art of making a decoy look like a more valuable strategic target.

Slew Time: The time needed for a weapon to re-aim at a new target after having just fired at a previous one.

Soft Kill: See Functional Kill.

Space Mines: Hypothetical devices that can track and follow a target in orbit, with the capability of exploding on command or by pre-program, in order to destroy the target.

Spartan: Nuclear-armed long-range midcourse interceptor used in Safeguard/Sentinel systems.

Sprint: Nuclear-armed short-range interceptor used in Safeguard/Sentinel systems.

SS-18: Largest ICBM in current Soviet inventory, credited with carrying ten RVs, but capable of holding many more.

Stimulated Emission: Physical process by which an excited molecule is induced by incident radiation to emit radiation at an identical frequency and in phase with the incident radiation. Lasers operate by stimulated emission.

Structured Attack: An attack in which the arrival of warheads on their diverse targets is precisely timed for maximum strategic impact.

Synthetic Aperture Radar (SAR): A radar technique involving the processing of echoes of signals emitted at different points along a satellite's orbit. The highest resolution achievable by such a system is theoretically equivalent to that of a single large antenna as wide as the distance between the points most widely spaced along the orbit that are used for transmitting positions.

Terminal Phase: The final phase of a ballistic missile trajectory, lasting about a minute or less, in which the RVs reenter the atmosphere and detonate at their targets.

Thermal Kill: The destruction of a target by heating it, using directed energy, to the degree that structural components fail.

Threat: The anticipated inventory of enemy weapons. The inventory includes nuclear weapons and their delivery systems as well as decoys, penetration aids, and other BMD countermeasures.

Track File: Information stored in computer memory containing position coordinates and velocity components of a target. Refers to such information concerning offensive weapons during their trajectories (e.g., boosters, RVs, decoys).

Tracking: The monitoring of the course of a moving target. Ballistic objects may have their tracks predicted by the defensive system, using several observations and physical laws.

Transition: The period in which the world strategic balance would shift from offense-dominance to defense-dominance.

Warhead: A weapon, usually a nuclear weapon, contained in the payload of a missile.